The Wire-to-Wire
REDS

John Erardi and Joel Luckhaupt

CLERISY PRESS

Published by Clerisy Press
P.O. Box 8874
Cincinnati, OH 45208-8744
www.clerisypress.com

Cover and interior designed by Stephen Sullivan
Edited by Jack Heffron

ISBN 978-1-57860-465-4

The photographs in *The Wire-to-Wire Reds* appear courtesy of the following: The Associated Press: Pages 110, 182; The Cincinnati Reds Hall of Fame and Museum: Pages 8, 157, 207 (NLCS program), 244. Photos taken by Zia Portrait Design; The *Cincinnati Enquirer*: Front cover (top center, bottom left, bottom center). Back cover. Pages 24, 82, 103, 107, 134, 141, 150, 153, 160, 161, 174, 190, 205, 208, 212, 213, 219, 222, 223, 235, 248, 249;

All other photos appear courtesy of The Cincinnati Reds.

Printed in Canada
Distributed by Publishers Group West
First edition, first printing

John

To Chris and Gina, who after years of guiding me through
one book crisis after another with their tech-savvy,
emerge from backstage.

To Barb, whose good humor made another
book-writing lark possible.

And to Big Daddy, who when I told him in 1966
that I'd just seen a blind former big leaguer named
Specs Toporcer walk onto the field at an old-timers game,
told me how as a kid he had watched Specs play—
and opened my eyes to everything.

Joel

To Sara and Alex, who didn't know what they were getting
into when I asked if they minded if I helped to write this
book. Your support made it possible.

To Dad and Mom, who never made me believe that I
couldn't do anything I put my mind to.

Contents

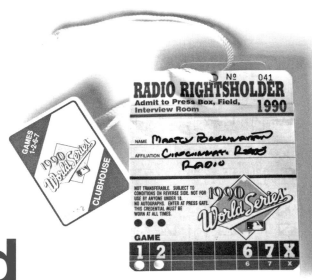

Foreword

by Marty Brennaman

The 1990 World Champion Reds are my favorite team ever, and that includes the Big Red Machine.

And Lou Piniella may well be my all-time favorite manager, which is really saying something, considering how much I liked Sparky Anderson, Pete Rose, and Dusty Baker.

It's hard to believe that we're talking twenty years ago, isn't it? That, to me, is shocking. But I'll say this: The timing for this book is perfect. Nobody gave that team a chance to win. If Lou says he thought that team could win the division, he's a damn liar. I certainly didn't think it could. And not only did they win, they went into first place on opening night and never vacated it. They caught people early by surprise,

and by the time people in the division and the league woke up, it was too late.

Lou had a quality you don't see in many people. He was extremely intense, and yet he had a very pleasant way about him off the field. He was very personable, amiable, approachable. The fans picked up on that quickly, almost instantaneously. He has said on more than one occasion that Cincinnati was his favorite place of all the places he's ever been as a player or a manager. Anita, his wife, felt the same way.

The fans loved the way he got after it; they were starved for it. That incident where he picked up the base and threw it? People loved it. They loved him. They hadn't seen that in a manager in a long time. Every now and then Sparky Anderson would do something

Marty Brennaman and the late Joe Nuxhall called the 1990 Reds their all-time favorite team.

like that, but to continually have a quick trigger and go out there and battle like hell for your team and throw your hat and kick the dirt at home plate—let's face it, a lot of that was show business—but it still was the essence of what this guy was about.

I believe that one reason this team played so hard for him is that he showed by his actions that no single individual was more important than pulling out all the stops to win a game. He'd pinch-hit for guys with no regard for their egos because he was trying to win.

Over the years I've dealt with managers, and privately I'd say to them, "Why didn't you pinch-hit for so-and-so?" The answer would be, "I can't pinch-hit for *him*. He's a regular player. If I pinch-hit for him in that situation, I lose him."

You know what? Lou wasn't worried about losing a guy. He did what he felt was needed to win a game, everything else be damned. His personality was so overwhelming that players knew he'd cut his arm off to win. And they knew that if he pinch-hit for them, no matter who they were, "He's not doing it as a slight to me; he's doing it because he genuinely feels the pinch hitter has a better chance of hitting this pitcher right now than I do." Beyond that, Lou didn't care.

Do I believe this team underachieved in the years leading up to '90? Yes. They'd finished second for four straight years, and in '89 came all the injuries and Pete Rose being suspended and banned for gambling. Four straight second-place finishes? At some point, you've got to get lucky and win.

If there was a knock on Pete—and I'm sure Pete would disagree with this—he was in a tough spot as a player-manager. He could only go out and argue so much for his players because he was in the lineup playing. Lou didn't have that problem. I heard players complain when Pete was managing: "Why the hell should I care? He doesn't go out there and fight for us." But, with Lou, every single guy on that club knew he had their back. That's important. You get inside a player's psyche, and they'll tell you: "If I know my manager is going to come out here and fight for me

and defend me, then I'll bust my ass every second. But if I know I got a guy sitting in the dugout who's going to be passive, and I'm hung out to dry by myself arguing my cause, I'm not going to care as much." That's just the way it is.

The players also saw how painful it was to Lou when the team lost. This wasn't a guy who paid lip service to how badly he wanted to win. He went out every night legitimately and unequivocally expecting to win, believing he could go 162–0. Most managers want to win, but there aren't too many who will turn over a food table after getting beat. There'd be food on the ceilings and on the walls—Lou just didn't care. He was aggressive with a capital "A." He didn't rein it in. When he put on that uniform every night, it was batten down the hatches. Most of the players, if not every one of them, had never experienced a guy like that. They respected it and played like it.

But the reason it's my favorite team is because I've never been around a team that had better chemistry. Blacks, whites, Hispanics, no cliques. Everybody had each other's back. They had the best coaching staff I've ever been around. Everything about that team fit. And when Billy Hatcher came in here in spring training of '90, he and Lou grew into a level of respect that perhaps nobody else achieved. Ever since Billy retired and Lou moved on, Lou's had Billy with him almost everywhere he's been.

Not only did the '90 team have good starting pitching, they had three guys in the bullpen who were absolutely nuts. They all threw a thousand miles an hour, and all three would bury a fastball in your ribs if you looked at them funny.

Norm Charlton is the one I call the true Nasty Boy. People were legitimately afraid of him. That collision he had with Mike Sciosia? Sammy Perlozzo was throwing up the stop sign at third base, and Norm never even looked at him. After the collision, Charlton got up and walked away, and Scioscia was a little slow getting up. That epitomized it. Rob Dibble's a big guy; Randy Myers wasn't big, but he threw hard. Norm Charlton? He'd fight you.

There was that time in 1989 when the Reds were playing in New York on a Sunday afternoon, and it was four thousand degrees, and the Mets had a guy named Tim Teufle who just beat the Reds to death. They could've thrown the ball behind him, and he'd have hit it for a line drive. Dibble hit him with a fastball right in his numbers. It took his breath away. Both dugouts emptied, and there was some fighting and people got thrown out.

So now the game ends, and the phone rings in the Reds clubhouse. Charlton answers it, and it's Darryl Strawberry, and Strawberry wants a piece of Dibble. And Charlton says, "You're not going to have the opportunity to get a piece of Dibble, but you can have all of me you want." They were on their way to face off in the runway between the two clubhouses, but somebody had tipped off a couple of security guards and they made it go away before anything could happen. That was Charlton. You were going to have to go through him to get to anybody else.

He was like Don Drysdale, who'd bury a fastball in your ribs, and then walk halfway into home plate, so that if you wanted some of him you didn't have to come all the way out there. Opposing hitters might challenge Dibble, they would challenge Myers, but they wouldn't challenge Charlton.

He was one of the brightest guys on that team, too, but he didn't want people to know it. He was a baseball player through and through. It was a team full of bright guys: Barry Larkin, Hal Morris, Joe Oliver, Eric Davis, Todd Benzinger, Billy Hatcher, Paul O'Neill, Chris Sabo…. The list goes on and on.

My respect for Eric has done nothing but grow over the years. No matter all the teams he played for, he's a Red through and through. I felt for a long time that he was a soft player, susceptible to injury, that there were times when he could have gone out there and played and didn't. And yet he was smart enough to figure out what the new manager was all about, and he realized that he maybe had to go out and do some things he wasn't inclined to when he played for Pete.

I've said it before: Eric's as good a player as I've ever seen when he was at the top of his game. And I think that he saw in '90 as spring training unfolded that with the tweaking the front office had done—adding Hatcher, giving Mariano Duncan the second base job—that maybe he didn't have to go out there every night thinking he needed three hits and two home runs and a great defensive play for the club to win. And I think that was good for Eric, and that he saw it even more clearly when he went on the disabled list in May and saw the way the club continued to play and win without him.

If I ever write a book, I'm going to list my Top Ten favorite players, and a lot of it's going to have to do with guys who understood my job and didn't get all ticked off if I was critical of them. I'll never forget a time—it might have been '90, might have been after—the Reds were at Riverfront, and the other team was leading, 2–1. Davis leads off the ninth inning and hits the ball to right field, toward the line. When he left home plate, I'm sure he had the idea of going to second. He rounds first, the right fielder gets to the ball incredibly quickly,

and throws him out at second.

And I buried him on the air. "Bad play. You can't let yourself be the first out of the inning, and you can't be the last." And they wound up losing the game. The next day I'm in the clubhouse, and Eric comes up to me and says, "We need to talk." I say, "About what?" He says, "I heard what you said last night. What I did was right." I said, "No it wasn't." We stood there and argued for five minutes, but it never got heated. And finally I said, "Look, we could stand here from now until the cows come home. You think you made the right play, and I thought you made a bad play. You're not going to convince me otherwise, and I'm not going to convince you. Let's turn the page." And that was that. Next day, it was like nothing ever happened.

Ron Oester, same way. He played a huge role on that '90 team, even though he wasn't a starter. If you said something Oester didn't approve of, he'd come to you, rather than talking about you behind your back like most players do. I respected the heck out of those guys.

Talent-wise, Barry Larkin was off the charts. There wasn't anything he couldn't do. What he did on opening night in Houston—tripling off Charlie Kerfeld in the eleventh inning to win the game—set the stage for the rest of the year. As talented as Eric Davis and Paul O'Neill were, I think you have to have one guy that the team individually and collectively, consciously and subconsciously, rallies around. Sure, a successful team rallies around its manager—Lou's personality became the personality of the club—but you have to have one guy, at least one, who you as a team are going to follow, a guy who is going to play the game not only with the God-given abilities he has, but is also going to play the game the right way. Larkin was that guy. He played the game as brilliantly as any player who ever put on a uniform. He never made a mistake. He could run the bases, field and throw, hit for power. He intuitively understood how the game was meant to be played; he had the whole package. As time goes by, you realize how few teams today are as fundamentally sound as that team was. As a group, they rarely made a fundamental mistake.

Lou had an expectation of how good you should be as a player, and you may not agree with it, but more often than not he was right. The one guy that Lou eventually grew exasperated with—but in '90 was just trying to get the most out of out of—was Paul O'Neill. That's how O'Neill wound up with the nickname, "Big." It came from Lou, who called him that right to his face, in front of the other players: "Big Blanking Paul O'Neill." Lou believed Paul should be more of a run-producer, should pull the ball, should take advantage of that short porch in right field and hit home runs and drive in a lot of runs. But Paul was a guy who moved the ball all over the ballpark and was an outstanding hitter to begin with. He realized that Lou wanted him to do something he frankly did not want to do. Paul felt like he contributed to the club more by maintaining his approach at the plate. I give Paul credit: Despite his conflicts with Lou, he produced. He never went into a shell when it came to producing.

No team's ever won without a guy behind the plate who knew what he was doing. Joe Oliver impressed everybody early in the year with his ability to throw people out. It fell in line with every single aspect of that team. They played ball Lou's way: aggressively. Joe not only had the ability to throw, he had the *desire* to throw. A lot of guys have the ability, but for whatever reason they don't want to. The biggest single thing he did was develop a close relationship with the pitchers, and he did it quickly. They knew he was the man. They respected the fact that he was busting his ass on every pitch to make them successful. And he also had an outgoing personality—still has it today. He's one of my all-time favorite players. Pitchers loved pitching to him, and his teammates loved playing with him.

And those '90 Reds had role players. Lou would bring out the best in everybody. He would put you in situations where you could succeed. The bench players knew their roles; they knew the guys in front of them were better players.

Luis Quinones? Besides being a hell of a pinch-hitter that season, he was a character. When Reds traveling secretary Joel Pieper would come down to the clubhouse, Luis would shock him and make everybody in the clubhouse laugh by dancing naked in front of him. It became a ritual. Joel got a little gun-shy and would be looking to avoid Luis, but Luis would hide and pop out of somewhere just like he came into the world. Funniest thing I ever saw. And that was all part of 1990, too.

Well, sit back and enjoy. I hope you enjoy the season as much as I did. Keep reading—you're going to feel like you're there.

Introduction

by John Erardi and Joel Luckhaupt

JOHN ERARDI: The 1990 Reds were the first—and only—team that I was integrally involved with covering as a sports writer that went on to win it all.

I had watched the Big Red Machine in its best days when I serendipitously arrived in town as an *Enquirer* news intern in May 1974, but the only writing I did about that team came later, when its individual stars began being considered for Cooperstown.

Or, in the case of Pete Rose, who had been brought back to town in late 1984 to show the young players how to win and to "put some butts in the seats" and maybe ultimately run down Ty Cobb's all-time hit record, I chronicled with a book.

By 1985, I was a rookie sports writer, enticed from city-side to write about Rose's pursuit of Cobb, which is when I first learned—in March of that year, well ahead of almost everybody, I think—of Rose's betting on baseball from, of all people, Rose's own mother. She told me, off the record, that "Pete lost a bundle on the Padres in the (1984 World) Series."

I admired Rose the player because of the passion with which he played, and I felt the same way about Rose the manager because of the way he filled my notebook.

But, by the early summer of 1986, I thought he should have retired as a player and made way (and time) for the younger guys. By the time Lou Piniella arrived for the 1990 season, I was glad there was a new sheriff in town, fully invested, the guys in the muscle shirts gone and the playing of baseball again earnestly pursued to the exclusion of everything else. And I think that was liberating to the players, too, and that Piniella's passion was contagious, and that the players knew how good they were and that Lou gave them that little bit extra that made winning not only possible, but required.

What was it that coach Tony Perez told Piniella when Sweet Lou asked him upon first taking the job, "What do they need, Tony?" The Big Dog had answered, "They need to be pushed."

I didn't feel that Rose's Reds played bad baseball, just that Piniella's played it with fewer mistakes and more in-your-face intensity and with a deeper knowledge of what it took to win, all because Piniella had instilled that in them—not by osmosis but by hands-on tutelage.

History tells us that if you're a Reds fan, you will win a World Championship once every fifteen or twenty or thirty years. Once every generation, in other words (or, in the case of the Big Red Machine, twice).

If you're lucky to live long enough, you receive one in your youth, one in your adulthood, and one in your golden years. That seems just about right to me. It's enough to make you appreciate it, but not so often that you're spoiled by it. Then, every so often, the victors from your youth (or your adulthood) return as conquering heroes, and you get to re-live it all over again. And right about then is when you begin thinking: "Gee, I wonder if the Reds could win it all again?"

And here we are.

If you know a kid, you're probably thinking, it's time they got theirs. If you're an adult with some kid in you, you're likely thinking it's time you got another one. And if you're a codger, well, then, there's no question you're thinking, "Man, wouldn't it be great to see another one?"

In June of 2002, I remember standing on the turf at Cinergy Field with Piniella when he came in with his Seattle Mariners and I asked him what it meant to him to have won a World Championship here with the 1990 Reds, and he answered, "What it means to me is that it might be the only one I ever win."

He used those words not because he didn't feel he was capable of winning another one, but because the passage of years had made him fully appreciate how rare and special and magical that season really was.

Had the '90 team been able to stay healthy with Piniella at the helm, I believe they would have won another World Championship sometime again in the first half of the 1990s.

And if they had done that, they would be regarded not unfortunately and unfairly as one-year wonders, but as winners of the same number of World Series as the Big Red Machine.

Nonetheless, the 1990 Reds made for a great spring and summer, and most of all October, when championship baseball returned to the Queen City, and my then fifteen-month-old son, Chris, mysteriously climbed out of his crib on his own the night the Reds won the NLCS, and I remember saying to my wife, "Geez, I wonder what he'll do if the Reds win it all."

JOEL LUCKHAUPT: They say you never forget your first time. My first Reds championship was 1976, but you'll have to excuse me if I don't remember much of it. I was barely five months old when the Reds swept the Yankees that year. By the time I was old enough to have lasting memories, most of the Big Reds Machine had moved on to other teams.

In February of 2010, I had the great fortune to attend Reds Fantasy Camp in Goodyear, Arizona. The coach on my team was former Reds catcher Joe Oliver, who was a rookie with the 1990 squad and a personal favorite of mine on that team.

Standing in the on-deck circle during one of the games, Oliver asked me why I chose to wear the number 23 on my jersey. I told him that I wasn't completely sure, but I'd always liked the number since Hal Morris wore it for the Reds. I suppose it helped me feel connected to that team in 1990, my first real championship team.

The camp was filled with guys wearing #5, #8, #13, #14, and #24. It made sense. So many of these guys grew to love baseball with the Big Red Machine.

Growing up in the 1980s, I always thought of the Big Red Machine as a tall tale, a myth of exaggerated proportion. That's not to say they weren't a great team—clearly they were—but they might as well have been a team in a book about Paul Bunyan and Davy Crockett because I never saw them play. Legends lose a bit of their reality over time, especially if you only know them through the stories of others.

For me, the 1990 team was real. Sure they had a mythic feel to a kid my age—Eric Davis's talent was awe-inspiring from the first time I remember seeing him as a nine-year old in 1985. But I actually saw these guys play. I followed them throughout the season, checking box scores every morning in the *Enquirer*, watching their highlights on ESPN, and going to games at Riverfront Stadium whenever I could. I didn't need others' stories to learn about them. I got it first hand.

When John and I first started researching this book, I was surprised that so many of my favorite memories about the Reds when I was growing up happened in this season. On top of that there are dozens of great stories that I think many Reds fans may have forgotten about already. It's a shame because this team really was something special, but for so long it has been overshadowed by the legend of the Big Red Machine.

That's why I wanted to write this book with John. I felt like my championship team deserved its day in the sun, out from behind the massive shadow cast by the great teams of the seventies. It needs to be more than just a few anecdotes about a hard-throwing bullpen and a big World Series upset. It needs to be made real again.

1

Sweet Lou

She knew where to look (New York) and what to look for ("Somebody to make the players squirm.")

Mid-October 1989, Las Vegas

Lou Piniella was on the Strip with a buddy when the telephone call came. "It's the perfect team for you, Lou," said the voice on the other end. The voice was that of Bob Quinn, newly hired as general manger of the Cincinnati Reds. "Think about it and get back to me."

Piniella finished off his gambling and a while later called Quinn back. "I'm interested," he said.

Marge Schott had a kindred spirit in New York Yankees owner George Steinbrenner. He was an outsized personality, and he wasn't part of the old boys club. George did things his way. He made front office

people squirm, made his managers squirm, made the players squirm. Marge liked that last part best of all.

She wanted results.

And if she wasn't going to get results, she wanted the players at least to be uneasy about it. She wanted somebody to have a boot up their rear ends.

She wanted a tough guy.

It's why she was interested in Dallas Green, Pete Rose's former manager with the Phillies, where Rose had won his third World Championship ring in 1980.

Every time she asked somebody, "Who's the toughest guy in baseball? Who's the toughest SOB in double

Before Lou Piniella was recommended to Marge Schott by GM Bob Quinn,
she "didn't know him from a Puerto Rican rum drink."

Marge Schott turned to confidante George Steinbrenner in remaking the Reds' top brass.

knits?" the answer always came back the same.

Dallas Green.

Marge liked Pete Rose—"The Pete and Marge Show" she called it—but Pete wasn't tough enough. If she had known that every September Pete asked his players, one-by-one, "Got all your money?" she would have been livid. But that's what Rose did, remembers Herm Winningham. *Got all your money?* In other words, *Got all your incentives?*

If you needed more at-bats, more innings, more whatever to reach the numbers at which your incentive bonuses kicked in, Pete almost always tried to make sure you got them. And he almost always could, because the club was never still in the race in September. Yes, the players loved Pete; Pete always made sure they got their money.

They loved him for other reasons too: for his legend, for his humor, for his decency, for his very *ballplayer-hood.* And they loved him for the fact that he never played favorites. Well, except one, and that was back when he was a player-manager: Pete always played Pete.

But what was the big deal, anyway, the players wondered. It wasn't like Pete was costing the team a pennant by making sure that guys got their money. You would have to have been *in* the race for it to become an issue. Rose's Reds had finished second four straight times before dropping to fifth in 1989. There wasn't an honest-to-goodness September pennant race in the bunch, not for the Reds, anyway. And, yes, that ticked off Marge. Every year, the attendance plummeted when school went back in session, and the Bengals would get the big crowds on home Sundays.

Marge had been owner of the team since Christ-

1980S REDS BASEBALL: A DECADE OF COMING UP SHORT

Heading into the 1990 season, the Reds had played ten seasons without making it to the playoffs. After a decade that saw them make the playoffs six times, including four World Series, a ten-year drought seemed like an eon for most Reds fans. This drought was made worse by the way the Reds achieved their failure. Here is a rundown of each season of that frustrating decade of Redlegs baseball:

1980 After winning their first eight games of the year and thirteen of their first seventeen, the Reds stumbled through May and June. They managed to regain first place for a day in mid-August, but they couldn't hold it for long despite going 27–19 down the stretch. They finished in third place, 3.5 games back.

1981 The Reds finished the season with the best record in baseball, but the mid-season strike led to a ridiculous set of rules that kept the team, which finished both halves of the season in second in the NL West, watching the playoffs at home.

1982 The only Reds team to lose one hundred games in a season, this group finished last in the NL West, twenty-eight games out of first.

1983 A slight improvement in record (74–88) didn't soften another last-place finish for the fans.

1984 Another ninety-loss season was helped only by the return of Pete Rose as player/manager in mid-August.

1985 Led by the big bat of Dave Parker and rookie Tom Browning's twenty wins, and energized by Pete Rose's drive to break Ty Cobb's hit record, Reds baseball gets a big boost. Unfortunately, though they won eighty-nine games, they only managed to get within 5.5 games of the hated Dodgers by season's end and finished in second in the NL West.

1986 The addition of youngsters Barry Larkin and Kal Daniels as well as a breakout season by Eric Davis weren't enough to keep the Reds from taking a step back, winning eighty-six games and once again finishing in second place, this time to the Astros

1987 Daniels and Davis both had huge seasons and Paul O'Neill made his debut, but the Reds fell short again, winning eighty-four games and finishing six games behind the Giants in second place.

1988 In a year that most pundits thought would surely be theirs, the Reds sputtered through the first half and were just 42–45 at the All-Star break. A 45–29 record in the second half—the second-best record in the NL—left many feeling certain that the second-place finish was a prelude to a championship in 1989.

1989 A 21–15 start put the Reds 2.5 games in front by mid-May, and by mid-June they were still just a half-game out of first. By July, however, the Pete Rose gambling investigation had taken over the clubhouse, and by August injuries had crippled many key players. Two ten-game losing streaks in July and September killed any hope, and the Reds finished a disappointing fifth, seventeen games out of first place.

New GM Bob Quinn's "one and only" choice for manager was Sweet Lou.

mas of 1984, four and a half months after then-general manager Bob Howsam, architect of the Big Red Machine, brought Pete back to town to considerable fanfare to both manage the team and to break Ty Cobb's hit record if he could. But mostly to manage and to put—as Rose phrased it—"fannies in the seats" of a fallen franchise.

Marge thought she and Pete would go on forever and that eventually he would bring her a World Championship. *Wouldn't that be grand? Marge, Pete, and the return of the Big Red Machine. What could be a better legacy than that?*

Marge knew she never could have fired Pete. But Pete and Major League Baseball had done it for her, when he got in trouble for gambling. Then she fired general manager Murray Cook, just because she could, and went looking for a tough guy to manage her team.

Even George told Marge that Dallas Green was a tough guy.

Steinbrenner hadn't gone into all the details, naturally, but Green had stood up to him. It didn't get Green anything but fired, of course, but there was no shame in that. George unloaded managers like he unloaded .220 hitters.

And now that Marge had hired, on October 13, one of George's former GMs, Bob Quinn, she figured she'd get her guy now.

The Reds offered Green the job. The papers had it in their October 17 editions. Yes, Marge had read the story. She hadn't cared much for the headline: "Baseball Veteran 'Hesitant' About Becoming Manager." The reporter who had talked to Green had even called her the night before at home—she knew how those reporters worked, calling her after she'd had a couple vodkas, hoping she would sink some ships with her loose lips—but she hadn't given the guy a thing. She told the reporter, "No comment, sweetie," when the reporter told her what Green had said.

Green was concerned that Schott—although he hadn't called her out by name; he had referred to "The Reds"—would not spend the money necessary to build a winning ballclub. He knew the team had talent. "Might be the best in the league," he said. But the old lady wasn't talking about winning the league; she was talking about winning the whole enchilada. Did she know anything about the Oakland A's? Was she going to open her purse to sign a bopper for left field?

And did the reporter know that Marge was insisting upon some of the coaching staff being retained? She wanted to maintain the connection with the Big Red Machine. She wanted to make sure that one or two of those guys were on the coaching staff. Green hadn't liked hearing that. He wanted carte blanche to hire a whole new staff, if that's what was needed.

"I think they need to go in a little different direction if they want to turn it around," Green said.

And as if *that* wasn't enough, what really frosted Marge is when Green said that he was concerned about the "little people," the baseball lifers who were making thirty or forty grand a year and would lose their jobs, sometimes one or two at a time, sometimes all at once, whenever an owner did something on a whim.

"When things go wrong, the little people—the ones who really care—are the ones the owners want

to fire," Green said. "I don't like the heartache I see. I don't like the pain that it causes people. I don't know if I want to be part of it again."

What is he talking about, the little people? I want to win a World Championship, and this guy is talking about the little people?

The guy's lost it, George.

Who else you got? Got another tough guy?

❖ ❖ ❖ ❖ ❖

Louis Victor Piniella was born at Centro Espanol Hospital in West Tampa on August 28, 1943. He joined his parents and his mother's parents and two of his mother's brothers and his uncle's wife in the three-bedroom house in a Spanish and Italian section of town.

Tampa was a port city back then, a cigar center. Lou's mother worked as a secretary for a cigar company, and his father sold cigars, cigarettes, candy, and household drugs store to store. Lou's grandparents raised Lou, while his parents worked.

My parents, of course, spoke English, but neither of my grandparents did, and I spoke only Spanish until I went to school. The nuns taught me English, but boy it wasn't easy. My tongue always seemed to be in the wrong place!

Lou's father and two uncles played together on a baseball team. They played once during the week, and in doubleheaders on Sunday. Lou's father was a pitcher. One day, little Lou watched as big Lou shook off the catcher's signals four times. The catcher ran

Family man Lou was to Marge's liking. L to R, background, are Bob Quinn, Marge, Lou's son, Derek, and Lou's wife, Anita.

out to the mound, and Big Lou decked him.

Little Lou would have done the same thing. Chip off the old block. *Tough guy.*

Yes, the guy who Bob Quinn wanted all along, right from the get-go, was Lou Piniella.

"Marge didn't know Lou Piniella from a Puerto Rican rum drink," Quinn said later. "But that's who I wanted. Lou was the perfect fit."

Marge was the owner, however, and as longtime baseball executive Gabe Paul had taught Quinn,

"With ownership comes proprietary rights." Marge had wanted Dallas Green, and so Dallas Green was asked. And, yes, Quinn could have worked with Green. Hell, he had even recommended Green to Steinbrenner, and Green was hired as manager of the Yankees for four months until George fired him.

A reporter sat down with Quinn three days after he got the Reds' GM job and didn't even bring up the name of Piniella as a candidate. The guy asked about Green, Doc Edwards, Hal Lanier, and Dave Duncan, but he hadn't asked about Piniella. *How could he not have asked about Piniella?*

"Marge didn't know Lou Piniella from a Puerto Rican rum drink," Quinn repeated.

Piniella didn't know much about the Reds club. But the people he spoke with after talking with Quinn agreed that the Reds had talent. A lot of talent. And it was the right age. Young, but with major league experience, for the most part.

Maybe not quite as much as you'd like, Lou, but you can mold 'em. They finished second four straight years. Tough year last year, but you know all about Rose. You got Eric Davis, if you can re-sign him, and you've got Larkin, best shortstop in the National League. Can bat him anywhere, one through three. The pitching staff is good. You've got a good third baseman in Sabo if he's healthy, and Benzinger's your first baseman unless you want to move him to left. You've always liked Duncan; he'll be your second baseman. You've got a good-looking young catcher in Oliver, a good handler of pitchers. One more bat, and you're off to the races. It's your kinda club. Didn't you always say the perfect club was a young club, but one with some major league seasons under their belt? This is that club, Lou.

Piniella liked the sound of that.

He'd even be willing to take a slight pay cut from his personal services contract with George.

Word leaked out of New York that Piniella was the front-runner for the Reds job. Late last spring, Steinbrenner had blocked the Toronto Blue Jays from interviewing Piniella when they were thinking about firing Jimy Williams. George didn't want Lou managing against him in the division. But George didn't block Lou from talking with the Reds because George loved Lou like a son.

Piniella flew to Cincinnati on Monday, October 30, 1989, and was picked up at the airport and driven to Marge Schott's house in Indian Hill.

On the way through downtown, he saw Riverfront Stadium on the right side as he crossed over the Ohio River. He hadn't been inside Riverfront in a while, and it wasn't for long at that—only two games, in the 1976 World Series. He vividly recalled Don Gullett shutting down his Yankees in Game One. In Game Two, his buddy Catfish Hunter returned the favor for eight-plus innings, before Tony Perez knocked in Ken Griffey with the game-winner in the ninth.

Lou got in and out of town cleanly; nobody in the media spotted him.

The next night, Tuesday, Halloween, a reporter called Lou and asked if he had been offered the job yet.

Marge's St. Bernard, Schottzie, "sat in" on Lou's job interview.

Piniella confirmed that he had met with the Reds' "hierarchy." (Lou was fond of fine-sounding words and would drop them easily into interviews and conversations, which often meant quote marks in the morning paper and rich memories years later by his players.) He met with the "hierarchy" for four hours at an undisclosed location.

"It wasn't Dayton," Lou said.

The reporter asked: "Was a St. Bernard named Schottzie (one of Schott's dogs) at the meeting?"

Piniella paused and then laughed. "Next question," he said, chuckling again.

He wouldn't say if Marge Schott was at the meeting—she had obviously told him not to—but later said he was "impressed" with her.

"She's a proud lady," he said. "She's very interested in bringing a winner to Cincinnati. That's her number one priority."

After a few more questions about how much money he wanted and how long a contract, Lou excused himself.

"Trick or treaters at the door," he said.

In the next day's *Enquirer* there was a lengthy story about the meeting at Marge's house, and a locally bylined story that quoted two of Lou's former players in New York—Tommy John and Mike Pagliarulo—who said he would be an excellent hire for the Reds.

"He's a tough guy, a tough person, but he's not tough to play for," Pagliarulo said. "Everybody likes Lou. But you don't want a confrontation with Lou He'll back you down."

Perfect, thought Marge. Just don't try to back me *down, sweetie.*

❖   ❖   ❖   ❖   ❖

Marge loved the way Lou came across in the press conference in the Crosley Room at Riverfront Stadium on Friday, November 3. Tall, dark, handsome, impeccably clad in a double-breasted, blue-and-black tweed sports coat and red silk tie. Her kinda guy. Looked sharp. Well-spoken, obviously no stranger to the microphone.

Man's man, thought Schott. Ladies' man, too. Knew what he wanted, intended to get it, and would have fun along the way. He drank life in.

He also could deliver a line…and get a laugh.

"I like to look at myself as calm, cool, and collected," Piniella said. "And that's a bunch of bleep, too."

Only he didn't say "bleep," even though that was how he was quoted the next morning.

Piniella was known even then for his candor—not in a slam-bang Dallas Green way but for candor presented tactfully. Everyone liked that the new man actually answered this question: "How much money will you be making?" Piniella said he was taking a pay cut from his Yankee job. Mrs. Schott shook her head, as though to cut off that answer at the pass. *Too late.*

And he had a sense of history—Reds history. He was *connected*, you see?

"As a kid, I used to sneak over (to spring training) and the nuns used to scold me," he said. "The priests over at (Tampa) Jesuit used to scold me, too—the high school right down from Al Lopez Field."

Marge might have felt she hadn't gotten quite what she wanted ("I'm not a Marine drill sergeant from Camp LeJeune," Piniella said) but clearly she had gotten a lot.

She had found a lieutenant with knowledge, enthusiasm, and devotion to duty. All he lacked was experience.

He was, the thinking went, Tony LaRussa without the résumé. He and LaRussa had played ball together in Tampa. "The difference," Marty Brennaman would say twenty years later, "was that after their games, Tony would go home, and Lou would go out and raise some hell with his teammates." LaRussa was signed to a big bonus by Charlie Finley but never made it as a big-league star. Piniella did. LaRussa got a head start on managing. Piniella was still hitting (.302) as a forty-one-year-old in 1984.

A "professional hitter," the New York writers called him. A professional outfielder, too. "Best slow outfielder I ever saw," wrote Yankee teammate Sparky Lyle in his book, *The Bronx Zoo.*

A mere six years before taking the Reds job, Lou was still a player.

"It was like he was one of us," Barry Larkin remembers.

One of the guys, with many of the same vices. Later, when Piniella was talking to reporters after the press conference, Schott asked him if he wanted a cigarette. Sure, Piniella said. Schott came back with one of her Carlton longs. In Piniella's hands, it looked like one of Chi Chi Rodriguez's extra-long golf fees. "This (the cigarette-giving) is going to be expensive," Schott said. "Here we go," said a reporter. The new manager just laughed.

Yes, the new skipper and the lady owner were getting along famously. This Piniella guy really was a smoothie. Nobody wrote about it, but you just knew:

Revisionist history is that Piniella's awarding Mariano Duncan the second baseman's job before spring training was a no-brainer. In reality, a lot of people in the Reds front office and clubhouse backed veteran Ron Oester for the position.

During that four-hour day with the Reds' "hierarchy" at Marge's house the previous Monday, Marge had herself a vodka or two afterward, and Lou had joined her with Jack Daniels and water.

A guy you'd like to have a beer with.

Of course, Lou would have you up and running the next morning. At the press conference, he spoke the words that were music to Marge's ears. "The philosophy that these kids learn in the minor leagues [is] an erroneous one," Lou said. "We want coaches that can go out and teach these players. Because if players don't get the job done, they'll be out here working [during the day before night games]."

Now you're talkin', sweetie.

❖   ❖   ❖   ❖   ❖

Piniella told the media he was leaning toward naming Mariano Duncan the Reds second baseman, although he expected Ron Oester to give Duncan a battle.

Anointing Duncan was a bold move. Oester had hit .294 since the All-Star break in 1989, and Duncan had played only fifty-two games at second base in his major league career. In Los Angeles, he had been almost exclusively a shortstop, and in Cincinnati he had played mostly shortstop when Larkin went down with an elbow injury at the All-Star Game.

"I've liked Duncan ever since he came up with the Dodgers [in 1985]," Piniella said, "and from what I'm told, he is a player who is just coming into his own. I like his ability, and I like his speed. There's no doubt about it; Duncan can run. Stolen bases is one of the things you want from a guy like that."

Although Duncan had stolen only fifteen bases in 1989—in limited playing time with the Dodgers and slowed by a hamstring injury after coming to the Reds—he had stolen thirty-eight bags in 1985 and forty-eight in 1986.

Duncan, for one, was surprised to hear he had the edge over Oester.

"With two weeks to go in the ('89) season, Murray Cook told me Ron Oester would be the second baseman in spring training," Duncan said. "That's why I was so surprised to hear when Lou Piniella said what he did. Now, I just have to prove I am the man for the job."

He said the Reds had already told him they wanted him to make better contact and to run—he'd been a strikeout artist since turning professional—and that he would be playing winter ball in the Dominican Republic to get ready.

Some of the Reds players felt that bypassing Oester was a mistake.

"Ronnie is a guy we need out there every day," said Reds closer John Franco. "People don't understand. He does a lot of things for this team that just don't show up in the box scores. He is very important to this club."

Soon it wouldn't matter what John Franco thought.

2

New Season, New Decade, New Reds

Winter, 1989–90, Cincinnati
Even to this day, twenty years later, Lou Piniella and Bob Quinn don't talk openly about it. They knew from their time in New York that Mets' closer Randy Myers might be available. The Mets had soured on him. Too much weightlifting, they felt.

If the Reds traded for Myers, the Mets would need a closer in return.

"How about John Franco?" Quinn asked them.

"Let's talk," they said.

Piniella and Quinn wanted to change the culture of the Reds clubhouse. John Franco is well regarded in Cincinnati, well regarded in New York, and one day is going to get serious consideration for the National Baseball Hall of Fame.

He just happened to be in the right place at the wrong time when Pete Rose was banned from baseball and a new Reds general manager and manager wanted to put their own stamp on the ballclub. Clearly, Quinn and Piniella wanted to get people's attention—the players, the fans, even the owner, Marge Schott.

It couldn't be a minor addition. It had to be a sea change. Something that rocked the baseball world: *Didja see what they did in Cincinnati?* But, most importantly,

"He'd better be good."
– Marge Schott on Eric Davis after he signed a three-year contract.

it had to have a damn good chance of making the ballclub better—World Championship better.

On December 4, Quinn denied reports in the New York media that Franco was about to be traded there.

"Those rumors are absolutely and totally false," Quinn said. "We plan to make every effort to keep our people.... From our perspective, we are not shopping John Franco. We want to sign John Franco."

Two days later, Franco was traded to the Mets for Myers.

"It makes sense, now that I think about it," says former Nasty Boy Norm Charlton, twenty years later. "At the time, we just thought it was money. Randy made less than Johnny. But think about it. Lou did the same thing in Seattle [in 1993]. I know. I was there. We [the players] even talked about it among ourselves. You have to change the culture."

Initially, Charlton didn't like the trade for Myers. A lot of guys didn't like the trade.

"Johnny was a popular guy in the clubhouse," Charlton recalls. "He was good to me, had taken me under his wing, explained things to me. I liked him immensely. He was a good guy and a hell of a closer, and I was upset that he was traded. But you know what? Trading him for Myers allowed me and Dibs [Rob Dibble] to blossom. It allowed us to be the idiots we were. And it gave us a persona [the hard-throwing Nasty Boys]."

Enquirer baseball writer Greg Hoard opined on December 17, 1989, that "the nastiest story of the winter in the wake of the trade that sent John Franco to the Mets [is the] New York papers implying that

Reds brass made a statement by trading closer Johnny Franco.

the Reds dealt Franco to cleanse themselves of all remnants of the Pete Rose scandal."

Hoard wrote that "at one point last summer, Franco was implicated as Rose's go-between with a New York bookmaker. However, no official action was taken

Closer Randy Myers gave Reds "fresh blood"

fice or the commissioner's office or anybody that 'You need to trade Franco,'" Quinn recalls. "We had an opportunity to get a hard-throwing, left-handed closer who we knew might be available, and we took it."

For his part, Franco told Hoard, "I don't think that (the rumors) had anything to do with the trade at all.... I still think the trade was made because of money. Marge didn't say that, but Marge is Marge."

The team was under siege. There was a skeptical, even cynical, tone in the press. The four straight second-place finishes and the 1989 collapse had created an acerbic climate.

Almost all of the focus by the media was on the money part of the deal: Franco, who was twenty-nine, had made $1,067,500 for the Reds in 1989 and would command a salary of at least two million dollars in 1990 through arbitration. And he would be eligible for free agency after the 1990 season. Myers, who was twenty-seven, made $300,000 with the Mets in 1989.

No matter how many times Schott and Piniella and Quinn said that money had "nothing to do" with the Franco trade, there wasn't a single writer in town who appeared to believe it. The players certainly didn't. Only Paul O'Neill gave the new regime the benefit of any doubt when he said, "I hope it's not like that. When you start looking at things like that, people start wondering if you really want to win."

His teammates were less generous.

Danny Jackson: "I don't put Myers in Franco's category. He can be, but he isn't right now. For three and half years, Johnny was the best [closer] in the National

against him. In fact, former commissioner A. Bartlett Giamatti went out of his way to stress that the investigation revealed no links to Reds players."

Bob Quinn confirms that belief twenty years later. "I never received any word from the league of-

MYERS-FRANCO DEAL A TIT FOR A TAT

When the Reds traded John Franco for Randy Myers in December 1989, it seemed like an odd deal to make. Franco had just finished third in the National League with thirty-two saves. His third straight year of thirty or more saves, including a league-leading thirty-nine in 1988.

Myers, on the other hand, had only just become the Mets primary closer in 1989 after sharing the duties with Roger McDowell in 1988 and had never saved more than twenty-six games in a single season.

Saves are just a surface statistic, however, and when you look deeper at the numbers, the comparison is much more favorable for Myers.

1987-1989	IP	ERA	WHIP	SO/9	BB/9	HR/9
John Franco	248.2	2.39	1.22	6.0	3.3	0.4
Randy Myers	227.1	2.69	1.22	9.9	3.4	0.6

At twenty-nine, Franco was coming off his worst season for strikeouts, walks, WHIP, and ERA since his rookie year in 1984. Relief pitching can be highly volatile and unpredictable—relievers notoriously fall hard off the cliff when they go bad. The Reds could have been concerned by what they saw from Franco in 1989, even if they'd never admit it, especially given the career that Franco went on to produce.

At three years younger and after being more effective in 1989, Myers looked like the better choice for the future, and that's not even taking their salaries into consideration. Probably the most attractive statistic for Myers over Franco was the strikeouts. He was just as effective, but he didn't depend as much on his defense to get tough outs. That's a very nice quality to have in a closer.

The new Reds regime may have been trying to change the culture during the 1990 off-season, but they weren't taking a serious downgrade to do it. In fact, both pitchers ended up being very effective in 1990, but history shows that the Reds made the right move for their squad.

League and one of the two or three best in baseball."

Chris Sabo: "It seems pretty obvious what the intent was. Why do you trade the best [left-handed reliever] for another left-hander? Sure it's obvious what they are doing. It's money; that's all it is."

Barry Larkin: "What did we get, a lefty for a lefty? I think it's pretty obvious what's going on. I will let the obvious speak for the obvious. I don't want to say too much because I'm not signed either."

Even former manager Pete Rose weighed in: "[Myers] can throw hard, but he doesn't have the same ability to get right-handers out [as the screwball-throwing Franco]." Rose added that Myers was a left-handed version of Rob Dibble and would have to be alternated with Dibble as the closer instead of being given the job exclusively.

Rose and Franco were *simpatico*.

"I'm surprised," Rose said. "Dibs can't pitch a lot. He has too much herky-jerky wear on his arm. Every year he's played ball, he's had a sore arm. It's bad mechanics."

In the end, though, it was only Myers who nailed it.

"It seems there may be more of a commitment to winning than there has been in the past," he said. "Maybe I shouldn't say more commitment, but they are definitely taking a different tack toward winning, a different line and approach. To trade a player of Franco's caliber proves that."

On December 12, Cincinnati's New York boys, Quinn and Piniella, got another New Yorker, a young, promising left-handed hitter named Hal Morris, in exchange for pitcher Tim Leary.

Everybody's a critic, though, when the home team can't get over the hump.

Why hadn't the Reds packaged Franco and Tim Leary to get a power hitter, asked Danny Jackson.

"Joe Carter would have been excellent," he said. "Now, he's been traded to San Diego."

Power alone, however, wasn't what Quinn and Piniella were after.

"The Yankees had this guy at first base named Mattingly," Quinn recalls. "We knew Hal wasn't going to displace Don Mattingly. So the Yankees asked what we had for starting pitching, and we traded them Tim Leary. They received a good pitcher. He immediately joined their starting rotation. But we felt we had a pretty deep starting staff and were getting a good young hitter in return. Lou knew Hal; he had worked with him."

Piniella knew Morris could hit.

"Morris will hit sixth for us, and Larkin will lead-off," Piniella told the *Enquirer*. Then later he said, "Preferably, I'd hit Larkin second."

Still later he told the newspaper that Duncan would be the Reds leadoff hitter.

None of that would wind up happening; Piniella was—and is—a fisherman.

"Always a bridesmaid, never a bride," is what Larkin recalls—to this day—Schott saying back then.

Yeah, why never a bride?

Danny Jackson wondered why the Reds hadn't packaged Franco and Leary to get a power hitter.

"That's what we need anyway, that guy that's going to be there all the time," Jackson said. "Joe Carter would have been excellent. Now, he's [already been traded to] San Diego."

Power alone, however, wasn't what Quinn and Piniella were after.

"The Yankees had this guy at first base named Mattingly," Quinn recalls. "We knew Hal wasn't going to displace Don Mattingly. So the Yankees asked what we had for starting pitching, and we traded them Tim Leary. They received a good pitcher. He immediately joined their starting rotation. But we felt we had a pretty deep starting staff and were getting a good young hitter in return. Lou knew Hal. He had worked with him."

"Morris will hit sixth for us, and Larkin will lead-off," Piniella told the Enquirer.

Then, at another point, Piniella told the *Enquirer* "preferably, I'd hit Larkin second."

At another point, he told the *Enquirer* that Mariano Duncan would be the Reds leadoff hitter.

None of that would wind up happening; Piniella was—and remains—a fisherman.

He said the team would be about three things: First, pitching; second, speed; and third, hitting.

On January 7, the Reds signed Eric Davis to a three-year $9.3 million contract.

The Reds had signed their power hitter. All's well that ends well.

Or was it?

Davis had ticked off some fans. Nothing new there, nothing intentional, but good ol' E.D. seemed to have a way of doing that. But this time he also ticked off some of his teammates, most notably Tom Browning, which was like ticking off everybody.

It happened when Davis suggested that the Reds needed to sign another hitter to protect him in the batting order.

Hold on a cotton-pickin' minute, Browning responded.

"How does [Davis] think it makes someone like Paul O'Neill feel—or any of his other teammates feel—who hit behind him last year?" Browning asked. "Not too good, I wouldn't think."

Then Browning brought up what everybody on the team knew to be an open sore.

"The thing he doesn't realize is that this is costing him [stature in the community]," Browning said. "I've known Eric since 1982. He's a good guy. He worries about not being received by the fans like he thinks he should, and not getting his due. Well, things like this don't help."

For his part, O'Neill tried to remain above the fray.

"I don't know what to say," he said. "I don't know if it was pointed at me or not. If it was, what can I say? I don't want to cause any conflicts of any kind on the team. We don't need that. I read what he said, but I'm taking it with a grain of salt."

Enquirer columnist Tim Sullivan wrote the next day that Davis wasn't making an unreasonable request:

DAVIS'S LARGE CONTRACT WAS WELL-DESERVED

In his first five seasons in the majors, Eric Davis had proven to be an elite talent within the league, though many fans weren't comfortable considering him an elite player. For one thing, the Reds had not managed to finish any higher than second place in the National League West while Davis was with the team. For another, Davis was labeled a "soft" player because of his inability to stay in the lineup due to injury, regardless of the fact that his injuries were often due to diving on the rock-hard turf or slamming into the walls in the outfield.

Despite Cincinnati's love-hate relationship with their center fielder, Davis's résumé through 1989 was indisputable:

- He was a lethal combination of power and speed. He and Rickey Henderson are the only players to ever hit twenty-five home runs and steal eighty bases in the same season when they both did it in 1986. In 1987, Davis became the only player to hit thirty-five home runs and steal fifty bases in the same year.
- Furthermore, as of the start of the 1990 season, he was the active leader in both slugging percentage at .530 and stolen base percentage at 86.9%.
- He had won three consecutive Gold Gloves in center field. Also he had won a Silver Slugger and was an All-Star two out of the three previous years.
- He finished in the top fifteen in MVP voting for four straight years.

- From 1986 to 1989, he batted .281/.377/.537 and averaged thirty-one home runs, ninety-one RBI, and forty-seven stolen bases. Impressive numbers considering he only averaged 132 games a season over those years.
- Even advanced metrics that have only recently been developed see Davis's tremendous value at the time. Wins Above Replacement (WAR), which estimates the number of wins a player contributes to his team taking into account both offense and defense, rated Davis as the eleventh most valuable player in the majors from 1986 through 1989. More importantly, though, Darryl Strawberry and Barry Bonds were the only players of higher value who were younger than Davis.

That last point is probably the biggest key to why Davis deserved the big contract. He was only twenty-seven years old when the season started, just moving into his prime. It was reasonable to expect Davis to continue to blossom, or at least maintain his level of performance for two or three more years. As Pete Rose put it, "If he has the type of year he's capable of having in 1990, he could have signed for four million a year, anywhere he wanted."

This is why Marge Schott felt it necessary to lock up Davis prior to the season even though he wasn't eligible for free agency until after the 1990 season. Despite her objections that other owners were "nuts" for giving out such exorbitant salaries, she knew that to be competitive, she had to be willing to spend on her best players. And it's hard to deny that Eric Davis was not only the Reds best player at the start of 1990 season, but also one of the best players in all of baseball.

"If Davis did not seek assurances that the Reds would continue to compete for talent, he would have shown Schott a blind loyalty she has not earned."

While that was true, it neglected the bigger point Browning was making: *It's our team, Eric. The team comes first. Don't insult your teammates.*

The players on that team possessed an exceptional closeness that no one outside the team realized. One could disagree about the best way to make a team better—yes, certainly, use whatever leverage you have—*but we need Paulie. Don't disrespect Paulie.*

Davis said he wasn't disrespecting anybody. But his comments in the paper a day earlier seemed to contradict that statement. He sought to rectify it.

"My comments were directed to a vacant spot that we have on the field," Davis said. "Paul's the right fielder, and I'm the center fielder, and we have to have another outfielder to make an outfield. We don't have a left fielder."

Better.

And really, that's all that Browning wanted him to say.

What Davis didn't realize was this: Piniella and Quinn were already looking for a left fielder.

Right from the get-go of the New Year, notice was served that the shadow of the Big Red Machine was still out there. Not that anybody doubted it. If you were a part of Reds Country, you knew what was the greatest team ever assembled, certainly the greatest group of position players that ever walked on a ball diamond. And it wasn't like the guys were ghosts. They continued to make news.

Why just last season—the very year that Pete Rose was banned from baseball—Johnny Bench was elected to the National Baseball Hall of Fame, by a whopping 96.4% of the vote, at the time the third-highest percentage ever, behind only Ty Cobb and Henry Aaron, far surpassing the 75% minimum required for election.

Next up, everybody knew, was Joe Morgan in early January 1990. Many felt Morgan would be a first-ballot electee.

When Ken Griffey Sr. had heard the previous season that Morgan wasn't sure if he would be elected on the first ballot, Senior had doubled over in laughter.

"You tell Joe Morgan that isn't the guy I used to know," Griffey Sr. said. "The Joe Morgan I knew didn't have any doubts about his ability—or how good anybody thought he was."

Lou Piniella knew all about the Big Red Machine, having played for the New York Yankees team that got swept by them in the 1976 World Series.

On January 9, Little Joe was elected to the National Baseball Hall of Fame on the first ballot, with 81.8% of the vote.

Piniella wasn't whiling away the time at his home in New Jersey.

He procured TV footage of last season's Reds games and watched to see who was doing what. Who swung

Marge and fans loved having former Big Red Machine stars like Joe Morgan and Johnny Bench around the ballpark.

at bad pitches? Who didn't take enough pitches? Did the leadoff hitter work the count? Were the hitters moving guys over by hitting behind the runners? Which runners could he put in motion? Could the middle-of-the-order guys get their bats on the ball? Who could get a runner in from third? How'd they go about doing that? Which outfielders hit the cutoff man? Who had the strongest arms? Could the catcher throw? Who were the most aggressive base runners? Were the Reds running enough? Could they run more? Which guys could handle the bat on the hit-and-run?

Piniella was disturbed by how much the Reds struck out—1,028 times to be exact, second most in the NL. Piniella knew that strikeouts were a part of the game. Power hitters, in particular, were prone to

whiff a lot. But the Reds didn't have many power hitters. *What was with all the whiffs?* You can't press the action if you're striking out. Piniella wanted to press the action. He could tell by watching the Reds run the bases that when they were healthy they had some burners. *Really, what was with all the whiffing?*

"Channel the ball up the middle or right-center or left-center," Piniella told Hal McCoy of the *Dayton Daily News.* "I have to make 'em aware that a ground ball to short with a man on third, with the infield back, will get a run in. A strikeout just strands a runner. They have to be aware of the game situation as opposed to just going up there and hitting.

"Hey, this club has some talent," he said. "We have some power (Davis, O'Neill). We have some contact

SALARIES WERE JUST BEGINNING TO BOOM IN 1990

On January 7, 1990, Eric Davis signed a three-year $9.3 million contract to remain with the Cincinnati Reds through the 1992 season, buying out his first two years of free agency. The contract represented the largest single contract in Reds history at that point. If it had been signed just two months earlier, it would have been the largest average annual salary a player had ever received. As it happened, at least five other players had signed larger average annual salary contracts by the time the 1990 season started. Davis, who was paid $2.1 million in the first year of the contract, wound up as the twelfth- highest paid player in 1990 and moved up to fifth-highest, single-season salary in 1991. However, by 1992 he was no longer even in the top twenty-five in baseball for single-season salary.

Such were the times in 1990. After suffering through some financial struggles in the early 1980s, baseball was awash in money when the 1990s started. Just over a year earlier, CBS had purchased the rights to broadcast weekly Major League Baseball games and the playoffs for a whopping $1 billion over four years. The contract with CBS represented a nearly $70 million a year increase over the previous contract that had been split between NBC and ABC. The CBS deal, along with an influx of money from burgeoning local cable sports networks, meant that owners had more money than ever, and the players knew it. The vast amount of money, combined with the punishment owners received for colluding to control salaries in the mid-eighties, left the players with more negotiating power than they'd ever had. This is why between February 1989 and the end of the 1990 season, Major League Baseball saw eleven players sign contracts that were the highest average annual salary at that point in time. It was the dawn of a new age in baseball contracts.

For the most part, the Reds had managed to avoid being overwhelmed by large contracts in 1990. Thirty-year-old Tom Browning was the highest paid player on the Reds at $2.125 million, good for ninth in baseball, but Davis and Danny Jackson ($1.15 million) were the only other millionaires on the roster. The lack of large contracts was mainly a side effect of the Reds having such a young squad. Browning, Rick Mahler, Ken Griffey, and Ron Oester were the only players on the roster with enough major league service time to qualify for free agency. This is how a team paying three players nearly $5.5 million can still maintain a team payroll of just under $15 million.

The Reds $14.8 million payroll was the twentieth-largest payroll in the majors in 1990. Oh how the times have changed since then. When you adjust for inflation, the 1990 Cincinnati Reds were paid just about $24.5 million, which is slightly more than 2009 Reds closer Francisco Cordero ($12 million) and starter Aaron Harang ($11 million) made combined. The highest paid player in the game in 2009, Alex Rodriguez, made $8.5 million more than the entire World Champion roster in 1990, even after adjusting for inflation.

People were flabbergasted by the large salaries that were being doled out in 1990, but as we've since learned, it was merely the tip of the very large iceberg.

hitting, we have some good speed. It is just a question now of fine-tuning this thing and getting it into a winning, cohesive situation. I've seen a lot of teams with talent that don't win and there are reasons for it."

The annual Reds caravan kicked off from Cincinnati with Piniella announcing that 1990 was going to be a different story for the Reds—and that Reds fans were going to like the ending.

"There's going to be some butt-kicking in the NL West this year, and it's not going to be Cincinnati's butt whose butt is going to get kicked," said Piniella, to whistles and hurrahs.

He also repeated a line that he first used in December that received a laugh when somebody asked him what he thought it was going to be like managing in the National League for the first time.

"It's not like I'm going to Russia to teach ice hockey," he said.

Also on the caravan, Rob Dibble came out throwing heat, this time against his former manager.

"For Pete Rose to always tell me to my face that he

could use me out of the bullpen as often as he wanted to and could count on me...and now to say behind my back what he did in the paper about me being herky-jerky and having 'bad mechanics' is like a stab in the back."

"One full year," said O'Neill on the caravan. "That's all that I ask."

He had been a major leaguer for two seasons now, but still didn't have a year that he had played start to finish and put up 530 at-bats. Last year, he had to rehab a broken left thumb and was sent to Nashville. The previous year he was stymied in the first half because he was platooned with Tracy Jones.

"I just want to be an everyday player, a guy that can help this team day-in and day-out," O'Neill said. His patience would be rewarded in 1990.

Meanwhile baseball fans would have to be patient as they awaited word on whether the lockout could be avoided and the spring training camps opened on time. Everyone was eager for baseball to begin, especially Lou Piniella and his new team.

 *FAST FACTS*

- With his twenty-four home runs and twenty-one stolen bases in 1990, Eric Davis became the first Reds player to post five consecutive twenty-twenty seasons.
- Randy Myers led all NL relief pitchers in 1990 with the most appearances of at least one inning without surrendering a run. Myers did that in forty-eight of sixty-six appearances. Rob Dibble was third in the NL with forty-two such appearances.
- Lou Piniella's teams were a combined 889–858 (.509 winning percentage) in games that he played in during his eighteen seasons.

3

Spring Training

Like everybody else, the Reds had only three and a half weeks to get ready for the season. Would their youth help or hinder them?

Jack Armstrong had already made up his mind. No way was he was missing his big league opportunity this time, player lockout be damned. The twenty-four-year-old from New Jersey took out a five-thousand-dollar bank loan, and with his wife and new baby he headed to Florida looking for somebody, anybody, with whom to throw.

He had been the Reds' number one draft choice three years earlier, June 1987, the same year the movie *The Color of Money*, starring Tom Cruise and Paul Newman, hit the big screen. And now the thought occurred to him—he was a hustler, a baseball hustler.

He began his quest in late February in Bradenton, longtime spring home of the Pittsburgh Pirates franchise, but there were no Pirates to be found, of course, just the Explorers of the Senior League, consisting of many former major leaguers, one of whom was bullpen catcher Randy Ladd.

"He took more flak than anybody," Armstrong told the *Enquirer*'s Mike Paolercio. "Why? Because he

Jack Armstrong was determined to make 1990 special, even before Spring Training started.

was willing (to work with Armstrong). I was kind of a challenge for him."

Armstrong then moved on to West Palm Beach, and finally to Plant City, home of the Reds, but there were no Reds there yet, so he sought out high school and college teams.

"I'd be driving around looking for some kind of baseball going on," he said, "and I'd walk over and say, 'You guys need a pitcher?' I'd start out lobbing my pitches until I got loose, then I'd go through (catcher's) gloves one by one. I was like the Paul Newman of the pitcher's mound."

A reference, of course, to Newman's Fast Eddie Felson character in the movie *The Hustler* (and later with Cruise as his pool-hustling protege in *The Color of Money*, gradually going through billiard players, not quite showing everything he had, just so he could stay "in the action" and eventually set up the big score.)

Armstong had to feed not only himself on that five grand but his wife and baby as well.

"I'll tell you, an eleven-pound boy goes through (a lot of) Similac, and we're not even talking about Huggies," he said.

Armstrong swore that at one point his little guy went through forty-four disposable diapers in only two days. We're not sure exactly what was going on, but the kid either had a serious case of the runs or was maintaining a shinier tush than the babes in *Sports Illustrated*'s swimsuit issue.

"I said the heck with this," Armstrong recalled, "(and I went to the supermarket) and loaded up two grocery carts full of Huggies. Everybody was laughing at me. I think I spent four hundred dollars."

But the new dad knew this: When the lockout ended, his son would have the softest butt in Florida, and dad would have the strongest arm.

One week before the first Reds players arrived in Plant City to begin informal workouts at the Plant City High School baseball field—always during school hours so there was no conflict—the Sean Connery-Alec Baldwin movie based on Tom Clancy's first novel opened at 1,225 theaters, including the Plant City Premiere Cinema 8.

It's title? *The Hunt for Red October*. It would become a catch phrase for the team later in the year, as the Reds hunted for their own long-awaited October success.

Tom Browning was on the tee of the eighth hole, a par four along the road, when he saw a car pull over and a strong-looking, well-tanned man with a big smile on his face begin walking toward the tee.

One other member in the foursome was up in the front of the tee with Browning. The other two guys were farther back on the tee, obscured from the road by tall palmetto bushes.

"Tom, Lou Piniella," the man said with a grin, holding out his right hand, which Browning shook firmly.

"Lou, how ya' doin'?" said Browning.

Browning knew something Piniella didn't; it made the pitcher very uneasy.

After Lou shook Browning's hand, he turned and saw…

THE LOCKOUT

The 1990 season stalled before it even started as the owners and the Player's Association reached an impasse while negotiating a new collective bargaining agreement. The previous collective bargaining agreement had expired with the final out of the 1989 World Series, and neither side wanted to work without a contract in place in 1990.

The prior agreement had been negotiated in 1985, and the players promptly saw the owners collude against them on the free agent market and agree to cut rosters from twenty-five to twenty-four players in order to save money. Of all of the issues on the table, the main one was trust. The players no longer trusted the owners to follow through on their agreement, which hardened their stance and made the negotiations much more contentious.

There were two main technical issues on which they could not reach an agreement, and both concerned salary arbitration. In the 1985 agreement, the players had surrendered a year of eligibility before a player could go to arbitration, pushing it from two years to three. The move was intended to help the owners, who were struggling financially. However, by 1990, the owners were no longer suffering from the same financial woes, and the players wanted to return the arbitration eligibility to two years. The owners would not oblige.

In fact, the owners wanted to put even more constraints on the arbitration process. They wanted to cap the maximum raise a player could receive through arbitration at 75 percent. In the prior off-season, players in arbitration had collectively received a 98 percent increase in salary. The owners felt that arbitration was more responsible for the dramatic escalation in player salaries than free agency. As they have done throughout history, the players fought any form of a cap on salaries.

The distance between the two groups led to the third player lockout in Major League Baseball history and the seventh work stoppage since 1972. The lockout delayed the start of spring training by thirty-two days, shortening camps to just two and a half weeks, from the normal six and a half, and pushing back the start of the regular season a week. The result was a collective bargaining agreement that created "Super Two" arbitration eligibility for players in the top 17 percent of service time with under three years of total service time. It also raised the league minimum salary from $68,000 to $100,000 and raised the owners' annual contribution to the player pension fund from $39 million to $55 million.

Reds player representative Danny Jackson came away from the experience mentally exhausted, saying, "There were no winners or losers. Everyone was a loser. The ones that lost the most were the fans. They're missing baseball."

The result of the lockout, however, would not be felt for another four years, as the trust between the players and owners continued to deteriorate and led to the much more damaging strike in 1994 that saw the cancellation of the playoffs and World Series.

Pete Rose.

The former Reds skipper, banned from baseball, was in the foursome.

Browning remembers thinking he would rather be anywhere than here right now.

"The whole atmosphere changed," he remembers. "When Lou turned after shaking my hand, he saw Pete, and their eyes locked. It was a very awkward moment. But what happened next surprised me."

"Pete, how ya' doin'?" Piniella said.

"Hello, Lou," said Pete, managing a smile.

"Pete, maybe some time I could sit down with you and talk about your team."

And that is when Browning knew.

Piniella, a man renowned for his fiery temper and antics on the field, had totally defused the tension. He had grace and charm, and he was quick on his feet.

At times, he might repeat a word several times to start a sentence, much like Eric Davis, who had stuttered as a child (and he would repeat a word to relax his vocal muscles), but Piniella did it while his mind was turning a mile a minute.

"That's the day I learned about Lou's vernacular," Browning remembers. "His vernacular was unbelievable. He had a good vocabulary for a ballplayer. You could tell he had worked at it a little bit somewhere along the way."

Enjoy the round, Piniella told Browning.

And then, to himself: *You won't be playing any more golf after spring training.*

On Sunday night, March 18, the lockout was over.

Camps would open Monday; the first "official" workout for the Reds would be Wednesday. On Monday, March 19, the first players trickled into camp in Plant City. The eight who arrived that day were Browning, Barry Larkin, Paul O'Neill, Joe Oliver, Rob Dibble, Jack Armstrong, Rolando Roomes, and Mike Roesler. The Plant City High School boys.

They were rarin' to go.

The next day, more showed up. Among the new arrivals was Ken Griffey Sr., taking batting practice in bright Hawaiian print shorts.

The Reds equipment truck hadn't yet arrived from Cincinnati, but players were working out in their own shorts and T-shirts, taking batting practice bareheaded or in their golf- and ball-caps.

"Tomorrow I hope we'll be looking like a big league baseball team," said Piniella, loud enough for Griffey to hear, and they both laughed.

They'd been Yankees teammates. The Yankees had done pretty well raiding the Big Red Machine, getting pitcher Don Gullett in 1976, and Ken Griffey Sr. in 1981. If you can't beat 'em, buy 'em. Lou and Senior had been teammates from 1982 to 1984, and Lou had managed Griffey during the first half of the '86 season.

Some of the younger players on the Reds—everybody on the Reds was younger than Griffey—asked "Gramps" what they might expect from Piniella.

"He's a straight shooter," Griffey told them. "You will know where you stand with him."

Griffey had been the Yankee left fielder for four

seasons—with two years to go on the contract that had lured him from the Reds—when Piniella told him that Dan Pasqua was taking over in left field.

"I knew the decision had been made in the front office, and Lou was carrying out orders," Griffey told Ritter Collett of the *Dayton Daily News*. "I appreciated Lou coming straight out with it. We wound up talking about it for maybe three days. He listened to me. He could have hemmed and hawed like a lot of managers, but he was honest with me."

Griffey told his Reds teammates to get ready to run, because that's the way Billy Martin had managed the Yankees, and Lou was a disciple of Martin.

"Billy didn't wait for things to happen," Griffey said. "A lot of thinking in the American League is to wait for the three-run homer. Martin had his guys running, trying to scramble for a run every time he had an opening."

Lou would push the action. It was a style that stood out in the American League, Griffey said, but would stand out less in the NL.

"I learned a lot from Billy," Piniella said. "I liked Billy. Liked him a lot. I liked the way he managed. He was very aggressive, and the players knew he was on their side. And he really understood the game. He hated to lose and I hate to lose.

"But don't look for me to be kicking dirt on umpires."

We'll see, thought some of the writers.

Piniella laughed when Collett told him that Griffey had described how Lou would bait the um-

pires in his Yankee days to get himself thrown out of the game.

"People may not understand there comes a time when you have to get yourself thrown out," Piniella responded. "You're making a point to motivate your players. But let's get this upfront—umpires do not win or lose ballgames for you. When we get a bad call, I'm not afraid to run out there and let them know. Most of the time, you have to go out to back up your players when something happens."

One thing you can count on, Griffey told the younger Reds, your new manager *will* have your back.

He would have *everybody's* back.

There would be no turds on the '90 Reds.

Turds. That's what Big Red Machine manager Sparky Anderson had called the players back in the day whose names weren't Rose, Bench, Morgan, and Perez.

Then, again, Piniella didn't have any Roses, Benches, Morgans, or Perezes.

"Once Lou got to see how close we were and what kind of chemistry we had," recalls Herm Winnigham, twenty years later, "he let everybody know their roles. You got the eight starters, it's a given. He let the rest of us know our roles. There was no star treatment. We were all in it together. That part was very clear from day one."

Three days later, Griffey walked into the Plant City clubhouse to find his cubicle filled with early birthday "gifts." A black T-shirt that read: "This is what 40 looks like." An aluminum walker. A bottle of "Over The Hill" pills. Samples of Polident, Metamucil, arthritic pain relievers, and Ben-Gay. Griffey was turning "Four-Oh" April 10, the day after Opening Day.

"Here," he said, handing the walker to Reds trainer Larry Starr. "Some of the young guys might need this."

Starr got the joke. A lot of those young guys had been on the disabled list last year, while Griffey was racking up 236 at-bats, way more than he expected. Every day somebody else was out of the lineup. Not Griffey. Gramps just kept on ticking.

March 21, Plant City

With a new manager in place and the Pete Rose scandal behind them, the Reds hoped for a fresh start in 1990. As Collett noted in the *Dayton Daily News*, "The atmosphere at the Plant City complex would be improved over last spring even if Mickey Mouse was in charge."

But even without "the mob of media strangers" stalking Pete Rose who was under investigation by Major League Baseball in the spring of '89 for his gambling habits, spring training had always had that Rose-colored flavor.

In the years Rose managed the team, he was the dominant figure. The players—even the standouts such as Davis, Tom Browning, and Barry Larkin—seemed to be in Pete's shadow. That wasn't by Rose's design, but when you have one of the all-time great players and a man who knew how to use the media, it was inevitable he would be front and center.

"Gramps" Griffey told young Reds what to expect from Sweet Lou.

"I think it's the manager's role to be in the background as much as possible," Piniella said. "Sure, the writers need to talk to the manager. But the players deserve to be the center of attention."

Because Piniella was a native of nearby Tampa

Tom Browning liked Piniella putting the players first.

season. He barely knew most of them. But he didn't seem worried about it. He felt confident. How could that feeling not radiate to the players?

Lou felt like a free man. He wanted the players to feel the same way, and he sensed that they would.

"I'm very relaxed here," he said "There's no tension. But there will be pressure to win. I'm not foolish enough to think I'll survive if the club doesn't win."

It was all about winning. Nothing was secure without winning. Unlike Rose, Piniella didn't have a lifetime contract.

"I didn't come here just to say I'm a major league manager," Piniella said, his dark eyes flashing. "I'm here to prove I can put a winning team on the field that can go into postseason play. It's important to me. Very important."

He made that clear. It was also clear that he was concerned about Eric Davis and Randy Myers, neither of whom had shown up yet.

"We need them here," Piniella said.

March 22, Plant City

Most of the position players, and many of the pitchers, who now gathered around Piniella, had come through the minors together and had played for Pete Rose for a year or two—or, in the case of Eric Davis, Tom Browning, and Ron Oester, even longer—and they were mostly young. They were all close.

If Piniella intended to win the World Championship, you would have had to go back twenty-one years to the Miracle Mets of 1969 to find a World Champion

and was of Spanish ancestry, local writers were interested in him personally, but the Reds writers and national media couldn't have cared less. The focus was on baseball, and the writers wanted to know what Piniella was going to do to get his players ready for the

with a younger group of hitters than the '90 Reds.

Based on a weighting of plate appearances, the Reds' average age on offense was 27.5 years old. Only the Atlanta Braves, who lost ninety-seven games, had a younger offensive NL squad that season. The Reds didn't have a starter in their regular lineup over twenty-nine.

The pitching staff was young too. At twenty-nine, Browning was the oldest pitcher in the rotation on Opening Day. Norm Charlton, Rob Dibble, and Randy Myers were twenty-seven, twenty-six, and twenty-seven, respectively.

Many of the Reds players had been scouted, signed, and developed under the scouts of the legendary Big Red Machine architect Bob Howsam and been trained in "the Reds way" by Howsam's minor league managers and assistants. Five of the eight position starters (Eric Davis, Barry Larkin, Chris Sabo, Paul O'Neill, and Joe Oliver) were homegrown, a high number. All were in their prime or about to enter it.

Myers, who wasn't a member of any of those fraternities, was the last to arrive to camp, late in the morning. He had been headed for a snowmobiling trip to Mount Saint Helen's when the lockout ended.

But he did share one bond with his new teammates.

He knew he was good.

He had gotten his confidence from elsewhere. Most of the Reds had their natural-born confidence topped off by Rose, who had more than enough for everybody. Catcher Joe Oliver had picked up on it right away. "Pete had a slight arrogance about him," Oliver remembers. And the Reds who played for him had a touch of that arrogance too, passed along by number fourteen.

Now, Piniella was going to give them a little something else: A New York swagger.

"He definitely had some of that," Oliver remembers. "All that Yankee tradition is a good thing, something to live up to and believe in when you're a (former) Yankee. Act like a winner. Play like a winner. Be a winner. Lou gave us that."

Piniella knew that the Reds franchise had it, but perhaps it lay dormant.

Lou had seen the swagger fourteen years earlier when he and his Yankee teammates had been steamrolled by the Big Red Machine in a four-game World Series sweep. These present-day Reds weren't too young to remember it.

In 1976, these Reds players were pre-driving age, wide-open, drink-it-in baseball age. If there were two things they knew growing up, it was the Big Red Machine and the 1977–78 World Champion New York Yankees of outfielder Lou Piniella. The new Reds had seen a lot of both teams, both on the NBC-TV Saturday *Game of the Week* and in the World Series on TV, four years in a row, 1975 through 1978. Nobody, n-o-b-o-d-y, represented that Reds-and-Yankees winning tradition better than the manager just departed and the one newly arrived.

As much confidence as Piniella and Rose possessed, there was something downright likeable about Piniella. Not that the players hadn't liked Rose—they had. But by all their accounts, he was a bit too easy on them.

Players immediately saw that Piniella didn't have Rose's arrogance, but he had every bit of Rose's confidence. More importantly, Piniella was going to make his players understand right away, because there was no time to build up to it, one fundamental concept.

"Accountability," Eric Davis remembers twenty years later. "You did it, so you are being held accountable. That's different than discipline. Lou made you accountable for your actions because what you did or didn't do affected the *team*."

The players were all ears. They already liked the guy. He was one of them.

Rob Dibble, who been there three days, noticed right away that Piniella had this ability to…*blend*. Almost like he was still a player. Not that he gave off the sense, like Rose did, that he still wished he was a player—heck, at times, Rose acted as though he was jealous of the players, because he could no longer do what they did, Todd Benzinger remembers. But Piniella was just *there*, taking it all in.

"It's funny how you keep seeing Lou in a group," Dibble said. "It's funny, because you don't notice him, but then all of a sudden he'll say something. He always seems like he's around."

Lou was a like an old prizefighter that way. Always moving and swaying, on his toes, not just rocking back and forth, but actually taking steps to and fro, like he was dancing, pressing you at times, falling away from you at others, but then always coming back in, leaning, leading, cantilevering. *There.*

Barry Larkin noticed that, too. It was like Lou was one of the guys, still a player—*we'll* do this, *we'll* do that—and yet you always knew he was in charge. Even when Lou would let somebody have it—coach, player, umpire—for some transgression, he would often wink at Larkin afterward and say, "teaching opportunity." Twenty years later, Larkin still remembers it, marvels at it.

And that is when you know that Piniella meant everything to Larkin, especially at that point in his career, when he was just starting to blossom and wanted something more. He wanted to win.

"I love Lou Piniella," he says.

Browning felt the same way.

"He would say things to me for the purposes of wanting everybody else to hear it," Browning recalls. "Maybe I pitched horses---, and I knew that, and he knew it, and he knew I could take any criticism he was going to dish out for everybody to hear. He used me as a sounding board. And he didn't make it personal— even though sometimes you had a hard time reminding yourself of that. He'd say something to you, and ten minutes later it'd be done."

And yet, on this day—team address day—Piniella seemed a bit nervous. "His hands were shaking," Todd Benzinger remembers. And he wasn't totally sure where everything was going, just that he intended to get it to where he needed to go.

Lou knew that this team had question marks.

How was Sabo's knee? Larkin's elbow? Rijo's

back? Danny Jackson's shoulder and big toe? What if those guys couldn't go? Who then? And who were the fourth and fifth starters? And what about the bench? It seemed thin. No wonder we fell to fifth when the regulars started dropping like flies. Could Oliver cut it for a full season? Was Armstrong ready for prime time? What about this kid Scudder? And Ron Robinson's right elbow? Could he relieve if somebody else started? Would Todd Benzinger—who'd had his hand broken by an errant pitch from a pitching machine only three weeks ago in Cincinnati—be ready for Opening Day? Benzinger hadn't even taken batting practice yet!

"Lou didn't talk long—two, three minutes, tops," Benzinger remembers. "He said, 'There are only three things you need to do: One, show up on time. Two, listen to everything I say. And three, play like hell.' Do those three things. That was pretty much it."

Actually, there were three other things, Browning recalls. "But Lou didn't list them as the 'three things to remember.' These other three things were 'You've got too much talent not to have won by now...I want to win, too...And I don't care if you like me. Okay, now here are my coaches.'"

Browning laughs at the memory. Short and sweet. *My kind of manager.*

That night, Benzinger went on WLW-AM radio, and the sports show's host asked Benzinger what Piniella had said.

"He told us, Show up on time, play like hell, and, uh, uh...I can't remember the third thing."

Benzinger's quote wound up appearing in *Sports Illustrated*. Pretty funny stuff. Especially since the part Benzinger had forgotten was "Listen to everything I say."

Only six days after the Piniella address, the first Grapefruit League games began.

"Usually we see ten days of live pitching before the first (spring) game," Eric Davis said. "We've had three."

"Haven't even taken infield yet," Piniella lamented.

But there were some good signs, things Piniella had hoped to see.

Jose Rijo threw two innings pain-free, which was huge because he had to shut it down in June of 1989. His aching back had made pitching impossible. But Rijo was ahead of the other pitchers, having thrown fourteen innings in the Domincan Winter League, and he looked sharp.

There was a nice crowd of 5,276 at the first game in Plant City, and the day was warm and sunny, just the way everybody envisions baseball to be in Florida in March. That much hadn't changed.

"Baseball is too big for people to say 'We're going to give it up,'" said Cincinnati native Ron Oester, speaking to the issue of whether there would be any repercussions from the lockout, which most of the fans blamed on the players. Most of the fans even referred to it as a players' "strike," which it wasn't. "Baseball is too important to fans," Oester said. "I don't think the lockout is going to hurt baseball a bit."

The Reds won their first spring game, 4–1. That was nice, too. Everything else being equal, Piniella would rather win than lose, even in the spring. But

Todd Benzinger called Ron Oester the one teammate he was afraid to let down.

most of all he liked the way his young Reds played. They were fast. They were efficient. The mere six days of practice had seemed to be enough for the position players. They were crisp, lively, and up in the bit. Like a good horse, they wanted to run.

"It was a good ballgame," Piniella said. "No walks, good defense, and timely hitting." *That is how we want to play.*

In late March of 1990, Barry Larkin was already an established star. Only twenty-five, he had already made two All-Star teams and won two Silver Slugger awards as the best-hitting shortstop in the league. He hadn't yet won a Gold Glove but only because the St. Louis Cardinals' Ozzie Smith still had "the name."

Back home in Symmes Township, not far from where Larkin was born, were his new house, his new wife (he had married Lisa, from the old neighborhood less than three months before), and Roscoe, his four-month-old Rottweiler pup. (If ever there was a metaphor for Larkin and the 1990 season, it was Roscoe.)

Right from the start, Larkin was ready to play. *He loved baseball.*

He loved *baseball* not just being a baseball player. There is a huge difference.

Barry and his brothers and his sister had been coached by their father, Bob, in the fundamentals of playing sports correctly, using all their athletic gifts—and brains—to beat an opponent, to never show them up and to never hot dog it. *Play the game correctly.* You owe it that, Bob had told them, or you are cheating the game and yourself.

Maybe that is why there are old-timers who swear they've seen a few Reds run the bases faster than Barry Larkin, but they have never seen anybody run them better.

For all of Reds announcer Marty Brennaman's criticisms of players over the years—and he's had his share with Larkin—he also pays him the highest compliment when he says, "I never saw him make a mistake on the bases."

The athlete that Larkin most resembled on the field was hockey star Wayne Gretzky, because Gretzky was the headiest, most anticipatory player his sport

Coming off of an injury, Barry Larkin was primed for a big year in 1990.

had ever seen, and also the most protected by his teammates. They knew what they had. And the Reds knew it, too. It's why Ron Oester absolutely blistered Rod Dibble one night in 1989 for throwing at a batter, unprovoked. *"Don't you know who's going to pay for that, you idiot?" Oester had roared. "They're gonna drill Barry!"* The Reds could not afford to lose Larkin.

Not as widely known about Larkin is the support he drew from his teammates. Although Larkin was confident in his abilities, he did not have the swagger that comes naturally to athletes with similar gifts. Nor did he possess the same grit or the flair that others gave to their games. But just as he learned how to play the game from his father, he hung close to Eric Davis to learn some swagger and to Oester for some blue-collar grit and to Jose Rijo for some élan and to Browning for the looseness without losing an ounce of competitiveness.

That was probably why Larkin learned Spanish to communicate with the Latin players. It wasn't just that he could be helpful to them but that they could be helpful to him. This characteristic is what made Barry a great teammate. To him, his teammates mattered more than they would ever know. In a sport renowned as the most selfish of team sports, Larkin had no conceit other than being as good as he could be. One hundred years from now, he and Davis and Rijo and Browning will be the players from that team the historians remember. But what matters twenty years after the fact is that these four teammates—Davis, Oester, Rijo, and Browning—are the ones Larkin singles out as his role models, the ones from whom he drew.

From these four, he winnows the list to two.

"Eric was the street guy, Ronnie the Cincinnati work-ethic guy," Larkin remembers. "I wanted Eric's swagger, and I wanted Oester's work ethic." He never did get Davis's swagger—some things you must be born with—but he did get Oester's work ethic.

Larkin loved and respected all his teammates, but the one to whom he was closest was Eric Davis. Larkin is only two years younger than Davis, and yet he says his relationship with Davis, who grew up in Freemont, California, in the inner city of Los Angeles, was not a typical friendship.

"Eric was more like an uncle to me," Larkin says. "I'd go out to LA and stay with him, and he'd show me around—where he grew up, what he'd overcome, the strong family he'd grown up in. Eric was a very, very confident player. He had no doubts about what he could do on a baseball field. I fed off that. I needed that. I learned the ropes from him."

Davis took a lot of "younger" guys under his wing, including Jose Rijo, who was three years his junior. Even though Rijo was an extremely confident athlete, there was the language barrier. So Davis was his uncle, too.

Davis had had an uncle of his own in the Reds clubhouse with Cincinnati native Dave Parker, who taught him about baseball and life.

"I have the courage to do spectacular things," Davis told the *Enquirer*'s Paolercio that spring. "There's a lot of guys who'd be scared to dive after a ball with the game on the line. They have a fear that they'd miss it. I don't have that fear.

"Some guys are scared to challenge the wall. I don't have that fear. Guys that don't believe in their ability to stretch a single to a double. I believe in my

Chris Sabo learned a lot from Pete Rose, but it was Lou Piniella who turned him into a power hitter.

ability to run, I believe in my ability to catch, and I believe in my ability to jump. I want to be that guy with the game on the line."

And that is exactly what Barry Larkin wanted.

There had been only one error, late in the game, by shortstop Jeff "Whitey" Richardson. As the fans listened to Marty Brennaman back in Reds Country on WLW-AM, they remembered Whitey. No fault of Whitey's. He had been part of the Triple-A lineup the banged-up Reds trotted out in the summer of '89 when they were making their run from first to fifth.

Whitey didn't know it, but soon those boos would no longer matter.

March 27, Lakeland

The only coach Piniella had worked with in the past was pitching coach Stan Williams. At one of the first meetings, the coaches picked up on the manager's intensity and goal.

"What's the wardrobe for Oakland in October?" one asked, good-naturedly.

March 28, Plant City

The Reds got rocked by the Astros 8–6. Tom Browning gave up a first-inning, two-run blast to Glenn Davis on a pitch on the outside corner. Davis hammered it like he knew it was coming. Browning filed this setback away. The Reds would play the opening series in Houston.

Randy Myers, making his "debut" as a Red, wasn't impressive. He walked a guy, gave up a run-scoring double, and recorded zero punch-outs.

Piniella didn't like the way the third game of spring training had gone. He ordered the players to run sprints in the outfield while he stewed near the foul line.

"Relax, skip," coach Sam Perlozzo told Piniella. "It's only the third game."

Piniella fired back, "Damn it, these guys have been here a week!"

Then Piniella realized what he said and began laughing. Perlozzo joined in.

Sweet Lou could be intense, all right. But he could laugh at himself. His ability to acknowledge and laugh at his own shortcomings was the one trait that his players would remember twenty years later.

March 29, Plant City

Hours before the Reds were to play an exhibition game in Plant City, Piniella was on a back field for two hours working with third baseman Chris Sabo and first baseman Hal Morris.

Asked later if Pete Rose had ever spent two hours in one day working with him, or even two hours total, Sabo grunted and shook his head no.

In his next seven at-bats of the spring, Sabo ripped six hits, four of them doubles.

"Lou has made a world of difference for me," Sabo said. "He noticed I had a problem with breaking balls. Now I see them all. Once I perfect what he taught me, there's no reason I won't hit .300. Pete couldn't break down a swing the way Lou does. He breaks it right down to the toenails."

Morris still calls Piniella "the best hitting instructor I ever had."

Larkin remembers listening to Piniella offer hitting instruction to Paul O'Neill.

"Can you dance?" asked Piniella, bat in hand.

"What?"

"Can you dance?" Piniella repeated. "Hitting is about balance and rhythm. You gotta get some rhythm."

Recalls Larkin, chuckling at the memory: "Paul looked at Lou like, 'What is this lunatic talking about?'"

Piniella soon learned that Eric Davis did understand the rhythm of hitting.

"He does things so effortlessly and gracefully," Piniella told the *Enquirer*'s Mike Paolercio, "people come to expect to see it all the time. It's not that easy."

Piniella also marveled at Davis's speed. "He's got that long stride...and (gets) around those bases as quick as anybody I've ever seen."

It was a mutual admiration society.

"When we talk," Davis said, "it's 'us' and 'we.' That's good, that makes everybody feel a part of the team to win."

No longer is the finger being pointed at Davis to lead the Reds to the pennant. The Reds' poor finish last year supported his long-held contention that most people ignored.

"I think everything was built around if I win, everybody wins," Davis said. "I tried to stress that it doesn't work like that. Look at the numbers I put up last year, and we finished fifth."

Piniella disliked the notion that "as Eric Davis goes, so go the Reds."

"That's unfair, that's unfair," Lou said, repeating himself, as he often did when he felt strongly about something and wanted to make sure his listeners got the point. "He's certainly our main cog here, but if he has a great season and no one hits around him, this club's not going to win. Yeah, we need a productive year from him. But we've got other people here that can carry the load.

"We look to Eric for leadership, but he shouldn't be the only one you look to for leadership. Larkin, Sabo, O'Neill, Browning—these are people that are very capable. We need leadership from more than one guy."

Before the game, Piniella told the players he was bothered by the way they had played the first three games—they were 1–2.

"We're sloppy," he said. "I don't like it."

Later that day, Paul O'Neill told Hal McCoy of the *Dayton Daily News*: "He's a sore loser, that's for sure. And that's good. Maybe he can motivate a few more wins around here. That'd be different, wouldn't it?"

Pitcher Rick Mahler, who at thirty-six had seen many managers pass through the big-league carrousel, observed, "Lou is constantly involved in everything. Even during practice workouts. In games, a lot of managers let their coaches move players around defensively. Lou does it himself."

Browning: "It's a new year and a different atmosphere around here. Lou is here with a whole new staff. He is real loose when he needs to be, but he stresses fundamentals. He wants to play good baseball, and he makes certain things are done the way he wants."

Pete Rose had told the writers more than once that the players should know the fundamentals by the time they get to the big club. Maybe that was true when he came up, but it wasn't true now.

Browning: "Our camp (is shorter) this year, but more regimented; it is demanded that you get your work done. Before, we had too many distractions."

March 30, Winter Haven

Sabo was pegged out at second base trying to stretch a single into a double.

"Good," he said. "I wanted to see if I could kick it in like I used to."

He could—and he did. It didn't matter that he'd been thrown out. Next time, he'd make it, he vowed. He knew his speed had returned. He smiled at the thought.

"I don't have the power of most third basemen, but most third basemen can't steal fifty bases like I can," he said.

Sabo was getting a good look in the leadoff spot.

Lou Piniella and Bob Quinn knew they had the talent to win now when they came to the Reds.

Piniella loved speed at the top of the lineup. He was aware of on-base percentage, but he believed he could get by with an aggressive hitter in the one-hole. Sabo batted leadoff in five of the Reds first six spring game and did fine.

Sabo had come up a little later than your average bust-on-the-scene major leaguer—he was NL Rookie of the Year in 1988 at age twenty-six—but he arrived in time for his prime years. That was the most important thing.

Larkin was twenty-five, Davis twenty-seven, O'Neill twenty-seven, Oliver twenty-four. Oliver had reported to camp in thinned-out condition as Lou awarded him the catcher's position. ("Sight unseen— he couldn't have picked me out of a police lineup," Oliver remembers.)

Ron Oester was turning thirty-four in May. And he knew that this was the main reason why Piniella had given the much speedier, twenty-seven-year-old Duncan the second baseman's job. Lou had said in the spring that "O" would get his at-bats, but Oester knew that if Duncan didn't fall on his face, the job would be Duncan's.

"I read it in the paper (in February back home in Cincinnati)," he said. "This season might be my last."

March 31, Plant City

The players were hanging out in the clubhouse, wondering if the overnight rain might wash out their game in St. Petersburg, wrote the the *Enquirer's* Greg Hoard. Larkin, Davis, and O'Neill were there, but they wouldn't be going to St. Pete even if the game were played. Piniella had told them they could stay behind and work out and take their cuts. This fact wasn't widely known in the clubhouse, but Piniella saw no need to share it with anybody but his coaches and the players involved.

Then the tranquil scene was ruptured by the roar of a two-cylinder engine. It sounded like a chainsaw on wheels. Randy Myers rode a tiny scooter into the clubhouse, and in his left hand, held high enough for all to see, was a six-foot black snake. The clubhouse boy and grounds crew scurried out of the room.

"It's rubber," said Rob Dibble, unaffected, as he resumed answering a writer's questions.

Myers laughed with delight. Moments later, he appeared at Dibble's locker, looking more like a guerrilla warrior than a pitcher. He wore a scarf tied around his brow and a black T-shirt with the inscription, "Gun control is holding it in both hands." Myers was known to have dummy hand grenades in his locker and to use ammo boxes for storage and a survival knife for a hat rack. His voice sounded like a mixture of Robert De-Niro in *Raging Bull* and Gerry Faust on a good day.

"C'mon, Dibs," he rasped. "They want to get our picture."

It was the making of the Nasty Boys—take one.

But nobody knew them by that name yet.

Davis remembers Myers saying all spring that the club was going to start out 15–0, go to 35–10, and ultimately win ninety-nine games in the regular season and then go on to win the NLCS and World Series.

Lou would have been happy with such a prediction.

The field was fine for the scheduled game in St. Pete. The players boarded the bus, and before it left the parking lot, a voice in the back piped up, "Where's the big three?" The big, well-tanned, unsmiling man in the lead passenger seat stood up, put his right hand on the overhead rack, and glared to the back of the bus.

"I manage the club," Lou Piniella barked. "I make the decisions. You worry about playing."

Reds advance scout Jimmy Stewart was on the bus. He later recalled, "Right then, they knew who was in charge."

April 1, Plant City

Dibble was struck on the ankle by a line drive in his first of two innings of scheduled work. He stayed in the game and worked the second inning, striking out three Detroit Tigers hitters. As the reliever came off the field, Piniella waited for him at the foul line between home and first base with arms crossed and proceeded to lecture Dibble in front of everybody.

What was it about?

"He didn't like my pitch selection, particularly the first pitch I threw that inning," Dibble said. "That's fine with me. Sometimes I need my butt kicked. Better that way than talking behind your back the way Pete used to do it."

Twenty years later, O'Neill recalls several such moments in Piniella's first spring with the Reds. "We'd be going along pretty comfortably, getting our work in, and Lou would see something he didn't like and

he'd tighten the screws," he remembers. "You got the very distinct impression he intended to win, and that he knew the mindset he wanted. He'd put a play on or say something just to let us know."

Piniella told Browning he would be the Opening Day pitcher in Houston. Afterward, Browning went out to play golf. He played golf every day of spring training, and he played on a lot of days during the regular season when he wasn't pitching. This year would be different, however. Piniella had already told him and everybody that there would be no golf once the season started. Piniella wanted the players to focus on baseball.

"That's all right," Browning reasoned. "I have my whole life to play golf."

April 2-3, Plant City

Pitcher Ron Robinson learned through the clubhouse grapevine that he was no longer going to start the fourth game of the season.

"I confronted Stan and he confirmed it," Robinson told the *Enquirer*'s Mike Paolercio. "He said (Danny) Jackson's starting the first game in Atlanta. You hear this and it makes you mad. Who I heard it from is not important. It's that I heard it and not from the right people. You expect the same courtesy you give them."

Later, Hal McCoy batted out his story in the Plant City pressroom: "Lou Piniella made an impact...and it thundered through camp like a Florida hurricane. When pitcher Ron Robinson whined about his status and said he absolutely refuses to work out of the bullpen, Piniella

BOB QUINN OFF-SEASON TRADE SCORECARD

Reds General Manager Bob Quinn made three trades prior to the start of the 1990 season, all of which had a major impact on the success of the team that year. Here's the breakdown:

December 6, 1989

To the Reds:
Randy Myers 27-year-old left-handed closer
Kip Gross 25-year-old right-handed
minor league starting pitcher

To the Mets:
John Franco 29-year-old left-handed closer
Don Brown 22-year-old minor league outfielder

Value Comparison after the Deal

Player	1990	As a Red	Career	Player	1990	As a Met	Career
Myers	3.1	4.3	12.1	Franco	1.9	12.8	12.3
Gross	0.0	0.4	0.4	Brown		*Did Not Play in Majors*	

The value number is Wins Above Replacement, which estimates the number of wins a player provides his team over what you can expect from the typical player in AAA.

This deal came down to the two primary players, Randy Myers and John Franco. Despite Franco recording a league-high thirty-three saves to Myers' thirty-one, Myers had a much bigger impact in 1990, mainly because he pitched nineteen more innings and gave up nearly a half-run a game less than Franco. While it's conceivable that the Reds still make the playoffs with Franco, it's doubtful that the bullpen would have had the same intimidation factor without the much harder throwing Myers. Franco provided much more value to the Mets over his career, but that's mainly because he stuck with the team after becoming a free agent while the Reds traded Myers after the 1991 season. Given the integral role that Myers played with the 1990 squad, and that Franco was making nearly twice as much money as Myers, this deal falls as slight advantage for the Reds.

December 12, 1989

TO THE REDS:
Hal Morris 24-year-old first baseman
Rodney Imes 23-year-old right-handed
pitcher

TO THE METS:
Tim Leary 31-year-old right-handed starting pitcher
Van Snider 26-year-old outfielder minor league starting

Value Comparison after the Deal							
Player	1990	As a Red	Career	Player	1990	As a Met	Career
Morris	1.5	11.1	11.3	Leary	1.5	0.1	-0.2
Imes	*Did Not Play in Majors*			Snider	*Did Not Play in Majors*		

The value number is Wins Above Replacement, which estimates the number of wins a player provides his team over what you can expect from the typical player in AAA.

Leary pitched decently for the Yankees despite a 9-19 record as his 4.11 ERA was tops among starters on the team, and his 208 innings pitched was fifty more than any other Yankee starter in 1990. However, despite only getting 336 plate appearances, Morris matched Leary's value in 1990 with his .340 batting average and .880 OPS. Given that the Reds had a surplus in the starting rotation and were able to get an excellent young hitter who contributed to the playoff stretch run in 1990 as well as for another seven years after that, it's hard to consider this deal anything but a big win for Quinn.

April 3, 1990

TO THE REDS:
Billy Hatcher 29-year-old outfielder
Mike Roesler 26-year-old right-handed reliever

TO THE PIRATES:
Jeff Richardson 24-year-old shortstop

Value Comparison after the Deal							
Player	1990	As a Red	Career	Player	1990	As a Met	Career
Hatcher	1.6	-0.2	-1.7	Richardson	0.0	0.0	0.5
				Roesler	0.1	0.1	0.1

The value number is Wins Above Replacement, which estimates the number of wins a player provides his team over what you can expect from the typical player in AAA.

Billy Hatcher was a critical piece to the Reds championship run in 1990, so it might be hard to believe that he had been acquired for a meager-hitting minor league shortstop and a less than impressive minor league reliever. Hatcher provided the Reds with coverage in both left field and center field when needed and was firmly entrenched in the first or second spot in the order for most of the season. He gave the Reds good defense in left and was an adequate replacement for Eric Davis in center. However, his defensive value had a steep decline after the 1990 season, which is why his overall value after the deal was negative. Even with that decline, it can't be denied that this deal was a huge success for the Reds. It seems like every move that Bob Quinn made for the 1990 season turned to gold.

squashed him underfoot like a June bug."

"Pitchers are not going to tell me how and when to use them," Piniella shot back. "That's the wrong approach with me to start with. I'll use them the way I want."

Piniella's message rippled through the clubhouse, and if there was ever any doubt who was in charge, the doubt was obliterated.

Paul O'Neill: "Man, he really let Robby have it, didn't he?"

"That's the way it is going to be," Piniella said. "That's the way it has to be. Players have to know who is in charge or things won't work."

Soon, it wouldn't matter what Robinson thought.

April 2, Bradenton

Billy Hatcher was having trouble getting to sleep. Midnight passed, and he was still awake. About one o'clock, he fell asleep.

Which is when the phone rang. It was his wife.

"It's time, Billy," she said.

Billy looked at the clock. He knew the flight schedules to Houston. He'd be on the seven a.m. flight.

April 3, Kissmmee

Norm Charlton was steaming. Late in the game, he firmly tagged Astro Eric Anthony on the way to first base and took a sharp elbow to the ribs from Anthony, and then got in his face, telling Anthony that he would brook no such nonsense in a spring training game.

It was a portent.

"We had a lot of fights that year," recalls Barry Larkin, adding that it had started in spring training. "Our attitude was, 'They wanna fight? Let's fight.'"

Opening Day was only six days away, and yet the benches had already emptied, Charlton was in the middle of it, and in the dugout, Lou smiled and took note.

"I'd heard that he's spunky on the mound," Piniella said. "I like that."

Six games ago, Piniella had told the players he didn't like the way they were playing. They buckled down and won all six games.

Stan Williams, the fiery former pitcher, loved it.

No matter how much Skip pushes the players, runs them, prods them, they can't get enough.

"We can't get the guys to complain," Williams said.

April 3, Houston

Hatcher was in the delivery room when the phone rang.

"Billy, we traded you to the...." said Pirate manager Jim Leyland.

"Okay, Jimmy, I'll talk to you guys later, okay?" Hatcher answered. "My wife's going into labor right now."

And with that, he hung up the phone. His wife, Karen, was giving birth to Chelsea, who arrived later that evening. Billy and his son, Derek, drove home together.

"About then, it hit me," Hatcher recalls. "I'd been traded...but to who?"

A few minutes later, Reds general manager Bob Quinn called Hatcher to welcome him aboard, and

Lou Piniella cultivated a unique relationship with his stars as he extracted greatness out of them.

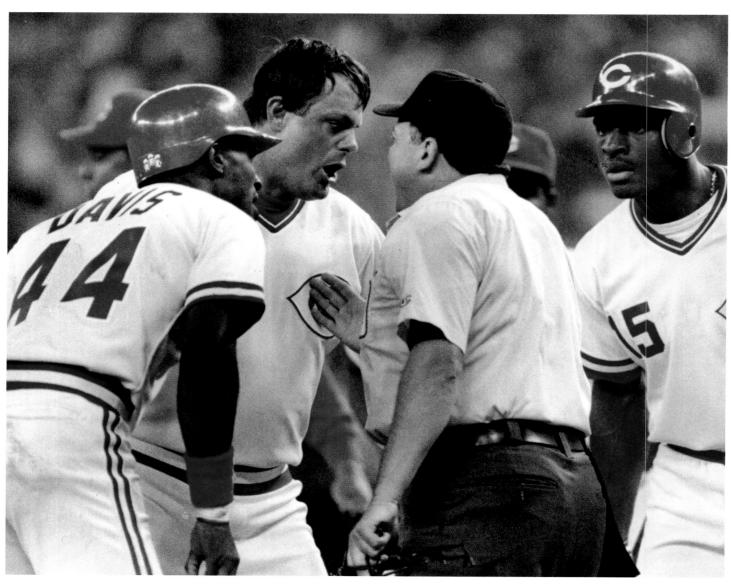

Lou Piniella was ejected from this game on June 22, when Terry Tata reversed his safe call at home plate on what would have been the game-winning run.

The Reds' aggressive style of play from early in the season returned during the playoffs against the Pirates.

CINCINNATI REDS 1990

IT'S A WHOLE NEW BALLGAME

CINCINNATI REDS

SEASON
TICKET
CALENDAR

Only a rookie in '90, Joe Oliver impressed his manager and teammates with his ability to handle the pitching staff and kill the opponent's running game.

Rob Dibble's erratic behavior on and off the mound intimidated hitters.

Randy Myers and Rob Dibble brought the heat together from Opening Day to the World Series.

The Reds victory over the Braves on September 27 brought their magic number to two.

(Left) Few players went first-to-third better than Barry Larkin. (Below) Danny Jackson had a quiet season but came up big with two wins against the Pirates in the NLCS.

The '90 Reds were aggressive while running the bases and just as aggressive about shutting down their opponents' speed.

Reds brass saw Billy Hatcher as the "missing piece" when they traded for him six days before Opening Day.

then the phone rang again. This time it was Reds owner Marge Schott.

"How's the baby?" she asked.

"Fine," said Hatcher, realizing Leyland must have called the Reds to tell him Hatcher was in the delivery room.

"This is a great thing!" Schott told him. "You're having a baby, you just got traded, and we're going to win the World Championship this year!"

The Reds announced the Hatcher trade. Piniella said Hatcher would play left field, maybe in a platoon, and bat leadoff. Somebody told Piniella Hatcher had been caught last year with a corked bat.

"Really? He's a cheater?" asked Piniella. "I like that!"

April 4, Plant City

The Reds lost 10–8 to the Cardinals, but Larkin had three hits and two stolen bases. He felt it coming on. Davis and Sabo each stole a base. Lou had everybody running like crazy. Get used to it, fellas.

Hatcher arrived at the Holiday Inn in Plant City at 10:30 p.m.; it took him until two to fall asleep.

When Oester heard about the trade, he made a few phone calls to his buddies in baseball to find out more about Hatcher. Oester knew Hatcher, of course, but mostly as an opponent who he admired for his all-out play. But Oester wanted to learn more. Could Hatcher take a joke?

What if a racial phrase were used? Could he take that? Yes, Oester was told; Hatcher could take it.

April 5, Plant City

Oester made sure he was the first one the locker room, so that Hatcher couldn't beat him there. Oester told Reds equipment manager Bernie Stowe what he planned to do.

Which is how it happened that at 7:30 a.m. when Hatcher walked through the front door of the Reds complex carrying his Pittsburgh Pirates equipment bag, he heard somebody say, "Hey, Bernie, who's the new little colored boy?"

Hatcher, momentarily taken aback, scanned the clubhouse and spotted the veteran Reds second baseman with a big grin on his face. The first words that came to Hatcher's mind were "Why you son of a...." And then they both burst out laughing.

Which is when Todd Benzinger, who also happened to be in the clubhouse early that day, turned to somebody and said, "It's going to be a fun year."

Even then, Benzinger knew there was a little "something" about this team.

"If there was one person you wanted to play good for besides yourself, it was Oester," Benzinger recalls. "He'd been there ten years, he was a hard-ass. I saw him get on Dibble in the clubhouse one time after throwing at a guy. Oester was nose-to-nose in Dibble's face, practically spitting in it. 'Who the f--- do you think you are? We're trying to win a f------ game and you're pulling this s---?' I remember thinking, 'I don't ever want a guy like Oester to do that to me.'"

Benzinger says that "on a typical team, you have two or three guys who are real leaders, one or two or three guys who are bad apples, and everybody else is in neutral. One of Lou's abilities was he would light a fire—he'd figure out which buttons to push—under the guys that were more or less content to play in neutral. And I was one of those guys. When you got a guy who not only wants to win, but a guy who absolutely hates to lose—that's Lou—it's got to affect you."

Piniella, recalls Benzinger, wasn't a guy like Dusty Baker (Benzinger later played for Baker in San Francisco) "to buddy up to you, put his arm around you and say 'Listen, here's your role.' Players like that. 'This guy is thinking about me; he's got my thoughts; he understands my situation; he's really concerned about me.' Lou wasn't like that.

"But I think it's good to keep a big-league player on edge a little bit. You don't know what the manager's thinking; he's not going to be approachable; all you know is he wants to win in the worst way. 'I'd damn well better do what I can do to help him win, because he's going to be all over my case if I don't.' So yeah, fear is a great motivator. There was definitely some of that with Lou. Some of, 'We don't know what this lunatic might do.' So we didn't have any bad apples, we had two or three leaders, and then Lou lit this fire under the rest of us. We played for the guys around us—very rare. And it all started in spring training."

But Benzinger also remembers wondering about Eric Davis.

The previous season was Benzinger's first with the

*Todd Benzinger had no expectations for 1990, but was intriqued by what Piniella might bring...
and how Eric Davis might react.*

Reds. Davis had been up full-time since 1986. Benzinger was the only regular not to spend any time on the disabled list in '89. He had played 161 games.

"With about two weeks to go in '89, Eric and I were the only everyday guys playing, and he got his hundredth RBI in San Diego, and the next night he didn't play," Benzinger remembers. "The night after that, I was getting ready to go on the field, and I said, 'How come you're not playing?' He said, 'I got my hundredth RBI. I'm done. You should be done, too. What are you playing for?' I said, 'I don't have a hundred RBI. I'm at seventy-six. I'm trying to get to eighty.'

"So, while I didn't have any expectations for us as a team in '90—we had just finished fifth, we were coming off four straight second-place finishes before that—I remember thinking, 'Eric was kind of a selfish player last year, kind of me-first. If we're in this thing, if the heat's on, I wonder what kind of guy Eric's going to be then. I wonder how Eric's going to affect us.'"

❖   ❖   ❖   ❖   ❖

Piniella, wasting no time, gave Hatcher the steal sign. Hatcher, losing his footing, was thrown out.

HATCHER GAVE THE LINEUP FLEXIBILITY

When the Reds traded for Billy Hatcher, Lou Piniella said, "He's going to hit leadoff." At Redsfest in 2009, Piniella said, "Getting Hatcher allowed us to hit him leadoff and move Larkin to the three-hole."

But that's not quite how it happened, at least not in the beginning. Chris Sabo was such a hot hitter at the end of spring training—and he continued to hit after Hatcher arrived—that Lou left Sabo in the leadoff spot when the season started. And he raked.

Piniella, who clearly wanted Larkin in the three-spot, batted Hatcher second by default and everything worked out. Three good hitters, three rabbits, three guys making things happen. Coming into the season, Larkin was the only real threat of the three to get on base consistently, but through the first forty-five games of the season, all three spent nearly as much time on base as off. Larkin led the way (.427 OBP through 33–12), but Sabo (.391) and Hatcher (.378) gave the heart of the Reds order plenty of opportunities to drive in runs.

By the middle of the season though, the offense was struggling, and Piniella had to shake things up. At that point, Sabo led the team in doubles and home runs, and while he was still getting on base (.374 OBP at mid-season), Piniella needed his pop lower in the order. By mid-August, Sabo was hitting fifth or sixth, depending on the pitcher, and Hatcher was given the majority of starts in the leadoff spot, just like Piniella had planned.

The beauty of the Hatcher acquisition was that it created many more options. Without Hatcher, the Reds likely would have been stuck with Sabo batting first and Larkin batting second. It's not a bad combination, but Hatcher's presence meant that the more rounded players could move around in the order. Hatcher was a more traditional speedy leadoff hitter, and that may have been what Piniella thought he was getting in the deal, but he really got flexibility.

And Lou took advantage of it, using 125 different lineups during the season. That's about twenty-five more than Sparky Anderson had to use with his World Championship teams. But that's how the Reds were built in 1990—interchangeable parts where everybody could take on the role they were given and perform. The Reds weren't a great offensive team in 1990, but the balance throughout the order made them a formidable opponent.

"That's okay," Piniella said. "I wanted to see him run just this one time."

The Reds looked lousy—they made eight errors.

Piniella hated errors. Almost as much as he hated his pitchers issuing walks. Hatcher had made an error. *What's with Hatcher?*

After the game, Piniella told the writers loud enough for everybody to hear that he was pissed off that Norm Charlton had made a low, hard throw that handcuffed first baseman Benzinger on a comebacker to the mound, allowing a runner to score.

"That's the second time I've seen that happen," snapped Piniella, referring to an earlier throw by Dibble. "There's no need to throw that hard. Get the ball to the first baseman in orderly fashion and come back to the dugout."

Orderly fashion. There's that Lou vernacular again.

But Sabo had two hits and Larkin three.

Larkin remembers Piniella talking to his players that spring.

"Let's take it to these sons of bitches" in the National League, said Lou, "and not let them breathe."

Lou's attitude was starting to rub off. Nobody felt it more than Davis.

And if Davis could have just one wish for this year?

"I'd like to drink champagne in October. I know it won't be from a wedding, because I'm already married," said Davis, laughing. "I dream of that kind of stuff. You see the guys run out on the field, you know the excitement and joy they're feeling. I always picture myself pouring champagne on people's heads and jumping for joy and everybody's watching. That's prime time. That's where I want to be."

April 6, Plant City

Tomorrow, the Reds would break camp. Piniella was sitting in the manager's office taking writers' questions early in the day when somebody asked him about the difference between being manager of the Reds and manager of the Yankees.

"It's much more relaxed," he said. "I like it."

Earlier in camp he had joked with the writers about being free from the meddling of Yankees owner George Steinbrennner.

"We used to have a 'George Patrol' with walkie-talkies over at Fort Lauderdale (the Yankee camp), and when George was spotted coming in, that was my cue to go out to the furthest diamond," Piniella said, smiling at the happy memory. No more calls on the red phone from George.

"Hey," one of the writers said to Piniella, "the phone in your office at Riverfront Stadium is red."

"We might have to change that then," said Piniella, brown eyes twinkling. "I might pick up the phone one day and it's George by mistake. They (the Yankees) might have an off-day and we're playing (and here, Piniella imitates Steinbrenner's voice): 'I can't bother Bucky (Dent, Yankees manager), let me call Lou.'"

The writers cracked up.

So did Sweet Lou.

The season was about to start. He couldn't wait.

In a mere three weeks, he had put his stamp on the ballclub. His insistence on accountability had transformed the culture. And rather than the players being shackled by the new order, they were liberated by it

No longer did they have a manager who shrugged his shoulders when players beefed. If a player messed up during a game, no longer did their manager overlook it. When writers asked after a game why a player had fouled up, no longer were they told, 'Go ask him and come back and tell me what he says.' "

Suddenly, under Piniella, everything mattered. His down-to-earth genuineness—combined with his street cred and his caring—made those around him follow.

Let's take it to 'em....

4

9–0

Nobody knew, except Lou Piniella, what was about to unfold. And even he wasn't totally sure.

April 9, Opening Day, Houston

As soon as Astros slugger Glenn Davis stepped into the batter's box, the Reds had the edge.

"I was not going to let him beat me," Tom Browning recalls twenty years later. "I was going to come inside, and if I hit him, so be it. But he wasn't going to beat me on the outside half. He hit five home runs off me that spring on pitches on the outside. That wasn't going to happen again."

Lou Piniella could have said those words himself, had he been a pitcher.

He wasn't going to let you take bread off his table.

He applied that philosophy not only to his opponents but to his teammates, players, coaches, even the people in the front office. He wasn't manipulative about it; he didn't ask people to do his bidding. Rather, because of his natural way with people, he appealed to the desire most people have to strive together in a common mission. That it happened to be *his* mission, too, well, that was secondary. He wanted you to strive because you felt you owed it to the guy in the foxhole next to you. And he'd be in that

The Reds spent a lot of time celebrating victories over the first two months of the season.

foxhole with you. Piniella was the lieutenant you'd run through hell for.

Ball one, inside. Second pitch, inside, Davis hit by pitch.

Browning had not intentionally hit Davis but later noted, "It didn't bother me that I hit him."

When the Astros Bill Doran came to the plate with two out in the bottom of the first and ripped a Browning pitch into the left-field corner, Reds left fielder Billy Hatcher knew Doran would try to stretch it into a double. Who knew Doran better than Hatcher? Doran was the best man in Hatcher's wedding.

"Two outs, I knew he was going," Hatcher said.

Hatcher gunned down his best man with a perfect throw to Mariano Duncan.

The tone was set: *We run on you; you don't run on us.*

❖ ❖ ❖ ❖ ❖

Browning got knocked around in the bottom of the second, which started by hitting Davis. He then gave up a walk and a wild pitch to dig a 4–2 hole. Piniella didn't like what he was seeing. There was nothing he hated more than his pitchers walking hitters, and everybody within earshot knew it.

Browning already had an out when, on a 2-2 pitch, he came a little too far inside on Davis and hit him again.

"That one didn't bother me either," Browning remembers.

In the top of the fifth with the Reds trailing 4–2 and a man on second, Piniella called on Ken Griffey to hit for Browning. Griffey promptly cut the deficit with a sacrifice fly to right. Mariano Duncan, hitting eighth, had hit a two-run homer off Astros starter Mike Scott in the top of the second to give the Reds a 2–0 lead; now he tied it with a single in the top of the sixth.

The Reds' Tim Layana pitched a one-strikeout, hitless fifth; Norm Charlton a four-strikeout, three-hit sixth, seventh, and eighth; Rob Dibble a three-strikeout, two-hit ninth and tenth; Randy Myers a three-strikeout, no-hit tenth and eleventh, most notably drilling Glenn Davis again with one out and one on in the bottom of the eleventh following which Myers punched out Gerald Wilson and Franklin Stubbs. *Ballgame.*

Sixteen outs. Ten of them by strikeouts.

Man, these guys can bring it, thought the Astros.

Back in the early 1990s, Whitey Herzog said that if were starting a team, the first guy he would pick was Barry Larkin. The 1990 coming-of-age Larkin would have given the White Rat the best shortstop in baseball for the next five to seven years.

Larkin was not your typical three-hole hitter, but then, the Reds weren't your typical baseball team. Larkin was the team's best hitter, the best combination of batting average and some power, so in that sense he fit the three-hole. He was a terrific first-to-third base runner and the poster child for the 1990 Reds—young, fast, and confident. He was also handsome, well spoken (including in Spanish), and popular among his teammates.

Manager Lou Piniella particularly needed Larkin, and he had him. Oh, did he have him.

"I can't speak for everybody on the team," recalls Larkin, twenty years later, "but I can tell you this, straight out. I love the man. *I love Lou Piniella.* That's how much he meant to me. He came in here and he said, 'Losing is not acceptable.' Coming from him, I knew he meant it. I remember thinking, 'This guy is different.' I think every year you play for your teammates. But I was playing for Lou. When that happens, that's a helluva thing."

Bases loaded, 2–2 pitch, top of the eleventh. Larkin had hit .302 the previous season on two-strike counts, compared to the league average .175. Charlie Kerfeld tried to get a slider by him. Larkin roped it into right-center to clear the loaded bases and slid headfirst into third. Eric Davis singled him home to give the Reds an 8-4 lead.

Randy Myers and his teammates were getting cleaned up when a *Houston Chronicle* reporter told Myers that the Astros weren't happy about Glenn Davis being hit three times.

"Well, I've got the radar readings right here, and it says the last three of us all hit at least ninety-five on the gun," Myers said. "So if it comes down to that (a retaliation war), just let 'em know."

"That's pretty nasty," the reporter said.

"Well, we're pretty nasty guys," Myers said.

"And that," recalled Norm Charlton twenty years later, "is how the whole 'Nasty Boys' thing got started."

April 10, Houston

Opening Day belonged to the players, but game two belonged to Piniella. He would argue that every game belonged to the players, but late innings in close games in the National League have always belonged to the managers. The score was tied at one in the eighth inning when Todd Benzinger, batting fifth behind Eric Davis, walked, bringing up Paul O'Neill. Piniella flashed the bunt signal to third base coach Sam Perlozzo who flashed it to O'Neill.

He had been asked to bunt only four times in his previous 1,215 major league plate appearances spanning over three years, but he laid down a perfect one, to the first-base side. Pitcher Juan Agosto fielded the ball and tagged O'Neill, as Benzinger moved to second, and came around to score on a single to right field by Ron Oester, who had come into the game in the sixth inning as part of a double switch for reliever Tim Layana and second baseman Mariano Duncan.

The Reds were up 2–1, and the game was as good as over.

"O'Neill had understood, right from the outset.

"With our bullpen, if you get the runner over and in, that's the ballgame," he recalls. "That's Lou's style of managing, and it worked."

A generation later, the sabermetricians would scoff at having O'Neill sac-bunt in that situation. In a playoff game, maybe. But in the second game of the year? Take a bat out of a slugger's hands? No way. But Lou Piniella didn't know from sabermetrics. He knew from bullpens, and from professional hitters and from

9–0: HOT, HOT, HOT

HITTING

In the first nine games of the season, the Reds hitters were hotter than MC Hammer:

- As a team, the Reds hit .324, which would have been good enough for fifth in the National League on the season for all hitters with at least 350 plate appearances.
- Their .869 OPS (on-base plus slugging percentages) would, if done by an individual, have placed them thirteenth in the NL at the end of the season.
- The Reds had five players with at least thirty plate appearances after nine games who were batting over .320, led by Barry Larkin at .564 and Mariano Duncan at .448. Those two were first and second in the NL in batting average.
- The Reds had the top three OPS hitters in the NL in Duncan (1.274), Larkin (1.267), and Chris Sabo (1.183).
- Six players drove in a game-winning run in the first nine games. Larkin had three game-winning RBI and was joined by Duncan, Ron Oester, Eric Davis, Todd Benzinger, and Paul O'Neill, who each had one game-winning RBI.

PITCHING

The Reds pitchers were hotter than Julia Roberts:

- The pitching staff posted a 2.60 ERA during the first nine games, only allowing a .214 batting average while striking out seventy-six and walking twenty-six in eighty-three innings.
- The bullpen was better than advertised in the first nine games, posting 1.54 ERA in thirty-five innings. Led by Rob Dibble's sixteen strikeouts in nine and a third innings and Norm Charlton's twelve strikeouts in seven innings, they struck out forty-six batters (11.8 K/9) as a group, saved six games, and didn't allow a home run.

GENERAL

- The Reds trailed their opponent at the start of an inning just six times in their first eighty-three innings, and four of those were on Opening Day against the Astros.
- The Reds scored at least one run in the first inning in five of the nine games but didn't allow a first-inning run until the tenth game of the year.
- After the games on April 21, the Reds already had a four-game lead in the National League West.

WHAT A HOT START CAN DO

- A hot start doesn't guarantee anything. The two best previous starts by the franchise—8–1 by the 1919 and 1980 Reds—ended very differently. The 1919 team won the World Championship. The 1980 team finished in third place in the NL West. The Reds were the eleventh team since 1901 to start the season with nine straight wins. The previous ten teams finished the season with average winning percentage of .578, which is approximately a 94–68 record over 162 games. In many years in most divisions, that will at least put you in contention for the top spot. But despite the previous 9–0 teams having good winning percentages, only five of the ten made it to the postseason, and only the 1984 Detroit Tigers and the 1955 Brooklyn Dodgers won the World Series.

getting leads and holding them.

If the bunt was the chess match of the game, what happened in the ninth was the unbridled mayhem part. Billy Hatcher led off with a single, and then—teasing, teasing, teasing reliever Charlie Kerfeld with a big lead—drew an errant pickoff throw and advanced to second base. Was that a trace of a smile on Hatcher's face?

Barry Larkin knew he needed to hit the ball hard, preferably to the right side, run like hell, and hope Hatcher could score. The ball didn't get through, but Larkin was able to beat the throw to first, as Hatcher moved to third.

And now, here it came, the mayhem that Piniella had foreseen since first meeting these speedsters in Plant City. Kerfeld threw ball four to Eric Davis, and it got past catcher Craig Biggio, who ran it down and flipped it back to Kerfeld, covering home, but too late to have a play on Hatcher. And then, as big Charlie stood at home plate with ball in glove, and hand on ball, Larkin—who had never stopped running as he barreled around second on the passed ball—glanced toward home and saw that Biggio had thrown to Kerfeld and sprinted for third, where he landed with a headfirst slide.

The ball never left Kerfeld's mitt.

There were still no outs, the Reds had a runner on third, and they had scored on a single and an infield hit.

And that's when Astros second baseman Billy Doran, a Cincinnati native, who had grown up watching Rose and the Big Red Machine, understood: These were not the second-place Reds.

Tim Layana pitched the sixth and seventh, Dibble the eighth, and Myers the ninth, earning the save. The Reds won 3–2. Around baseball, it was just another one-run game. Doran knew differently.

April 11, Houston

Even in a game in which Jack Armstrong clearly had his best stuff, the Reds kept pushing the action. They led 1–0 going into the third inning when Billy Hatcher beat out an infield single to Astros third baseman Ken Caminiti, and Larkin blasted a rocket off Caminiti's chest for an error. Eric Davis ripped a double off the right-centerfield wall, scoring Hatcher and sending Larkin to third. When O'Neill hit a bounder down the right-field line, Larkin and Davis scored, giving the Reds a 4–0 lead. The Astros knew the situation was hopeless, because even if Armstrong faltered, Piniella would quickly pull him. He was managing like it was the seventh game of the World Series.

A generation later, Doran recalled the three-game series that opened the '90 season.

"After three games, we were absolutely deflated," he remembered. "They ran us ragged. That team left such an impression on us. I'd never seen anything like it. It was like, 'How on earth are we going to be able to compete with this team in our division?' I remember the guys in our clubhouse—me included—after those games just shaking our heads at their speed, at everything they had. It was obvious to us that they were special. They were so athletic, so young, and they had that great bullpen. There was something about that team right from the get-go. They jumped out of the gate like nothing I'd ever seen before."

April 13, Atlanta

As a twenty-six-year-old rookie, Chris Sabo hit eleven home runs in 1988, when he was named Rookie of the Year, made the All-Star team, and was nicknamed Spuds MacKenzie by Pete Rose after the bull terrier in the Bud Light commercials popular at the time. The next year, the year of Rose's travails, Spuds hit only six.

After watching him for two weeks during spring training in 1990, Lou Piniella told Spuds, "If you work at this new hitting technique I'm about to teach you, you will hit fifteen homers by accident," Piniella said.

Sabo had ended spring training on a tear, getting seven straight hits at one point.

Before the opening game of the series in Atlanta, Piniella and hitting coach Tony Perez told Sabo they had noticed in the last game of the Houston series that he had reverted to swinging with his upper body only, instead of his whole body.

"Essentially, it's better balance and weight shift—use all 190 pounds instead of just my arms," Sabo said.

On the night of April 13 in Atlanta–Fulton County Stadium, aka "The Launching Pad," Sabo again led off. He hit the second pitch out of the park and hit another one in the ninth, the first two-homer game of his career.

In between, in the seventh inning, with the score tied at two, Mariano Duncan led off with a walk, Tom

Chris Sabo hit four home runs in the first nine games.

Browning sacrifice-bunted him to second, and Sabo took the count to 3–2 and managed to lay off a pitch that was only slightly outside and slightly high. He and Duncan then executed a double steal, Hatcher walked to load the bases, and up stepped Barry Larkin. He hit a soft fly ball to Dale Murphy in right field, but Murphy—aware of Duncan's speed at third—rushed a one-hop throw to cut-off man Nick Esasky, who threw weakly home, as Duncan scored easily.

"I was (most) proud of the walk tonight," Sabo said. "That was a tough pitch to lay off on a full count."

Piniella pulled starter Tom Browning with one out in the bottom of the seventh and a runner on third.

"Do your specialty," Piniella told Dibble. "We need a strikeout."

Dibble obliged, striking out Lonnie Smith, and then striking out Esasky to end the inning. In the eighth, he struck out two more Braves and then Randy Myers came in for the save. The Reds won 5–2.

And what did "Sabes" think of his two-homer night?

"I'm no weakling," he said.

April 14, Atlanta

You know you're hot when you go three-for-four, with two doubles and three RBI, the game gets rained out, and it doesn't faze you. Your fine offensive night doesn't count in the books—the game lasted only three innings—but what bothers you is that your 9–4 lead doesn't count for anything, either.

That's how it was for Barry Larkin after his fifth straight multi-hit game.

But there was some anxiety about pitcher Danny Jackson. He had been struggling all spring. The Reds knew they had a potentially dominant starter in Jackson—he'd had an injury-plagued 1989, but the previous season he was 23–8, and he was only twenty-eight years old. But when he gave up four runs on seven hits in only three innings, the team was concerned.

Piniella knew the Reds offense couldn't keep this fast start alive by itself. The team's ace, Jose Rijo, had tendonitis in his throwing shoulder. Without him and an effective Jackson, the Reds were down to only three of their top starters—Browning, Armstrong, and Rick Mahler.

Piniella and pitching coach Stan Williams had an idea up their sleeve, an ace in the hole, but they hadn't told anybody yet—not even the ace in the hole.

April 15, Atlanta

Eric Davis always had power.

Ron Oester knew right away Davis would be able to hit a major league fastball even though Davis held his hands unusually low—like Muhammad Ali daring an opponent to try to hit him.

"But I didn't know if he'd be able to hit the breaking ball," Oester recalls. "That's the great equalizer."

Davis had not been a can't-miss prospect like his cross-town LA high school buddy, Darryl Strawberry, but Davis had interested scouts from a very young age. He was fast and could hit the ball a long way. His basketball skills were eye-popping—he averaged 29.2 points as a high school senior—but there was something about him as a baseball player. He was only in the tenth grade when Reds scout Larry Barton Jr. asked Ham Davis if his son, Keith, (Eric went by his middle name) wanted to play on a Reds' winter-league team against local college teams.

"Okay by me, if it's okay by him," said Ham.

Eric Davis – Slow start, but never lost his cool.

It was okay. Future Reds Frank Pastore and Joe Price also played on that team.

"Keith" was drafted in 1980 and played shortstop in Eugene, Oregon. He thought about quitting the next year because he was told to stay back for extended spring training, which meant he'd be returning to rookie ball. He also felt minor leaguer manager Jimmy Hoff—who a lot of baseball people liked, because

he was organized and efficient—hated him. But he was saved by minor league manager Greg Riddoch, who switched him to the outfield, eventually to center field. "It's like playing shortstop," Davis remembers thinking. "Angles, throws, backup plays, the way the ball comes off the bat."

By 1983, Davis was in his first big-league camp, wide-eyed. He recalls meeting some of the Big Red Machine—Johnny Bench, Davey Concepcion, and Dan Driessen. Davis also met former Reds slugger, Ted Kluszewski, who liked Davis, even though Davis didn't know it. Kluszewski liked everybody. And everybody thought the skinny new kid could someday be a real bomber.

On Easter Sunday, 1990, in Atlanta, the bomber struck in the seventh.

After Sabo, Hatcher, and Larkin (who was three-for-five, his fifth straight multi-hit game to raise his average to .522), each singled off twenty-four-year-old left-hander Tom Glavine to cut the deficit to 4–3, Braves manager Russ Nixon signaled for hard-throwing right-hander Dwayne Henry with two outs to face the .136-hitting Davis (three-for-twenty-two).

Davis took ball one and ball two, and then, on the fastball he knew was coming—Hatcher was on second and Larkin on first, and the force was in effect at any base—Davis began his swing like Ali with those hands held low, and he whipped the bat through the zone. As bat met ball, Davis knew it was gone, as did everybody else in the ballpark. It shot over the left-center field wall. The score was 6–4 and everybody knew the game was

DAVIS'S SLOW START DIDN'T HOLD THE REDS BACK

"April is the cruelest month."

T.S. Eliot wasn't writing about Eric Davis when he penned those words to start his masterpiece *The Waste Land*, but he might as well have been. Throughout his career, Davis was a notoriously slow starter, and 1990 was no different. He batted just .186 during April, the fourth time in six seasons he had batted under .200 in the season's first month.

In the past, a weak start by Davis meant a weak start by the Reds.

But the past didn't matter in 1990. Hot starts from Barry Larkin, Mariano Duncan, Chris Sabo, Todd Benzinger, and Billy Hatcher showed Davis that he didn't have to carry the team for them to be successful.

It wasn't that Davis no longer mattered. It was that this was now a complete team with players picking each other up on a daily basis. Everyone embraced their roles, and that took a lot of pressure off Davis, who knew that, even after signing the big nine-million-dollar contract in the off-season, it couldn't be all about him.

The time would come when Davis would have to take the team on his back. The Reds would need him to be a superstar, and he would handle the role. But another slow start and a particularly cruel April didn't mean that the Reds were set up for another season of falling short. His teammates made sure of that.

ERIC DAVIS IN APRIL

Year	AVG	HR	RBI	Team Record
1985	.152	3	4	10–10
1986	.185	3	6	5–12
1987	.364	7	16	15–7
1988	.179	2	7	11–11
1989	.241	6	16	13–9
1990	.186	1	8	13–3

over. "I like guys that are good, hard fastball throwers," Davis said. "You don't have to think as much. You've just got to be short and quick and that's what I kept telling myself up there—short and quick, short and quick."

Sabo, who had six homers and twenty-nine RBI in eighty-two games in 1989, now had half those homers (three) and a fifth of those RBI (six) in a sixteenth of those games (five). He had tapped into Lou-Mo.

The big outs were secured by Rob Dibble. He was called on in the seventh, when relievers Tim Layana and Norm Charlton had loaded the bases. Dibble got pinch hitter Mark Lemke to hit a comebacker for a force at the plate, and then Dibble got Lonnie Smith to fly out and end the threat.

How sweet it was for Piniella. He had been pulling mightily for Davis.

"I said this spring it was unfair to put the burden on one guy alone," Piniella said. "Everyone's capable here. We can beat you with power and we can beat you with speed."

OLIVER SHUT DOWN SOME OF THE BEST IN 1990

Joe Oliver loved to throw out runners. And he was good at it, particularly in 1990. He didn't waste any time establishing his reputation as a rookie. If you were going to steal a base when he was behind the plate, you were going to have to earn it.

Through the first twenty games of the 1990 season, Oliver threw out twelve would-be base stealers while only eight runners were successful. And he took down the best base stealers in the National League: Roberto Alomar twice (twenty-four steals in 1990), Ron Gant (thirty-three) Larry Walker (twenty-one), Tim Raines (forty-nine), Marquis Grissom (twenty-two), Vince Coleman (seventy-seven), and Willie McGee (thirty-one steals). That's seven of the top thirty speedsters in the league.

Though he did slow down a bit afterward, Oliver was right at the NL average for catching runners the rest of the season, but his reputation had been established. Few runners even attempted to steal after those first twenty games. Overall, he found himself second in the league in caught-stealing percentage at the end of the season (minimum five hundred innings behind the plate):

Catcher	SB	CS	CS%
Tom Pagnozzi (STL)	40	28	41%
Joe Oliver (CIN)	64	34	35%
Darren Daulton (PHI)	78	41	34%
Joe Girardi (CHC)	80	34	30%
Benito Santiago (SD)	60	25	29%

The best thing about Oliver's success was that it took away the very thing the Reds hitters were trying to use against their opponents—speed. Being able to use speed to beat a team while simultaneously taking it away from their toolbox had to be demoralizing.

We run on you; you don't run on us.

And nobody had those things wrapped up in one body like Davis did.

April 16, Atlanta

Billy Hatcher in 2010: "I remember as an Astro playing against the Reds and thinking, 'These guys are a very talented team, but they get to a certain point and stop.' I didn't know if they were getting tired or what."

In 1990, there wasn't much chance of that happening with Hatcher sandwiched between leadoff hitter Chris Sabo and third hitter, Barry Larkin, who was loving his RBI role with Sabo and Hatcher getting on base so much.

Right from the start, opposing pitchers would struggle.

Here they come again.

Sabo singled, and Hatcher laid down a perfect bunt single to the left side. It was then that Larkin dubbed Sabo and Hatcher "The Rabbits."

"In the first inning, if those two rabbits hadn't

been running, my ground-ball single would have been a double play instead of the game's first RBI, scoring Sabo," Larkin said.

Paul O'Neill, who had come into the game hitting .267, was back in the lineup, having had the previous night off against left-hander Tom Glavine, singled home Hatcher and Larkin to give the Reds a 3–0 first-inning lead.

Sabo, Hatcher, and Larkin combined for nine of the Reds' thirteen hits in the 5–3 victory. Larkin had four of those hits, including a first-inning, hit-and-run RBI after Sabo's single and Hatcher's bunt.

It's hard to imagine that you could start off as hot as Larkin did in 1990 and not remember it, but he doesn't. Maybe having 9,057 plate appearances blurs the memory. But he remembers well the team's hot start.

"Lou's idea was to press the sons of bitches and not let up," Larkin recalls. "We loved it."

In the ninth inning, Hatcher again bunt-singled down the third-base line, and Larkin singled, scoring Sabo, giving the Reds some breathing room when the Braves scored twice in the ninth. Those were Hatcher's first two of ten bunt hits in 1990, tying him for third-most in the NL with another rabbit, the Cardinals' Vince Coleman.

April 17, Cincinnati

The Reds, at last, played their "home opener"—two words that go together in every major league city but one, where they are, in fact, redundant. Because of the lockout, the first week of the season was wiped

out. Rather than push the schedule back, the league moved those games to different parts of the year.

Joe Oliver, the twenty-four-year-old rookie catcher, brought the 38,384 fans to their feet in the first inning of that first game at Riverfront Stadium when he threw out Roberto Alomar, one of the best base stealers in the game. Tom Browning then faced defending batting champion Tony Gwynn with two outs and nobody on base, instead of one out and Alomar at second. When Oliver threw out Alomar again in the fourth, he made the first out of the inning, depriving a formidable heart of the order (Gwynn, Jack Clark, and Joe Carter) of a potential RBI in a tight game.

"I don't remember throwing out Alomar twice in the home opener," recalls Oliver twenty years later, "but I do remember how much we were taking away teams' running games and running ourselves."

The Reds tried to steal two bases and got them both; the Padres tried to steal two and got none.

So far that season, the Reds had stolen nineteen bases, the opposition three.

It was as much a reason as anything for the Reds being 7–0.

This wasn't math, it was a mindset: We will eat your lunch, kick sand in your face, and take your girl, and there's nothing you can do about it.

Browning pitched six innings of six-hit, one-run baseball—the run coming, as it so often did with

Teammates' aggressiveness unleashed rookie Joe Oliver to play the same way.

Browning, on a solo shot. And then here came two of the three Nasty Boys, first Norm Charlton with four punchouts in two innings and then Randy Myers in the ninth, ending it with a punch out and a ground out, appropriately, to Barry Larkin.

"The electricity was there," said Larkin, "especially in the ninth when everybody was standing. It was loud."

The game drew less than a full house, but the people appreciated what they had seen—a baseball game the way it was meant to be played, with fine base running and excellent fielding and taut pitching, and the slightest margin of error (those two caught-stealings, really) deciding it all.

The Reds were in the Padres' grill, pushing and shoving and grinding and never letting up, playing flawless baseball, the way it hadn't been played over the course of a full season here in fifteen years.

And the fans were hungry for it. This was a team they could root for because these guys were young and fast and good and confident, and they were led by a man who was a cross between a drill sergeant and the best symphonic conductor in the world. He got his guys to play.

It was also a coming-out game for Charlton, who had struggled in Atlanta.

Nasty.

The fans would get to see the third Nasty Boy tomorrow—in all his splendor.

April 18, Cincinnati

Paul O'Neill found himself on the bench the day after the home opener. He had come into the game hitting only .217 (five for twenty-three), but had worked with Tony Perez before the game on driving the ball and felt better about his swing. He was eager to put it into practice.

And so, it was pure Piniella that when San Diego Padres manager Jack McKeon relieved his left-handed starter, Dennis Rasmussen, with right-handed Rafael Valdez (making his major league debut) in the third inning, the skipper said, "Paul, grab a bat."

The Reds had walked-and-singled their way to a 3–0 lead in the first inning, but the Padres had responded by walking-and-singling to tie the score in the second inning off Danny Jackson and took a 5–3 lead in the top of the inning on a two-run homer by Joe Carter.

Is it unorthodox to call upon a pinch hitter in the third inning? A little bit. But Piniella was nothing if not unorthodox. He had printout after printout of statistics and matchups in the Reds dugout ("It looked like a library in there," said bench coach Jackie Moore) but when it came to matters of the gut, Piniella was a regular Paul Prudhomme.

O'Neill singled to get things rolling. Then Duncan blasted a two-run homer to tie the game.

In the fourth inning, after Barry Larkin led off with a single and Todd Benzinger followed with a walk, O'Neill drove them both home with a shot into the wind over the right-field wall, and the Reds led

8–5. It was can't-touch-this-time, and the Nasty Boys smelled it.

Piniella was eager to lock horns with Padres manager Jack McKeon. Piniella didn't like McKeon because Piniella believed that after the 1972 season in Kansas City McKeon had talked the Royals front office into firing then-manager Bob Lemon and elevating himself into the manager's job. As a Royal, Piniella had been American League Rookie of the Year in 1969; he played for Lemon the next three years and admired his manager, a decent and compassionate man who had been a Hall of Fame pitcher in Cleveland.

"(McKeon) was a champion second-guesser," wrote Piniella in his 1986 autobiography, *Sweet Lou.* "Second-guessing is a baseball disease. It destroys more clubs than sore arms. McKeon helped sour the front office on Lemon and greased the skids.... I didn't like his manner, his tone of voice, his sarcasm—and the feeling was mutual. He didn't like me very much. I just couldn't play for the man."

The drama continued in the seventh inning when McKeon told the home-plate umpire that Rob Dibble's uniform jersey sleeves were cut too wide. McKeon knew that Dibble let people get under his skin. McKeon was trying to use that to his advantage.

Piniella knew the type. He was one of them.

"He's just trying to rattle you," Piniella told Dibble. "Put on Stan's jersey (Reds pitching coach Stan Williams) and show them what you got."

As though Dibble needed firing up. He always pitched like his hair was on fire.

"That was the first time in three years anybody's checked me," Dibble said. "They were just trying to rile me. It pumped me up."

And O'Neill? He had a perfect night, four-for-four: Three singles, the three-run bomb, and he also scored twice.

April 20, Cincinnati

In U.S. District Court, Pete Rose pleaded guilty to two counts of filing false income tax returns, a dark day figuratively and literally. The Reds were rained out.

April 21, Cincinnati

The Reds liked their chances again this night. They had Jack Armstrong on the mound, and they were facing Braves right-hander Marty Clary. They came in hitting .320 against right-handers.

There was talk in the clubhouse of what would happen if the Reds could win out this weekend and run their record to 10–0. Some guys would shave their heads; others would join them at 15–0.

"I wasn't asked on this one," Piniella said, "but I'll jump in there with them. If we win fifteen straight, I'll shave my head, too."

Piniella was one of them—just more intense. Well, more intense than all but a couple.

"We'd be out having a beer or whatever and the subject would turn to Lou," recalls Billy Hatcher. "We'd say, 'What is it with this guy? We're winning, and he's not happy. What would he be like if we were losing?'"

DUNCAN'S SURPRISE SEASON

When the Reds traded Kal Daniels and Lenny Harris to the Los Angeles Dodgers for Tim Leary and Mariano Duncan in July of 1989, Leary was considered the key acquisition for the Reds. Duncan was a speedster who had racked up one hundred stolen bases in 125 attempts but had done little else offensively in the big leagues. Given that his primary position was shortstop and the Reds had Barry Larkin for years to come, it looked like Duncan would be only a switch-hitting bench player and insurance at shortstop.

Then Lou Piniella named Duncan the starting second baseman in January of 1990, though Duncan had a career .235/.285/.330 (AVG/OBP/SLG) line coming into the season and had only started twenty-six games at second base in the big leagues. Piniella said the decision was based on an opinion he received from a trusted Yankee scout as well as on the idea of having Duncan's speed in the eighth spot in the batting order. Even the trusted scout couldn't have predicted the numbers that Duncan put up for that year.

His impact was felt immediately as he batted .448 during the 9–0 start. More importantly, his hits were well timed. Twice he gave his team the lead with a hit, and two other times he tied the game during those first nine games.

Twenty-five games into the season, Duncan led the National League with a .400 batting average, and he was leading the majors with a 1.137 OPS. His surprising results weren't limited to the hot start, however, as he finished the season with a .306 batting average and an .821 OPS, the latter number being over two hundred points higher than his career mark to that point.

Defensively, Duncan wasn't much to look at. For someone who had very little experience at second base, he could have been much worse, but he was worth about six runs less than the average second baseman on defense, and that definitely took away some of his value as a player.

Still, it's hard to imagine where the Reds would have been without his production. Only Ryne Sandberg and Bill Doran outdid Duncan offensively as a second baseman in the National League. Perhaps the most telling statistic is that Duncan batted .338 in high-leverage situations—spots in the game when a hit historically has the most dramatic effect on a team's chances for winning. He came through when the team needed him most.

Duncan fell back to earth in 1991, mainly because his batting average when he put the ball in play dropped from .340, a number that was unsustainable, to a slightly below normal .277. Luck just wasn't on his side anymore, and with Bill Doran signed for a three-year/$7.4 million contract following the end of the 1990 season, the Reds granted Duncan free agency after 1991.

He had another brief stint with the Reds in 1995 after he was picked up off waivers in August. Unfortunately, he was unable to recapture the magic of 1990 as the team sputtered in the NLCS against the eventual World Champion Atlanta Braves.

Eric Davis planned to be one of the first to shave his head. In fact, he packed a set of clippers. So did Barry Larkin. They were both amateur barbers. When the moment came, they'd shave each other's heads, and then shave whoever else wanted to join in.

"I hope my wife can adjust to it," said Davis. "I hope a lot of wives can adjust to it. There are going to be some ugly ballplayers."

"I look good (bald)," said Jose Rijo. "I look sexy."

There was some good-natured quibbling over what they had discussed among themselves in spring training: How long of a winning streak would it take before they would start shearing their locks? And what constituted a shaved head? Did every last follicle have to come off?

How ugly might it get?

"We may never know just how ugly," wrote Tim Sullivan in the *Enquirer*, noting that if the agreed-upon number was fifteen wins in a row, the streak would be historic, because the modern record for consecutive victories at the start of a season was thirteen, and it was shared by the 1982 Atlanta Braves and the 1987 Milwaukee Brewers.

The Reds didn't want to be like either of those clubs—neither had made the World Series.

"We're going to run into some tough luck, some great pitching," Tom Browning predicted. "But right now we've got a lot of confidence. We feel like when the streak ends, we'll just pick up another one."

The way Saturday's game started off, it appeared the Reds were going to get one game closer to what-

ever the number was for head-shaving. The Reds got two runs off a combination of an infield hit (Sabo), a stolen base (Hatcher), a tag-up (to third, by Hatcher, on a deep fly ball to center by Larkin), two walks (Davis and O'Neill), and a ground ball to third (Benzinger).

Jack Armstrong pitched six innings, allowing only five hits and one run and striking out seven, and lowering his ERA to 1.95, tops among the team's starters. The Reds won 8–1. For his success so far (3–0), Armstrong in part gave credit to Piniella.

"Lou has a good way about him," Armstrong said. "He doesn't say too much in words, no lectures. But he'll give you a look here and there, and a compliment at the right time."

April 22, Cincinnati

The Reds' fabulous nine-game winning streak was ended—as Browning predicted it would be—by great pitching. Tom Glavine would be the Reds nemesis on not just this day, but for the next twenty years. In his career, the only team he would be beat more than the Reds (27–12, .692) were the Phillies (29–17, .630).

"Glavine had me off-balance all day," Larkin said. "He pitched me in, he pitched me out, he pitched me up, and he pitched me down. I came up in a couple of situations to help the team out and I didn't come through." His nine-game hitting streak ended.

Tom Browning's undoing was a first-inning, three-run bomb by Dale Murphy—the first time the Reds hadn't scored the first run of the game that season—

but by the fifth inning the Reds had the crowd buzzing again. Eric Davis and Todd Benzinger hit leadoff singles in the fifth (they were stranded on Paul O'Neill's strikeout and Joe Oliver's double-play ball), but Mariano Duncan got everybody back on their feet with a leadoff triple in the sixth, but he, too, was stranded. When Benzinger smashed a solo shot in the seventh, everybody figured, *Here we go.*

And in the eighth, that's the way it began, the clapping hands flashing on the Riverfront Stadium scoreboard and everybody joining in. The bases were loaded with two outs when Larkin stepped up.

Here we go, thought Piniella. Got the man up there we want.

In Larkin's locker sat his barber clippers; he had brought them to the ballpark anticipating victory number ten.

But reliever Mike Stanton got him to ground into a fielder's choice to end the inning.

"I was hoping (the streak) would never end," said Billy Hatcher. "The fans were beginning to think we were invincible."

"I didn't think we'd go 162-and-oh." Piniella said. "It was just a question of when we'd get beat." And, then, as always, Piniella laid some of what Browning refers to as "Lou vernacular" upon it. "I'm certainly attuned to the fact that the vast majority of our schedule is ahead of us," he said.

Larkin, as always, put his finger on it. It wasn't so much the lack of hitting in high-leverage situations as it was the lack of enough high-leverage situations.

"We made things happen (during the streak)," he said, "but (today) we did not get many people on base to make things happen."

"The heck with the loss," said Eric Davis. "I wanted to sees some ugly-looking guys in here."

 ## *FAST FACTS*

- Barry Larkin is the only player since 1954 to start the season with multiple hits in each of his team's first eight games. His twenty-one hits after eight games is the most during that span. He did this despite the fact that the April 14 game against the Braves was rained out after Larkin already had three hits.
- The 1990 Reds were the twelfth Reds team since 1901 to play the entire season without having their record dip below .500 once. Through 2009, the Reds have not done it since.

5

The Habit of Winning

A great start, but other teams have jumped from the gate and burst to the front. How long would it last? What if a key player got hurt? What would happen then, Sweet Lou, to this fast horse of yours? The answer to those questions was simple: 33–12

April 24, Philadelphia

Eric Davis slid into third base and felt his right knee twist, just as the umpire signaled safe.

Damn!

And in Philly, of all places. Davis had owned Philadelphia since his first full season in '86. There was just something about the place. The fans gave him a rough time, but it was almost always good-natured. They knew a ballplayer when they saw one: *How come we ain't got nobody running into walls like this dude?*

Davis was a gamer. The misconception about him was that he was "soft." Even Ron Oester, the quintessential gamer, thought so; Pete Rose did too; radio broadcaster Marty Brennaman agreed. Damn near every Joe Bag of Donuts from Batesville to Batavia thought it.

"I remember (as a player) at times being mad that Eric wasn't in the lineup," says Ron Oester, who played second base for eleven seasons with the Reds. "I'd be thinking, '*He's not in the lineup again today?*' But he's

Trading for Billy Hatcher became an even bigger deal when Eric Davis went down as now they had a viable center fielder to back him up.

WINNING WITHOUT ERIC DAVIS

During the late 1980s, the Reds depended on Eric Davis to drive the team's success, but the 1990 team didn't need to wait around for Superman to save the day. They kept winning.

Billy Hatcher had been playing left field before Davis got hurt. He split time between left and center field while Davis was on the mend and didn't miss a beat, batting .333 with four doubles and three triples.

The same can't be said for the other replacements. Herm Winningham, who saw more time in center field with Davis out, batted .255 but only managed a .291 on-base percentage and a .314 slugging percentage in Davis's absence. Rolando Roomes produced just eight hits in forty-one at bats while striking out twelve times. The Reds released him less than a month after Davis's return.

Mariano Duncan, however, continued his torrid pace, batting .357 with three doubles, a triple, and two home runs to lead the Reds offense. Joe Oliver hit half of his eight home runs on the season during the twenty-three-game stretch while driving in sixteen runs. Todd Benzinger hit .301 with fourteen RBI. Paul O'Neill and Chris Sabo each hit three home runs with O'Neill matching Oliver's sixteen RBI for the team lead.

The Davis injury showed this team what it meant to win as a team. Nothing is easy when your star player goes down, but compiling a 16–7 record in his absence showed them that they could depend on each other to get the job done.

---

the only one who knew how his body felt. Maybe he felt, 'If I go out there and can't do the things I usually do, maybe I'm hurting the team.' And the fact is, he went out there hurt a lot. You look at his frame. He was strong, lean, no body fat. He was more susceptible to injury because of that."

Oester, and all Davis's teammates, respected his abilities.

"I saw Darryl Strawberry, and Ken Griffey Jr., in their prime, and neither of those guys could do all the things as well as Eric could do them," says Oester. "He had the best five tools of anybody I'd ever seen, before or since."

The injury in Philadelphia was typical for Davis.

He'd been hustling. He didn't absolutely need to steal this bag. He was having a poor April (.167, only one home run), but when had he ever had a good April? He'd always been able to make it happen with his glove and his legs, even when he wasn't hitting.

The Reds were trailing 2–0 in the second inning when Davis led off with a single and stole second but noticed the dirt was mushy where he made his pivot and took that explosive first step, the one that kept him from being thrown out on a stolen base attempt in his first season as a Red.

It would take more than a Philly grounds crewman with a heavy hand on a hose trigger to slow down Eric Davis, however, and he slid safely into second base. He took his lead and got a read on pitcher Ken Howell, who had a history of throwing wild pitches because his slider was so sharp it would dive in the dirt and get past the catcher. If Davis could get to third, he could waltz home on one of those. He knew the baseball rule: Don't ever get thrown out at third base for the first or third out. There were two outs. He went anyway. He beat the throw but paid a price. He knew he hurt his knee but acted as though he hadn't, and when the Reds' half-inning ended he headed for center field. He didn't go back out for the third.

Two days later, he was put on the disabled list. Prognosis: Out. Minimum three to four weeks.

Sweet Lou was going to find out now how fast his horse really was.

May 9–10, Pittsburgh

The Reds continued to roll, but the Pittsburgh Pirates were playing well, too. Fans already wondered if this spring match-up foreshadowed one in the fall for the NL pennant.

In the first inning, Piniella argued when Mariano Duncan was called out on a close play at second base. Within two innings both third baseman Chris Sabo and Duncan would be ejected: Sabo for a *strike two* call; Duncan for slamming his helmet at the umpire's feet.

"He (umpire Charlie Williams) probably doesn't like me, and I don't give a darn," said Sabo, as only he could say it. "He can get me the rest of my career. I don't give a darn. He won't get me out of the game."

Duncan said less but did worse, reaching around third-base coach Sam Perlozzo to push third-base umpire Mark Hirschbeck in the chest.

Not wanting to add to the ejections, Piniella stayed under control, prompting a call from his wife, Anita, who was usually telling him to cool it. "You didn't argue enough," she told him.

The next day, after the 6–2 loss, Lou could only shake his head. "When I managed the Yankees and got thrown out, my wife would say I was acting like a little kid," he said. "You can't win."

Clearly, the players were taking on the personality of their manager back when *he* was a player. They were doing what he had done, not what he was now telling them to do. Or maybe that was just who they were—young, feisty, and in your face, even if you were wearing blue.

Pirates closer Bill Landrum had earned the save in the previous night's game against the Reds, pitching three shutout innings, and was unable to resist a shot at the increasing notoriety of the Nasty Boys. Afterward, he said, "They can talk about the Reds bullpen all they want. I'll take our bullpen. They're a good bullpen, but they've got nothing on us."

Reds hitters discussed the comment before that night's game. And so, when the Reds entered the eighth inning tied 2–2, Todd Benzinger had practically composed the punch line even before he delivered the punch: a triple that scored Barry Larkin to ignite an eight-run inning.

"I had a feeling we'd do what we did tonight," Benzinger said. "I didn't think Pittsburgh would beat us twice in a row. They'd be talking about Murderers' Row if they did." Then he added, "It feels great to do something like that against the best bullpen in the league."

The Reds were 19–6. Even more impressive: thirteen of those victories and only three of the losses were on the road. *That* is what worried their opponents. The Reds came into your town and ransacked the place.

The seven-game lead over the Los Angeles Dodgers was the biggest margin a Reds team had held since the Big Red Machine ended the 1976 season with a ten-game lead over Da Bums.

May 11, Cincinnati

Chris Sabo is not your typical bird. And he would prove it—again—on the Friday night opening of a three-game series with the Cubs.

There was no place like Riverfront Stadium on a Friday night to open a weekend series after a successful road trip. If there was one time the old joint still felt like the 1970s, it was in April and May of 1990.

Despite spotting the Cubs a 5–0 first-inning lead—Scott Scudder got knocked out of the game only two outs into the first inning—the Reds relievers (Tim Birtsas, Rick Mahler, Norm Charlton, and Rob Dibble) held the Cubs right there. Meanwhile, the Reds hitters chipped away at starter Greg Maddux to cut the deficit to 5–4 going into the eighth inning.

The Reds loaded the bases against closer Mitch "Wild Thing" Williams, and up stepped Sabo, who in his industrial-strength goggles appeared ready to weed-whack the south forty. Instead, he smoked a double to left-center to clear the bases.

After the game, he acted like it was no big deal. He was just doing his job, like all those blue-collar workers from Detroit where he grew up.

"What can I say?" he said. "It fell in there. I was just trying to put the ball in play. I hit it good but not that good."

Twenty years later, Paul O'Neill would note, "To Sabes, it never was a big deal."

On the field or off, Sabo was a bit different—unemotional, supremely confident and yet without a trace of ego. His words sounded strange because we expect athletes to be full of themselves. And, yet, every time somebody refers to Sabo as "a throwback," somebody else responds with Joe Morgan's line: "Throwback to when? There was nobody like Sabo when I played."

In other words, there was never before a guy like Sabo, and there never will be one quite like him again.

May 13, Cincinnati

Lou Piniella is fond of saying that on the '90 team, "everybody could run but Oliver."

Oliver didn't need to run on May 13. With his team leading 5–2, he hit a bases-loaded triple that became significant when the Cubs tied the score at nine, and again when the Reds were leading 10–9. Then

Chris Sabo's famous Rec-Specs gave every boy in glasses hope that one day he could be a big leaguer too.

Oliver hit a three-run homer, and the Reds won going away, 13–9.

It capped a seven-game stretch in which Oliver hit four home runs and drove in fourteen runs. If you want to know how a team starts out 33–12, look no further than your rookie catcher who is not known for his pop to begin popping them out of the ballpark. And he was throwing out base runners better than anybody in the league—fourteen of twenty-six, including that day against the Cubs when he nailed Shawon Dunston trying to steal third. Joe Oliver was only a month into his rookie season, and he already had a career day.

May 18, Cincinnati

Paul O'Neill hit a solo shot in the ninth inning to give the Reds a 1–0 victory over the St. Louis Cardinals. Ron Robinson and Norm Charlton combined for a shutout.

"Yeah, I remember that one," says O'Neill, twenty years later. "Ken Dayley to left, pitch away." He also remembered Davis getting hurt in late April. "Philly, right?" he asks. "I played with Eric all through the minors. Every year, the only question with Eric was 'How many games can we keep him on the field?' because you knew if you kept him on the field he was going to put up the numbers and help win games.

When he went down in Philly, I remember thinking, 'Is everything going to change? Are we going to be able to keep winning?'"

But the Reds proved to be more than any one player.

"Teams get in habits—and winning is one of them," O'Neill says. "We were in the habit of winning in that stretch. When we kept playing well and winning (after Davis went down), we came to expect to win."

May 19, Cincinnati

Jack Armstrong wasn't having trouble with the Cardinals until he got to the sixth inning, when they loaded the bases. That's when he realized he had popped one too many chunks of Bazooka in his mouth, something he did at the start of every inning.

"I get a tackiness on my fingertips from the bubble gum," he said. "(But) I had too much Bazooka in my mouth, and my fingers got all sticky. I threw the first pitch, and I started panicking and started aiming the ball. Then I went to the rosin bag, and I took a little from there and it got even stickier. I knew I was in trouble."

Pitching coach Stan Williams came out to give him "a breather." But a breather isn't what Armstrong needed.

"I need a garden hose to get this Bazooka off my fingers," Armstrong told Williams, with a smile.

Armstrong also dispensed some good advice to teammate Rolando Roomes. "He is a heck of a fastball hitter but sometimes has trouble staying back on

Jack Armstrong—a little too much Bazooka.

breaking pitches and off-speed pitches. (Cardinal) John Tudor is the consummate off-speed pitcher. I went up to (Roomes) and told him, 'Keep your hands back and thrill me.' The first two guys get on, and he goes out and hits it in the second deck."

THE MYTH OF THE CAREER YEAR

One of the myths that remain in people's memories of the 1990 Reds is that they all had career years. In fact, none of them did. But few had off years, and a couple had very good years.

CATCHER
Joe Oliver: He had a good year for a rookie, but he was better for the Reds in 1992 and had his best offensive season in 1995 with the Milwaukee Brewers.

FIRST BASEMEN
Todd Benzinger: 1990 could be considered his worst season offensively as he battled an injured wrist and hand most of the year. He had much more power with the Red Sox in 1988 and the Reds in 1989.

Hal Morris: This may have been his best year, but he produced at least three other comparable years in 1991, 1994, and 1996. This was hardly a career year.

SECOND BASEMAN
Mariano Duncan: It was arguably his best year, but he was just as good with the 1996 New York Yankees when he won another ring.

THIRD BASEMAN
Chris Sabo: He had a breakout power year, but he was even better in 1991 when he hit more home runs and had a higher average, on-base percentage, and slugging percentage.

SHORTSTOP
Barry Larkin: Breakout season, no question. But 1990 was not even among his five best years. Those would be 1991, 1992, 1995, 1996, and 1998.

LEFT FIELDER
Billy Hatcher: Good year, not great. He was better in Houston in 1987 and 1988. That's why the Reds got him. They wanted the Houston Hatcher, and the Cincinnati Hatcher in '90 was close.

CENTER FIELDER
Eric Davis: Ha! In 1986 and 1987 he was far better.

RIGHT FIELDER
Paul O'Neill: Don't even get us started. The man won four more rings as a Yankee. All four of those Yankee ring years were as good as, if not better than, his 1990. Even as a Red, 1990 was probably only his third or fourth best season.

PITCHERS
When you look at the pitching staff, the only career year that pops out is Jack Armstrong, and he really had a career *half* a year.

In the end, it wasn't a collection of career years that put the Reds into the playoffs in 1990. They were a group of talented players who executed well for a manager who wouldn't let them ease up. They could have been winners for many years, but taking a pennant is hard to do once and nearly impossible to do year after year.

Hal Morris nearly left baseball in 1990 to become a doctor.

The Reds won 4–0, the first shutout of Armstrong's career.

May 30, Cincinnati

Hal Morris almost quit baseball before he had a chance to become, well, Hal Morris.

"They needed to clear a roster spot when they traded for Glenn (Braggs)," recalls Morris, although actually the Reds were clearing a spot for Mariano Duncan—this was ten days before the Braggs trade. "I had an option left, so they sent me down because they could. After three or four days, I called my dad and said, 'I think I'm coming home. I'm thinking of going to medical school. This isn't going anywhere. I led the league (Triple-A) in hitting last year, and I was second the year before, and now I'm back (in Triple A).'

"I went in to talk to (Nashville manager) Pete Mackanin and told him what I was thinking about doing. He said, 'We ought to talk to Bob Quinn before you do anything.' Bob said, 'We're going to get you back up here (to Cincinnati) within twenty days.' At the time there was a rule that if you were in the minor leagues for less than three weeks, you never lost any major league service time. I said, 'That's fine.'

"I was down there for nineteen days, and it was a blessing because I got a lot of at-bats and got my swing together. It was the best thing for me. When they called me back up, I went directly to Montreal. Todd (Benzinger) was swinging in the on-deck circle, and one of the little French-Canadian batboys ran by him, and Todd checked his swing to avoid hitting him and hurt his hand. I was in the lineup that night. If I would've had to sit for another week or two, I might not have swung the bat as well. But I'd had those at-bats in Triple-A, and I was ready."

SPEED WAS A DEADLY WEAPON

If you ask the players from the wire-to-wire team what set them apart, almost to a man they will say, "We were aggressive. Everyone in the lineup but Oliver could run."

They attempted the fifth-most stolen bases in the majors. When they got on first or second base with the base in front of them open, they were thinking about stealing. And, more importantly, so was the pitcher.

"Lou put a lot of trust in his players," Billy Hatcher recalls. "He figured, if you have to think before you do, you're going to be a step slow. We didn't have a lot of meetings, so the guys who could steal bases just did."

While they were an aggressive team, they weren't foolish. If they attempted to steal, they usually made it safely. A team typically needs to be successful on 65 to 70 percent of their stolen base attempts to boost their run production. The Reds were successful 72 percent of the time. Only the St. Louis Cardinals attempted more steals and were successful at a higher rate.

There's more to running the bases than stealing them, however. Baseball Prospectus rates runners on all aspects of base running, including taking an extra base on a hit or out, advancing on wild pitches and passed balls, as well as on avoiding extra outs on the bases. The Reds rated as the third-best base-running team in the majors in 1990, behind only Milwaukee and Pittsburgh. In particular, the Reds excelled at advancing the extra base on hits as well as on outs. They rarely took their foot off the throttle and were always looking for ways to get that extra base.

Individually, according to Baseball Prospectus, the Reds had the best overall base runner in the league in Barry Larkin. He wasn't just an outstanding base stealer—he was thirty of thirty-five in stolen base attempts in 1990—he was also one of the best at advancing on a hit. He epitomized Piniella's aggressive strategy.

Chris Sabo was rated as the fourteenth-best base runner. Billy Hatcher tied for the team lead with thirty steals, and Mariano Duncan led the NL with eleven triples. Eric Davis, despite having a bad knee most of the season, stole twenty-one bases in twenty-four attempts. Heck, even Joe Oliver stole a base in '90, one of only thirteen swipes in his career. It was an aggressive strategy that knocked opponents back on their heels, leaving them wondering, as Bill Doran did after the first series of the year, "How are we going to beat these guys?"

June 3, Los Angeles

As zero after zero went up on the Dodger Stadium scoreboard, Tom Browning thought that he might notch his second complete game of the season. In his eleven starts since opening day in Houston, when he lasted only four innings, he had not gone fewer than six full innings, and twice he got into the eighth inning and twice to the ninth.

He loved those Nasty Boys, because he knew they were the potential difference between winning it all and winning most of it, and he wanted to win it all. Still, he didn't like coming out of games.

"Lou never said much to me when he came out there," he says. "He'd put his hand out, and you'd hand him the ball. I loved to go nine innings, but it was hard to do with (the Nasty Boys) behind you. Seventh inning on, any kind of trouble, you were usually out. Lou would give you opportunities to get out of situations in the sixth inning, and maybe sometimes even in the seventh. He leaned on the starters more than you might think. Of course, he wanted to shorten the game. If he could get through it with one guy out of the bullpen, he loved it. But if he had to use all three of them, he did."

The one thing Piniella couldn't stand was a walk. He hated nibblers. He wanted his pitchers going right at guys, and when they didn't, he let everybody in the dugout know what he thought with every word in the book and some they hadn't heard before.

"Being on the bench in the games you're not pitching, you'd hear what Lou would say about the pitcher who was out there," Browning recalls. "It would make you think, 'Man, what's he say when *I'm* out there?' I'm sure all the pitchers thought that."

After the combined shutout of June 3, though, Lou showed a rare bit of optimism, but he made clear there would be no coasting.

Lou Piniella was the man in charge, and superstars, rookies, and even the "nasty" players followed his lead.

"We know there's a lot of baseball left to be played," he said. "The players are well aware of it. We've got to keep our mind on business, and that's the hunt for red October."

The Hunt for Red October. There it was again. The title of the movie that hit the theaters right before spring training camps opened. Maybe it *was* an omen.

The team was 33–12. The players didn't know it at the time, but those numbers would become embedded in their minds. On occasion the players might forget the date of their wedding anniversaries, but they would never forget 33–12.

Everybody knew about 9–0. But it would take until the end of the season for them to recall 33–12. For some of the players, it would take even longer than the end of the season, but eventually everybody knew those two numbers.

That was their record after the game on June 3.

Ten games up on the second-place Padres.

Would the winning ever come to an end?

 ## FAST FACTS

- The Reds had eight winning streaks of four games or more, including separate five-, six-, and nine-game streaks all before the All-Star break.

6

Welcome Aboard, Braggsie

Lou Piniella and Bob Quinn liked but didn't love their bench, and they didn't like Paul O'Neill playing every day against left-handed pitchers. They envisioned the ten-game lead being cleaved in half like one of Joe Nuxhall's liverwurst-and-onion sandwiches. A Reds scout headed for Milwaukee.

June 9, Cincinnati

Question: Why would you trade for a right-handed right fielder other than to platoon with Paul O'Neill?

Answer: You wouldn't.

On one hand, Lou Piniella felt O'Neill could hit for more power; on the other hand, he felt O'Neill was too emotional. It's tough not to see the contradiction there—Lou calling *anyone* too emotional. It was almost as if he were watching himself play. *Man, if only I'd had his talent.*

Piniella wanted to get more out of O'Neill—wanted him to be as good as Piniella thought he could be.

Paul O'Neill was determined to be the player he thought he should be, even if his manager didn't agree.

When conventional teaching methods didn't work, Piniella began to goad him. "Big Blanking Paul O'Neill," Piniella began calling him, right to his face, even in the presence of his teammates.

Barry Larkin remembers thinking, "I had the feeling that Paul wasn't used to the tough-love treatment." That would fit with the way O'Neill writes of his father in his autobiography, *Me and My Dad*. O'Neill was already trying his damnedest. He didn't seem to be one of those guys who needed a fire lit beneath him.

"He rode O'Neill so hard that I couldn't figure it out sometimes," Glenn Braggs remembers. "Paul could be ripping it up, but if he had a bad at-bat—oh, man. 'Big O'Neill.' Here it comes. When Paul had a bad at-bat against a lefty, Lou would really get on him. Paul just blew him off most of the time. Not to his face, but just in doing things the way Paul wanted to do them, instead of the way Lou wanted him to do them."

Former manager Pete Rose was fond of O'Neill. Rose nicknamed O'Neill "Jethro," as in Jethro Bodine on *The Beverly Hillbillies* TV show. Rose drew a lot of his nicknames from TV. He called Tom Browning "Otis," as in the moon-faced town drunk on *The Andy Griffith Show*, because Browning was equally easygoing and a dead ringer facially.

Braggs believes it wasn't a matter of Piniella not liking O'Neill.

"Paul was one of those low-key guys," Braggs explains. "But he was one of our main guys, our left-handed hitter. Lou felt he needed to ride him. I think it got under Paul's skin a little bit, made him push a little harder. But Paul gave his all every day, anyway."

O'Neill was a solid right fielder who looked like he was going to get better. Among the players who made the Reds go, he and Sabo and Hatcher and Duncan were only a half-notch behind Davis and Larkin. Some Reds fans felt O'Neill was a little over the top with his helmet-throwing, but baseball people knew he could play.

Of course, he was going to have to improve to wrench his way into the top half of the league's right fielders, a group loaded with talent: Darryl Strawberry, Bobby Bonilla, Von Hayes, Tony Gwynn, Andre Dawson, Larry Walker, and on and on.

Piniella felt O'Neill could be one of those guys if he'd pull the damn ball.

O'Neill refused. *I'm a good hitter with power, not a power hitter*, he thought.

Piniella wasn't going to go easy on anybody; he intended to win the World Championship.

"Get me Braggs," he told Quinn.

❖ ❖ ❖ ❖ ❖

Some fans believe the Piniella-O'Neill conflict did not begin until after the 1990 season. They're wrong. Ron Oester, who was not around after 1990, recalls the tension vividly. Reds announcer Marty Brennaman confirms it. Everybody has their theories for what caused the tension: Piniella saw himself in the temperamental O'Neill; Piniella didn't see enough of himself.

"I think Lou saw Paul's potential," says Hal Morris.

Lou Piniella saw the potential for greatness in Paul O'Neill, but the two fiery personalities were never able to mesh.

"Lou was the best hitting instructor I ever had, so he would've known what he was looking at with Paul."

Todd Benzinger speculates that maybe O'Neill wasn't ready for that level of instruction.

"You can't say Lou didn't help him here, although Paul would be the last to admit it," Benzinger says.

"Paul was young. Lou had the expectations of a father when it came to Paul. But it wasn't a father-son, care-about-you kind of thing. That didn't exist. If it did, they'd be really close right now. It never developed that Paul really cared for Lou, or vice versa. I think if we didn't win a World Championship, twelve or fourteen guys might show up at our reunions, but half of them would probably hate Lou."

Twenty years after winning that championship, neither Piniella nor O'Neill has anything bad to say—at least not publicly—about the experience. The only complaint O'Neill will raise involves Piniella's style of communicating.

"It (the abrasiveness) gets tired after a while," he says. "Whatever you did wasn't quite enough."

But, in 1990, when the Reds were breaking quickly from the gate and O'Neill was trying to become the player he wanted to be, he says he wasn't giving undue attention to how hard Piniella was on him.

"What I remember about Lou is his intensity," O'Neill recalls. "I truly believe he wanted me to do well. He wasn't being malicious. He saw something in me that hadn't come out yet

O'Neill says he still talks to Piniella when he sees him, which he occasionally does in his work as a New York broadcaster. Piniella says his only goal was to always get the best out of O'Neill.

It took less than half a season for Piniella to grow disenchanted. Simply put, the Reds acquired Braggs because they didn't like the way O'Neill hit against lefties.

The Reds gave up Ron Robinson and Bob Sebra to get Braggs and Billy Bates, but to them it was worth it. Even though O'Neill was hitting well against lefties to that point in 1990, at times he appeared hapless—

and those times stuck in Piniella's craw.

For the first two months of the season, O'Neill hit better against left-handers (.297/.342/.486 in eighty plate appearances) than he hit against right-handers (.257/.336/.398 in 128 plate appearances), but coming into the '90 season, with just under three full seasons behind him, O'Neill hit poorly against lefties: .193/.251/.313 in 274 plate appearances. And Piniella did not like what he saw. He turned out to be right. O'Neill never did learn to hit lefties. His career line against them was .248/.312/.387.

Determined to prove he could take a team to the postseason, Piniella would not allow a perceived weakness to keep him from his goal. And so, the Reds acquired Braggs, who they felt was everything O'Neill wasn't: right-handed, unflappable, and powerful. He wasn't a great power hitter, but he could hit the long ball and was a dead pull hitter.

There are differing theories on why—two years later, on November 3, 1992—the Reds parted with O'Neill, trading him to the Yankees for Roberto Kelly. But there can be no question that an underlying reason for it was that Piniella had stopped believing he could get the best out of O'Neill.

Todd Benzinger recalls working out with O'Neill after a game in Pittsburgh, probably in early 1991. "They had this little weight room next to the manager's office, a thin wall between them," Benzinger recalls. "We heard Lou on the phone, talking to (Bob) Quinn. We started listening to what (Lou) was saying. We couldn't help it. He was screaming. *'We gotta trade blanking O'Neill. You wouldn't believe what he did in the outfield!* Paul was taken aback. You know how it is when you laugh, but you're embarrassed. It typified the way things were. Usually, it's not that (blatant). But it doesn't have to be that (blatant) for you to know how the manager feels about you. You can tell when a manager doesn't really like you."

Why does Benzinger think that Lou didn't like Paul?

"Paul was blessed with great talent," Benzinger says. "I think Lou saw some somebody with a similar temperament to him and saw a six-four kid who could hit home runs, and Lou wanted him to hit thirty. When things didn't go the way Lou wanted, Paul wasn't going be like a lap dog. It's why he doesn't come back to reunions."

Piniella followed O'Neill out of town after the 1992 season but remains a beloved figure in Cincinnati. O'Neill became a beloved figure in New York. Trading him was a mistake for the Reds, and everybody knows it. O'Neill, who had been painted as a problem, wound up being a solution, winning four more World Championships with the Yankees.

"Lou knew what a phenomenal player Paul was and how much better he could become—which Paul did, but he became that player in New York," Morris says.

From the moment he set foot in New York in 1993, O'Neill was a star and a quiet leader who the fans grew to love. He hit over .300 six years in a row. In Cincinnati, he had never hit better than .276. In strike-shortened 1994, he hit .359 and won the batting title.

"When Paul won that batting title, I noticed he was doing some of the things in getting his weight transferred that Lou was trying to get him to do here," Morris remembers. "He was getting his head behind the ball; he was coiling. He had developed this little move that was producing exactly what Lou wanted."

But O'Neill remained true to himself. In New York, he never came within three home runs of the twenty-eight he hit for the Reds under Piniella in 1991, the worst year of his career, in his mind. His batting average dipped to .256. O'Neill sacrificed who he was—a line-drives-to-all-fields guy—to be close to what Lou wanted, a thirty-homer guy.

And O'Neill vowed never again to make that tradeoff.

Certainly, he would never again strike out that much—107 times. You can imagine what those strikeouts did to the temperamental O'Neill. It's also easy to imagine what O'Neill's failure did to Piniella, who had always been able to make hitters better.

Even after the two departed Cincinnati they continued to butt heads. One of the most revealing encounters occurred in 1994, when one of Piniella's pitchers in Seattle threw a particularly tight pitch to O'Neill that touched off a brawl.

"I had Paul O'Neill in Cincinnati for three years," Piniella told the *New York Times*. "He was a crybaby over there every time they threw the ball inside on him. Pitchers knew it, so they frustrated him. What he has to do is step up there, hit a ball off the left-center-field wall like a man, and that stuff stops. But we weren't throwing at Paul."

Baloney. The Mariners were doing what Piniella

BRAGGS-ROBINSON TRADE SCORECARD

To the Reds:
Glenn Braggs 27-year-old outfielder
Billy Bates 26-year-old second baseman

To the Brewers:
Ron Robinson 28-year-old right-handed starting pitcher
Bob Sebra 28-year-old right-handed reliever

Value Comparison after the Deal

Player	1990	As a Red	Career	Player	1990	As a Brewer	Career
Braggs	1.2	3.2	3.2	Robinson	3.0	2.3	2.3
Bates	-0.2	-0.2	-0.2	Sebra	-0.5	-0.5	-0.5

The value number is Wins Above Replacement, which estimates the number of wins a player provides his team over what you can expect from the typical player in AAA.

From the start of spring training, Ron Robinson was unhappy. The six-year veteran wanted to be a starter, but the Reds couldn't find a spot in the rotation for him. By June, he had made only six appearances, including five starts. His last start with the Reds was a disaster in San Francisco (giving up eight earned runs in less than four innings), but it's likely that his persistent complaints in the media sparked his exodus.

The deal for Glenn Braggs gave the Reds some needed balance in the outfield. Braggs was able to cover right field versus tough left-handers and play left field when Eric Davis needed a day off. It was his back-up role that limited his value with the team. He batted .299 for the Reds and played excellent defense but only made 231 plate appearances. And while Robinson had an excellent season with the Brewers (12–5, 2.91 ERA), the Reds were in a position to deal pitching, and Braggs filled a large hole on the bench. In terms of value, this was a reasonably balanced trade, but given the memorable moments that both Braggs and Billy Bates provided in the playoffs, many Reds fans believe this was a huge win for the team.

would have done if he'd been managing against O'Neill in 1990: He'd have thrown inside, not only to get into O'Neill's kitchen but into his psyche as well. They'd have tried to get him to snap. Pineilla is as old school as they come and always has been. His approach: Find the weakness and hammer it unmercifully.

"I get tired of this guy crying every time we come inside on him," Piniella told the *Times*. "I'm sure other pitchers come inside, and his reaction is the same. When you see a player get frustrated, lose his concentration, and go crazy like that, what the heck do you think is going to happen?"

Most Reds fans remember Glenn Braggs' muscles, but they may not remember that he hit .339 against lefties after the trade.

O'Neill responded, "I'm getting sick and tired of this. It's been going on for four years. It's the same garbage."

Mariano Duncan, a Yankee infielder in '94, echoed his teammate's frustration.

"He started this nonsense," Duncan said. "He's the biggest jerk I've ever seen in my life."

Phooey, said Piniella.

"Mariano played with Paul for three years, and he saw how Paul reacted when he got knocked down," Piniella said. "And when he got knocked down, we retaliated and knocked somebody else down. We protected him."

Piniella admitted then—finally—that he was hard on O'Neill in the early 1990s.

"I was tough on Paul when I had him in Cincinnati," Piniella said. "I was trying to make him a man.

ON TOP OF THE WORLD, THE REDS LET DOWN THEIR GUARD

When the Reds reached 33–12, the best forty-five-game record in franchise history, they faced something they hadn't faced to that point—expectations. Going into the season, only one team in history had won as many as thirty-three of their first forty-five games and failed to make it to the World Series—the 1911 Detroit Tigers. While that fact, along with a ten-game lead, should put a team at ease, the baseball season is long, and titles aren't locked up in June. Manager Lou Piniella certainly felt that the team was a bit too relaxed.

"When we left Dodger Stadium, I think this ballclub felt we'd won the division," Piniella said of the Reds' three wins in a four-game series in Los Angeles at the start of June.

The Reds limped through the next nine games, managing just one win. When they lost the second game in a row to the Giants on June 5, it was the first time all season the Reds had lost a series. Heck, it was the first time they'd even lost back-to-back games to the same team. The Giants finished the sweep the next day, and then the Reds lost five of their next six to the Houston Astros and Atlanta Braves, the teams with the two worst records in the National League.

The primary culprit in the losing streak was the offense, which scored more than three runs in a game only once during the nine-game stretch—a 6–1 win over the Astros on June 7. They batted only .212 and only held the lead for twelve innings in the nine games. It wasn't a matter of not having momentum from game to game. They were unable to get any momentum going even within a game.

For a team that played so well in April and May, it's not unreasonable to expect a drop-off for a few games. But a string of nine games that saw their lead cut from ten games to five served notice that even though a division title was in sight, the Reds still had to work hard to get there.

He cries all the time. Outside of that, I got no problems with Paul."

Cincinnati native Jim Leyritz, a member of that '94 Yankees team, added, "I'd like to see Paulie get him—my money is on O'Neill."

Lou responded, "If (O'Neill) wanted a part of me (during the brawl), he could have had it," Piniella said. "'I was out there. I wasn't ducking."

On and on it went. Then, and now, Piniella concedes nothing when it comes to O'Neill. He was just trying to make him better.

But that inability to make O'Neill as good as Piniella wanted ultimately got O'Neill traded. It was Piniella's greatest—and perhaps only—significant failure as manager of the Reds.

But in 1990 nobody was worried about that.

They were trying to win a championship.

❖ ❖ ❖ ❖ ❖

Glenn Braggs was eager to get going. The trade was announced on Saturday, June 9, and by Monday night Braggs had arrived in Cincinnati and announced he was ready to meet his teammates the next day at the ballpark. He didn't say anything about his moustache to a reporter. He didn't intend to say anything to anybody about it. His teammates in Milwaukee had reminded him about the Reds' no-facial-hair policy, but he figured he would make somebody on the Reds tell him first. He said he was excited to be joining a pennant race. Although Braggs had never played in a pennant race, the Reds scouts had every reason to believe that he would do just fine.

June 12, Cincinnati

As soon as Braggs met his new teammates, he liked what he saw.

"A great group of guys, mostly my age group, and I think we're going to fit in well together."

Starting in place of O'Neill, he got two hits in the doubleheader, but the Reds lost both games to run their record in the last nine games to 1–8. Braggs was still sporting his moustache.

"We've got to get to this soon," said Ken Griffey Sr., referring not to Braggs' moustache but to losing. "If we don't, we're going to be looking up instead of back."

June 13, Cincinnati

By the next night, Mariano Duncan and Rolando Roomes had seen enough. Before the game, they made Braggs shave off his 'stache.

It wasn't long before Braggs became a believer that the team had pennant potential. He opened the second inning of the game against the Braves with a triple to right-center field off Steve Avery that ignited a two-run rally to tie the game at 2–2. He got three more hits in the 13–4 rout that broke the five-game losing streak

"When I look back and see pictures of myself in Milwaukee," recalls Braggs, "I ask, 'Why did I even have that peach fuzz on my face?'"

 *FAST FACTS*

- The Reds were only two games over .500 versus the NL West in 1990 (46–44). They were 45–27 against the NL East.
- The Reds were only the second World Champion to have an eight-game losing streak during the season (the 1953 Yankees lost nine in a row). The 2006 Cardinals also matched the streak, twice.

7

The Collision

The three-week period before the All-Star break was one of the many remarkable times in the 1990 Reds season. Their most dynamic player was hitting .183, their potentially best pitcher was headed to the disabled list, and the most versatile Nasty Boy roared through a stop sign at third base as Dodgers catcher Mike Scioscia, the human career-ender, awaited.

The season hung in the balance.

June 14, Cincinnati

Billy Hatcher was sitting in the trainer's room watching Eric Davis's pre-game ritual, when the idea came to him.

"Eric was getting his (forearms) taped and I was teasing him, so I taped my hands like his," Hatcher said. "Then I got Lark's high-tops and put them on like Eric does. I put on a shirt with his '44' and then all the gold chains."

He also rigged a big knee brace inside his right pant leg. He took his E.D. stance, hands held low, legs spread wide, and gave all the Davis mannerisms.

"Hatcher...took his place in the batting cage to hearty laughter from his teammates," wrote the

A former football player, Norm Charlton never backed down from a fight or a collision, even if it was with a man many believed was made out of bricks.

111

Enquirer's Rory Glynn. "Several hours later, Hatcher, looking more like Kirby Puckett, banged out four hits from that same spot to hearty applause from the Riverfront Stadium crowd."

"See how they mess with me?" Davis laughed.

His teammates loved to bust his chops; they knew he could take it. When Davis was on the DL, somebody hung in his locker a sign with an arrow on it that read, "This way to the field." Hatcher swore that trainer Larry Starr was responsible; Davis pointed at Hatcher and said, "That was *him*."

Davis enjoyed these pranks. He needed to laugh. He came into the June 14 game hitting .183—three points *worse* than he was hitting when he tore up his knee on April 24. The Reds had begun the year 9–2 with Davis in the lineup, went 16–7 without him, and were 11–11 since his return May 19.

"If you're scoring," wrote the *Enquirer*'s Tom Groeschen, "that's a .606 winning percentage with Davis and .696 without him."

"Eric Davis is not one to show emotion on the playing field," wrote the *Enquirer*'s John Erardi. "No flaps up or down, no home run trots by way of Poughkeepsie, no response to the fans even though the boos have now dipped from fair, beyond cruel to taunting."

"When you get a large contract," Davis said, "people think you're supposed to tear up the world right away. It just doesn't work that way. You get paid for what you've done. You try to go from there."

The man's calm in the raspberry storm was darn near beatific.

❖ ❖ ❖ ❖ ❖

In the June 14 game with the Braves, the first big play came in the sixth inning, when the Braves loaded the bases with two outs and were trailing 3–2. Dangerous Ron Gant—*Ronniegant* Larkin called him, running his name together—stepped into the box. He was third in the league in slugging percentage and had doubled in the third inning.

He ripped a one-hop shot to the left of third baseman Chris Sabo, who dove, speared it, and threw a strike to Mariano Duncan covering second base. It was an outstanding play under pressure, and the Reds were still up 3–2.

"The ball sort of surprised me because the turf was wet and it scooted on me," Sabo said. "If I had to throw to first base, I probably couldn't have made the play. Gant runs too good."

"Sabes was much underrated defensively," Paul O'Neill remembers twenty years later "Those old hockey goalie skills came into play. Very, very quick reactions."

O'Neill, who was hitting .293 against left-handers and leading the team in RBI, nonetheless found himself on the bench to start the game. Braggs, the right-hander, was playing in his spot. But, as always, O'Neill said the right things.

"Glenn's been swinging the bat great, and you can't take him out of the lineup," O'Neill said. "Lou is here to win baseball games, not to keep me happy or anybody else happy."

In the bottom of the ninth, with the score tied at three, the first two Reds made outs. O'Neill walked and Hatcher went to the plate as Larkin headed for the on-deck circle. Piniella said to him, "You're going to win it for us."

Hatcher singled O'Neill to third and advanced to second on the throw.

Larkin settled in but fell behind the count 0-2 to Joe Boever. In these situations, Larkin always gave the impression that the pitcher was in trouble, not him. "I concentrate more when I have two strikes," said Larkin. "I was going to bunt the first pitch, but it fell off the table and I couldn't do it."

He ran the count to 2-2 and then slammed a pitch to center. O'Neill slapped his hands and trotted home as the fireworks flew and the crowd roared.

"Maybe this is what we need," O'Neill said. "These close games have a tendency to pump teams up." The next night he went four-for-four with three RBI to lead the Reds to a 6–3 win.

June 15, Cincinnati

Lou Piniella was in a bad mood. He didn't like the line of questioning from reporters prior to the game. Someone asked about a broadcast report that suggested the Reds were working on a trade involving Eric Davis. Then Piniella really got hot when asked when he was going to play Ron Oester.

Piniella erupted, reaching for a lineup card and sailing it across the table: "You fill out the lineup card and if he goes oh for four and we lose, you take the responsibility!"

He'd been annoyed by the local media's portrayal of the recent losing streak and finally blew up.

"They told me in New York I'd have an easier time of it here with the media. But (expletive deleted), they're tougher here!"

Piniella said there was no truth to the Davis rumor: "I'm involved in every trade, and believe me, there is no substance to that whatsoever."

June 16, Cincinnati

On the night that Chris Sabo revealed he had finally forsaken his 210,000-mile Ford Escort—it was in his driveway and wouldn't start—Eric Davis hit a 441-foot bomb off of Houston's Jim DeShaies en route to a 6–2 victory for the Reds on the eve of Father's Day.

Actually, Sabo hit one, too. As did Larkin and Benzinger and Braggs. They were looking like the '56 club with Big Klu, Robby, Wally, Gus, and Ed-gar, as Joe Nuxhall used to call catcher Ed Bailey.

The story, though, was with Larkin, Sabo, and Davis, whose homers were back-to-back-to-back.

Neil Hohlfeld described it in the *Houston Chronicle*: "After each homer, a fireworks display is set off over the right-center-field wall. In the fifth inning, when Deshaies gave up consecutive homers to Chris Sabo, Barry Larkin and Eric Davis, the hardest-working men in the stadium were the guys who reload the fireworks display. Nine pitches, three homers, lots of noise and color."

Later in the game, Benzinger hit a solo homer off

reliever Larry Andersen. According to the IBM Tale of the Tape, the five Cincinnati homers traveled a total of 2,050 feet. For those scoring at home, it was Braggs (403 feet), Sabo (407), Larkin (381), Davis (441), and Benzinger (418).

And what about Sabo's Escort? Was he going big-time now, because he'd hit a few home runs? (He already had thirteen, two better than his career best as a rookie.) Sabo responded, "Some guy loaned me a car—it has air-conditioning."

June 17, Cincinnati

The Reds hit four more home runs, two by Eric Davis, as they beat the Astros 7–1.

"They flat-out kicked our butts," said Houston's second baseman Bill Doran. "It just keeps going on, doesn't it?"

June 22, Cincinnati

With two outs in the bottom of the ninth inning, with Eric Davis on second base and Paul O'Neill on first, and with the Reds trailing 6–5, Todd Benzinger smashed a line drive to center field, scoring O'Neill easily to tie it, but Juan Samuel's relay throw and Eric Davis arrived home at the same time. Dodgers catcher Mike Scioscia had home plate blocked like Fort Knox.

Scioscia gloved the throw and tagged Davis.

"Safe!" signaled umpire Terry Tata.

"He didn't touch the plate!" yelled Scioscia, holding up the ball and pointing to the plate—not so much as a grain of dirt on it.

"Out!" signaled Tata.

Piniella rushed from the dugout and threw a fit, signaling safe repeatedly, throwing his hat and kicking dirt. Davis argued wildly also. Piniella was ejected.

The Reds protested, and the Dodgers went on to win in the tenth. With this episode would begin one of the most interesting weeks for the Reds since their 33–12 start.

From the far end of the Reds dugout, in the section know as "the bullpen" (the Reds had no separate facility for relievers), Nasty Boy Norm Charlton watched Scioscia block the plate. A former Texas high school quarterback who had also been a hard-hitting defensive end, Charlton didn't say a word. But he decided what he would do if the opportunity arose.

June 23, Cincinnati

It was a Saturday, and even though the Reds players didn't know it at the time, they loved playing on Saturdays, going 16–9 on that day during the 1990 season.

The Reds went into the fourth inning down 3–1 but scored eight runs in the bottom half to bury the Dodgers 11–6. Reliever Tim Layana, who pitched four innings of one-run ball (with three strikeouts) in relief of Tom Browning, got the save. These Reds were always ready to play on Saturdays

June 24, Cincinnati

The Reds finally took a stage befitting their success—a nationally televised contest against the Dodgers on

PURE POWER WASN'T THE REDS GAME

Despite the five home runs on June 16, the Reds were not a power-hitting team, at least not in the traditional sense. They finished the year only seventh in the National League with 125 long balls. That doesn't mean they were weak. In fact, they were above average at both getting on base and hitting for power. In the NL, the only club that had both a better on-base percentage combined with more "power" than the Reds were the Pirates, which foreshadowed an evenly matched NLCS.

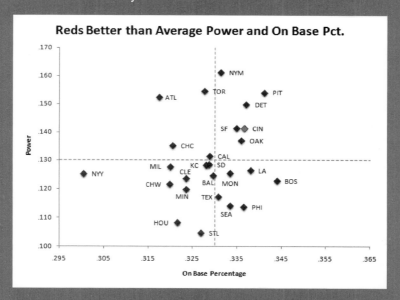

Power is calculated as Slugging Percentage minus Batting Average. It accounts for the number of bases a hitter typically gets per at-bat above and beyond a single.

The Reds were a well-balanced offense. They were good at almost everything and weren't bad at anything. If they had one exceptional skill, it was team speed, which made up for some of their lack of power. This chart would imply that they did not lack power, but some of that "power" was actually their speed allowing them to stretch a single into a double and a double into a triple. For instance, they were second in the majors in ground-ball doubles. Aggressive running gave them power.

What truly makes up for a lack of power is pitching and defense. The Reds were 38–20 after the game on June 16 because they out-pitched the opposition, not because they out-singled them. They didn't need to score as many runs as their power-hitting opponents because they allowed fewer runs.

Of course, you'd rather have a big bopper than not. But if you've got enough pitching and defense, a lack of power is less damaging.

ESPN. It was the first scheduled Sunday night game in team history. The Reds had a nine-game lead in the NL West, but the Dodgers were riding a five-game winning streak and had Fernando Valenzuela on the mound. The Reds countered with Rick Mahler.

When Norm Charlton took the mound in the seventh inning, the Reds were up 8–4 and Charlton batted for himself in the bottom of the inning. There were two outs, and Todd Benzinger was on first base when Mike Hartley hit Charlton with an 0-2 pitch.

Who wrinkles a pitcher at the plate on an 0-2 count with two outs unless that pitcher is Babe Ruth?

Charlton slammed down his bat, shouted angrily at Hartley, and headed for first base.

When Joe Oliver doubled down the left-field line to score Benzinger from second, everybody in the Reds dugout knew what might happen if the ball got into the corner, but they also figured that third-base coach Sam Perlozzo would stop Charlton, not wanting to risk a pitcher colliding with the renowned plate-blocker, Mike Scioscia.

Charlton, wearing his warm-up jacket, roared into third and turned the corner at full throttle despite the emphatic "Hold!" thrown to the skies by Perlozzo.

"I was concerned when I saw him coming," said Lou Piniella. "He's too valuable to lose, and Scioscia has put a few people on the DL."

DL? Not if Charlton got to Scioscia first. And Charlton was counting on beating the throw.

"I saw the ball roll into the corner, and I know guys have trouble coming out of there with it," Charl-

Norm Charlton was nicknamed "The Genius," but his intensity on the field was anything but scholarly.

ton explained. "When I hit third, he (left fielder Chris Gwynn) didn't have the ball, so I kept going."

In the dugout, the Reds were rooting for Charlton, not just because he was their teammate but because so many of them "owed" Scioscia.

"The guy had practically broken my ankle awhile

back in a collision at home," remembers Paul O'Neill.

"I'd been trying to get Scioscia for a long time too," Herm Winningham remembers. "Earlier (in my career)...I got caught in a rundown. I stopped, and Scioscia (jammed a glove in his face) and busted my lip. I said, 'I'll get you.'

"So we go to LA, and I get a chance. I ran right through the stop sign, and I hit Scioscia so hard. Helmet, facemask, my helmet, and we all hit the grass. I jump up and he's still on the ground. I go in the dugout and sit for about ten seconds. Then I got up, went inside the clubhouse and laid on the floor. Oh, you talk about a hurt puppy. But he was still on the ground because he was reaching one way and it was almost like I blindsided him."

The Reds knew that the 205-pound Charlton would pack a wallop, but they also knew that the 230-pound Scioscia would be more than able to take it. And he wouldn't give up even a sliver of home plate.

Charlton decided he wasn't going to try to slide.

"I figure if I slide he's going to kill me," Charlton said. "If you slide into Mike Scioscia, you're going to die."

Charlton later told one group of reporters he did not see Perlozzo's stop sign.

"If I'd seen the stop sign, I would've stopped," he said.

Baloney.

If Charlton had been looking at Perlozzo, he would have seen the sign. And even if he hadn't been looking, he'd have seen it in his peripheral vision. He didn't "see" it because he didn't want to see it.

And so he charged toward home, toward the very spot where Pete Rose had leveled Ray Fosse twenty years earlier in the 1970 All-Star Game. Charlton was playing for the team, for his guys, and nobody was going to get in the way of the 1990 Reds. Not even Mike Scioscia.

KA-BOOM!

Charlton drove his left arm and shoulder—his pitching shoulder—into Scioscia just as the horsehide met the rawhide. Scioscia crumbled and lay sprawled on the dirt. The ball came to rest in the right-side batter's box.

Charlton "hopped up, then stomped proudly to the dugout as if he were Hulk Hogan," wrote the *Enquirer's* Tom Groeschen.

"I thought it was a clean play," Scioscia said. "I have no problem with that at all. He was running and trying to score, and if I'm going to block the plate, guys are going to run into you. I don't think Lou Piniella really wants one of his top relievers doing that, but it's good baseball."

Charlton felt a slight, dull pain in his pitching shoulder as he headed for the high fives of his teammates.

In the top of the eighth, he gave up back-to-back leadoff singles, but then ended the rally with two strikeouts and a fly out. He earned the save, his second of the season.

June 25, Cincinnati

Charlton had an ice pack on his shoulder.

"It was a pretty dumb thing to do," Charlton told reporters. "I took a chance of getting hurt. You don't want a reliever out for the rest of the year for a run that was not that important."

He didn't mean a word of it.

A few years ago, in an interview for a book about Cincinnati's Opening Day tradition, Charlton expressed his true feeling about The Collision.

"It's funny that through my whole pitching career, that's the thing people bring up the most. It typified the way that '90 team played. It typified the fact that anybody on our team was willing to do whatever it took to win a ballgame. And if you were in the lineup, you played as hard as you could. That's pretty much the way we went about our business.

"My shoulder was a little sore after the collision, but I pitched the next inning. I never missed any time. I guess pitchers probably ought to play the game like a pitcher, but if I was on first again and Scioscia was catching and Joe hit a double down there, I think I'd try to score again. If I'm on base, I'm a base runner."

And home plate is mine.

Todd Benzinger was third on the team in RBI in the first half, but saw his playing time drop with the emergence of rookie Hal Morris

June 26, Cincinnati

Eric Davis was named NL player of the week for June 18–24, during which he batted .476 with a .621 on-base percentage and .714 slugging percentage.

June 27, Cincinnati

Rob Dibble was at it again. Two weeks earlier, he had blasted Reds fans for getting on him for not running out a ground ball. A week after that, he blew his fifth save in twelve opportunities, and tonight before the game he said wanted to be traded somewhere so he

could be a closer. Reds general manager Bob Quinn responded to the statement with, "It's not worthy of comment." Which is another way of saying what Dibble's best friend on the team, Norm Charlton, had said about him: "Rob's got more problems than a run-over dog."

The Reds lost 8–3.

Between Dibble's first meltdown that month and his last, the Reds were 10–4, and the team had little to complain about. But, as usual, Dibble found something. He wasn't a bad guy, but there were times when he didn't think before he spoke. Too often he let his emotions cloud his judgment.

But he did have a good reason to be upset when the media kept bringing up his "five blown saves in twelve opportunities." Twenty years later, through the use of statistical analysis, we realize how specious is the category of "blown saves" for setup men. Dibble didn't blow five of twelve save opportunities. He actually had twenty-one "save opportunities" at that point in the season, and he had saved seven, held nine, and okay, technically he had "blown" five. But three of his "blown" saves occurred in the seventh inning. Can you blow a save if you can't earn a save? That's the problem with the "blown save" statistic. Setup men can "blow" saves even when it's not truly a save opportunity. In every one of his blown saves, Dibble had come into the game before the ninth inning with men on base, and the Reds won every one of those games.

Compare that to Randy Myers, who blew two saves when he entered the game with the bases empty, though it's not really fair to compare Dibble to Myers because they were used in different ways. Dibble had inherited forty runners by the All-Star break and came into the game twenty-two times with at least one runner on base. Myers came into the game just seven times with a runner on base by the break and had only inherited thirteen runners. Dibble did the heavy lifting, while Myers got the glory.

Both Dibble and Myers were a big part of why the Reds were so good. Dibble knew what was going

on as far as his role, and it bothered him that fans and even the baseball writers didn't realize how much of the load he was carrying.

Norm Charlton, the third Nasty Boy, knew his own role, but that was about to change.

"We're a starter short," Piniella told him. "Can you help out?"

"Sure," the big Texan said.

June 29, New York

Jose Rijo, who had struggled in his start the day before, was put on the DL. Scott Scudder was called up from Triple-A Nashville.

June 30, New York

A big crowd of 49,128—which included some Yankees fans curious to see Lou Piniella without an "NY" on his cap—left disappointed when the Reds beat the Mets 7–4, their only win in the four-game series. The victory stopped the Reds' three-game losing streak and the Mets' eleven-game winning streak. Piniella masterfully used pinch hitters and double-switches and fresh starters—pressing buttons that all paid off.

And red-hot Eric Davis hit a blast off the facing of the second deck to add an insurance run off Mets reliever Alejandro Pena. For the two-week period since June 16—when Davis crushed the 441-foot bomb off Jim Deshaies—he hit .408, with a .517 on-base percentage and .878 slugging percentage, seven home runs, and fourteen RBI in fourteen games.

E.D. was back.

Rick Mahler

Tim Layana

July 7, Philadelphia

Rick Mahler shut out the Phillies 5–0 in Veterans Stadium, a nice shot in the arm for the Reds who were doing all they could to build their lead on the NL West going into the All-Star break.

July 8, Philadelphia

The Reds righted the ship after losing three of four in New York by winning three of four in Philly to go 4–2 in the week before the All-Star break. Hal Morris was named NL Player of the Week for July 2–8.

The Reds took a 50–29 record into the break, the best in baseball and the best franchise record at the break since the 1976 Reds were 53–33.

Even the skipper felt good.

But he wasn't about to tell the players that.

IN MEMORY OF...

Two members of the 1990 squad are no longer with us to celebrate the twentieth anniversary of the championship—pitchers Tim Layana and Rick Mahler. While not as celebrated as some of their teammates, their contributions were still integral to the team's success.

Layana, a twenty-six-year-old right-handed relief pitcher, was taken by the Reds from the Yankees organization in the Rule 5 draft in December 1989. General Manager Bob Quinn was well acquainted with Layana from his own time with the Yankees. As a Rule 5 draftee, Layana had to spend the entire season on the Reds' major league roster or be offered back to the Yankees.

His primary pitch was a knuckle-curve that he learned from watching Burt Hooton on television, and he used it well throughout the season. He appeared in fifty-five games during the year and threw eighty innings, posting a 3.49 earned run average.

His performance slipped during the final month, and manager Lou Piniella left him off the playoff roster, much to Layana's disappointment. Many teammates expressed their displeasure at his being left off the roster by writing his number "43" on their hat or shoes. To his credit, Layana did not complain much in the media and was honored that his teammates thought so highly of him.

The '90 season ended up being Layana's only real success in the big leagues. He was demoted to the minors in April 1991 and bounced back and forth for the rest of the year. The Reds released him just before the start of the 1992 season, and he spent time in the Orioles, Giants, and Expos organizations during the next three years but only pitched two more innings in the majors after 1991.

He was working as a high school baseball coach in California when he was killed on June 26, 1999, in a car accident. He was survived by his wife, Tracey, and ten-month-old daughter.

Rick Mahler, a twelve-year veteran in 1990, was the most experienced pitcher on the Reds' staff. He had toiled for several years with the Atlanta Braves, putting together a couple of good seasons on some bad teams before coming to the Reds as a free agent in 1989. He went 9–13 with a 3.83 ERA in thirty-one starts that year.

In 1990, he played a swingman role, splitting time between the rotation and the bullpen. He was only 7–6 with a 4.28 ERA on the year, but he pitched a couple of gems when the Reds needed help, including the complete-game shutout against the Phillies on July 7 and a complete game against the Cubs on September 1. Those games provided relief for the rotation at a time when several members were struggling or hurt.

Mahler was on the postseason roster and pitched an inning and two-thirds of shutout ball in the Reds' Game Five loss in the NLCS. He pitched one more season in the majors for the Expos and Braves before hanging up his spikes with a career record of 96–111 and a 3.99 ERA.

Mahler passed away in 2005 from a heart attack while preparing for his second season as the New York Mets minor league pitching coach. He was survived by his wife, Sheryl, and five children.

8

All-Star Game

At the All-Star break the Reds were eight games in front of the San Francisco Giants. Five Reds—Jack Armstrong, Rob Dibble, Barry Larkin, Randy Myers, and Chris Sabo—had been chosen to the National League squad, the largest contingent of Reds All-Stars since 1979.

July 10, Chicago, All-Star Game

The Reds had five players selected to the All-Star Game for the first time since Johnny Bench, Joe Morgan, George Foster, Dave Concepcion, and Mike LaCoss represented the team in 1979. Jack Armstrong, who was on his normal rest on the game day, was given the start by NL manager Roger Craig. Craig also liked Armstrong because the American League lineup was heavy with right-handed bats.

Armstrong would be the first Reds pitcher to start an All-Star Game since Mario Soto was annointed in 1983. No Reds pitcher has had the honor since.

"My presence here reflects credit to a great team that I happen to be part of," Armstrong said at a press conference the day before the game. "We have a great new manager, a fine attitude, and I'm surrounded by great players and a fine catcher I've worked with for several years."

It was a big moment in Armstrong's career, one he had worked tirelessly to reach. And now he was primed to make his first big step onto the national stage.

"Five—and we could have had more," said All-Star Barry Larkin.

Jack Armstrong, seen here with Tim Birtsas, had a lot to celebrate in 1990, including his greatest professional accomplishment, starting the All-Star Game.

Major leaguers tend to be different from the average Jack, but Jack Armstrong was unique even among his peers. When asked what he'd be if he wasn't playing baseball, Armstrong would say, without hesitation, "a tuna boat captain." Responses like that led Todd Benzinger to compare Armstrong to Nuke LaLoosh from the movie *Bull Durham*.

"I'm reminded of a scene when Crash Davis tells Nuke LaLoosh that if he wins twenty games, people will call him a flake because of the different way he acts," Benzinger said. "But he told Nuke that if he doesn't win, he'll be just another bum."

At age twenty-five, Armstrong was doing everything he could to be that twenty-game-winning flake. His workout routine was legendary. He would run up to eight miles a day, swim laps for thirty minutes, and *then* do some weight training. He modeled his regimen after the intense workouts of Hall of Famer

ARMSTRONG'S FALL WAS AS QUICK AS HIS RISE

Drafted with the eighteenth pick in the first round of the 1987 draft—four picks ahead of future Hall of Famer Craig Biggio—Jack Armstrong came to the Reds with high expectations. Those expectations led to a quick move through the minors, and in a little over a year Armstrong made his major league debut.

He struggled through his first year in the majors, going 4–7 with a 5.79 earned run average. He started the next year in Triple-A and spent most of the year there, putting up a 13–9 record with a 2.91 ERA. When he was brought up to the big leagues in September, he was determined to stick.

Armstrong worked hard during the off-season and came out strong in 1990. He got the victory in eight of his first nine starts, and at the end of May he held a stellar 1.55 ERA. His success was a result of good control—he walked just over two batters per nine innings—good defense, and keeping the ball inside the park. He didn't allow his first home run until his twelfth start of the season.

At that point, it wasn't unreasonable to expect some slippage. His peripheral numbers were solid (2.2 BB/9, OHR, 17% line drive rate), but he was not overpowering (5.4 K/9), and any pitcher who relies heavily on his defense is going to expect his numbers to even out. His ERA in June was a much more realistic, though still pretty good, 3.79. His last start before the All-Star break was a seven-inning, five-hit effort in which he allowed just one run and got the win. He would win only one more game the rest of the season.

Pitching coaches don't like their guys pitching in the All-Star Game because starters don't go through a normal routine and tend to pitch all out in their short stint. Jack Armstrong's All-Star start went through a slight delay before the game began, and for two innings he threw as hard as he'd thrown all season. Baseball players, especially starting pitchers, are addicted to routines. When those routines change, sometimes bad results occur.

The All-Star break may not have been the beginning of Armstrong's struggles, but soon afterward his elbow gave out. His mechanics were slipping and so was his control. He found himself trying to blow it by everyone, and as he said, "That's the worst thing you can do."

Though he continued to feel pain in his elbow, he threw on the side to try to restore his natural rhythm. "I took my next turn, even though it was still stiff and that made it really bad," he said. "I pitched a few games with it like that, until finally in a game against Pittsburgh (August 19) Lou took me out because I couldn't throw at all, couldn't even get it to home plate. That was that."

From the All-Star break to the end of August, he managed to go just 1-6 with a 6.56 ERA. He was finally put on the disabled list at the end of August. When he returned in mid-September, his arm felt much better, but Piniella opted to use him out of the bullpen, where he pitched four and two-thirds innings without allowing a run.

He stayed in the bullpen for the playoffs and World Series but returned to the starting rotation in 1991. He was never able to capture the magic of the first half of 1990 again, and after going 1–6 with a 6.79 ERA in the second half of 1991, he was traded to Cleveland with Scott Scudder for Greg Swindell.

He pitched two more full seasons in the big leagues with Cleveland and Florida, which took him in the 1992 expansion draft. He had a 15–32 record with a 4.56 ERA in those two seasons and after a two-game stint with Texas in 1994, he was out of the majors for good.

Nolan Ryan. Former manager Pete Rose feared the rigorous workouts would cause Armstrong's body to break down as the season wore on.

Armstrong explained, "I wasn't allowed to do the things I wanted to do [under Rose]. The intense workouts [were] contrary to popular beliefs of baseball's old school people." He added that he didn't feel comfortable with Rose. "I kind of felt Pete and [former pitching coach] Scotty [Breeden] didn't have any confidence in me. If you're young and not secure about what you're doing, you start to doubt yourself."

Armstrong felt the support of Piniella, who didn't care about the workouts as long as he won games. His eleven wins were the most by a Reds pitcher at the All-Star break since Jack Billingham had fourteen in 1973.

His success had also won him the respect of his teammates.

"I took abuse because I didn't conform to what was considered the baseball norm," Armstrong said. "Now I'm accepted. With success comes acceptance in any realm."

"We razzed him hard," said Benzinger. "Lately? I haven't heard any razzing. Nobody makes fun of him."

❖ ❖ ❖ ❖ ❖

As you would expect in an All-Star Game, Armstrong had his work cut out for him. The AL lineup consisted of four future Hall of Famers in the first five hitters, and the one non-Hall of Famer was possibly the best player in the game at the time, Jose Canseco.

Leading off the damp night at Wrigley Field, Rickey Henderson flied out deep to right. Then Wade Boggs scratched out an infield hit to the left side, and suddenly Armstrong faced the hulking Canseco with a man on base.

Armstrong had enough adrenaline coursing through his veins to power a small city, but he clearly hadn't lost any of his confidence.

"I wanted to see what they had," he reflected. "I didn't have to pace myself. I just let go from the get-go."

He threw sheer heat to Canseco and got him to a 2-2 count before finishing him off with a change-up that the big right fielder couldn't wait on. Armstrong had his first strikeout. With a weak ground out to shortstop by Cal Ripken, the first inning was over.

In the top of the second, Armstrong was even more overpowering. The inning started and ended with foul outs by Ken Griffey Jr. and Sandy Alomar Jr., and in between he threw nothing but gas to first baseman Mark McGwire, striking out the second of the fabled Bash Brothers.

And just like that, Tunaboat Jack's All-Star experience ended. Two innings, twenty-six pitches, eighteen strikes, and strikeouts of two of the biggest power hitters in the game. On this night, he had proven he was worthy of being an All-Star.

❖ ❖ ❖ ❖ ❖

Chris Sabo had been to the All-Star Game before. As a rookie, he was chosen by Whitey Herzog as a backup.

Chris Sabo started back-to-back All-Star Games in 1990 and 1991.

He got into that game, which was played at Riverfront Stadium, but only as a pinch runner. As he likes to remind people, though: "I did steal a base."

This season's All-Star experience would be different. Sabo was chosen to start by the fans in 1990, nearly doubling the votes of his closest competitor, San Francisco's Matt Williams. Sabo's response to the news was understated: "I won the vote? Great. At least I'll get to bat in this one."

And while he did get to bat twice, neither was particularly memorable—a one-out ground out in the second and a leadoff ground out in the fifth, both with the bases empty.

The All-Star start for Sabo was well deserved as the begoggled one led all National League third basemen in on-base and slugging percentage, was second in doubles, home runs, and batting average, and was doing it all while batting leadoff for the majority of the first half of the season. Sabo felt vindicated by the good start and the All-Star vote. "Two times in three years on the All-Star team," he commented. "Not bad after all the preseason publications this year said I stink."

Two factors contributed to Sabo's breakout season in 1990. First, he spent the winter rehabbing his knee after arthroscopic surgery the previous season. The extra work on his legs built more strength in his lower half, which provided more power in his bat. Second, by working with Lou Piniella before the season he learned to properly shift his weight at the plate, allowing him to use his whole body, not just his arms.

Piniella told Sabo that if he continued to use his new technique, he'd hit fifteen home runs by accident. He had sixteen at the break, matching the most he'd hit in a season at any level since high school (he also hit sixteen in 1983 for the Michigan Wolverines).

But it wasn't just the increased power that got Sabo into the All-Star Game. Fans loved him from the day he entered the league. His flatop buzz cut and Rec-Spec goggles made him instantly recognizable. And his intense, maximum-effort attitude endeared him to the fans who longed for the next Pete Rose to play in a Reds uniform.

Sabo was never that simple to pin down, however. On one hand, his intensity indicated a bit of a chip on his shoulder. "Sometimes you wish he'd make it easier on himself," Todd Benzinger said. "He's got that attitude that he's got to get a hit. He gets five hits in a row, and the sixth time he's mad if he doesn't get another."

On the other hand, Sabo frequently tried to deflect press from himself in a possible attempt to lower expectations. "I don't consider myself one of the better players in the league, not by any stretch of the imagination," Sabo said. "I made the team as a utility player and I kept telling people that. If people think I'm going to be a superstar, that's where they are stupid."

The work ethic was a by-product of his upbringing. He was raised on the west side of Detroit. His father, Walt was as a plumber. "He worked hard all his life and he taught me to do the same," Sabo said. "He told me, 'As long as you produce, somebody will always want you.'"

This blue-collar work ethic is also why Sabo was intent on deflecting fame from himself. It's why even though he was in his third season in the big leagues, a season where he made $200,000, he still drove his 1984 Ford Escort that had over 200,000 miles on it and no air-conditioning. He hated to be the center of attention.

"He has simple ideas and simple ways," Benzinger said. "I remember Paul and I were talking about buying a house. Sabo said, 'What do you do in a house? You just sleep in it.' He's an odd character."

His teammates appreciated the character, however.

"He's probably the most underrated player on the team by the fans and the media," Eric Davis said. "But we know how good he is."

"He's such a quiet guy," Rob Dibble said. "Then, he takes the field and he's one of the meanest guys you've ever met. He doesn't talk a good game; he barely talks at all. But he's an incredibly tough competitor."

The irony of Chris Sabo is that his trying to stay out of the spotlight and not giving into the glamour of being a big league ballplayer made him so popular and memorable. He may not have been a superstar, but many fans loved him like one.

❖ ❖ ❖ ❖ ❖

Being selected to the All-Star team can melt even the hardest heart. It did for Rob Dibble. He had not spoken to the media for two weeks except to tell *USA Today*, "I want to be here for the fun, but after this year, I hope I get a look-see from another team."

His anger was directed mostly at some local radio talk-show hosts. The thin-skinned Dibble felt that he was being unfairly criticized by the media, especially on WLW radio, the Reds' flagship station. "(They're) attacking my family, my character, things (they don't) even know about."

Out of frustration, he shut himself off.

The joy of being selected to the All-Star Game, however, broke that silence.

"I wasn't going to let the media ruin my life," he said.

Rob Dibble changed the way people look at setup men in the bullpen.

from 1988 to 1993, his prime years, he hit only seven batters in more than four hundred innings.

"Rob dominates and blows hitters away," said Norm Charlton. "Nobody else has ever done the kind of things he's doing."

His attitude, however, grew tiresome at times. In a season that was mainly about the team, Dibble was the one most frequently spouting off in the paper about individual issues. His teammates were often annoyed by his antics, but they tolerated him because when you've got that bazooka in your bullpen and you're winning, you look past the flaws.

While they may not have respected his act, they did respect his performance, and so did the rest of the league. That's why he was selected to his first All-Star Game despite being primarily a setup man.

"He's a guy who puts up great numbers every year," said Randy Myers. "He's done the job, and for him to get credit, it shows people are looking at what he means to our team."

Dibble was looking forward to the game. "I may not get in the game, but I'd like to," he said. "If it came down to me against Jose Canseco, that would be great. I'd throw it as hard as I can and say, 'Hit it as far as you can,' and see who's the best man."

Dibble would get his chance against Canseco, but first he would have to deal with the situation created by the man who later would be known to Reds radio listeners as "The Cowboy."

Following a one-hour and eight-minute rain delay. Dibble strode to the mound in relief of San Francisco's

"But it was wrong of me to make everyone pay for the actions of a couple of guys who don't know the score."

And that, in a nutshell, is Rob Dibble—a volatile personality who one day could erupt in the clubhouse and the next day try to say all the right things. He managed that unpredictability to a tee and used it to intimidate his opponents. Hitters feared him—both for his amazing fastball and his explosive reputation. And yet,

ROB DIBBLE: REVOLUTIONIZING A ROLE

In 1960, Chicago sports writer Jerome Holtzman created a statistic that would give more credit to a reliever who pitched the ninth inning of a close game and preserved the win for his team. He called it a save, and in just over a decade later, the role of closer was firmly established.

One could argue, however, that the "save" marginalized the value of a quality middle reliever or setup man. Without the benefit of a sexy statistic like saves to put by their name, the non-closers in the bullpen were often overlooked.

Then came Rob Dibble.

When you throw the ball a hundred miles per hour and can hit the corners with a slider, you don't stay anonymous for long. Dibble was selected to the All-Star Game in 1990, despite accumulating only seven saves in thirty-six outings by the break and despite the fact that setup men were rarely considered for the midsummer classic. Before Dibble, only Ron Davis of the Yankees in 1981 was selected to an All-Star team as exclusively a setup man.

Dibble's selection was clearly deserved. Every-one knows about his gaudy strikeout totals—he led the majors in strikeouts per inning pitched every season from 1989 to 1992—but for a power pitcher, Dibble also had considerable control. According to a metric called "Situational Wins" which tries to properly value a pitcher's performance based on the situation in which he pitches, Dibble was the top reliever in the National League in 1989. The following year he was merely the second-best reliever in the NL behind teammate Randy Myers.

You could say that Dibble ushered in a new era for setup men, but he was a few years ahead of his time. He made his second All-Star team in 1991, but by that point he was the Reds closer and had twenty-three saves at the break. It would be another nine years before a setup man was be selected to an All-Star Game. Eleven more have been chosen in the following decade.

Rob Dibble helped to bring the setup role to the fans' attention. He rarely had trouble getting attention.

Jeff Brantley. Back to third base went Roberto Alomar; back to first went Lance Parrish. It was a familiar scenario for Dibble. Thus far in 1990, "Dibs" had entered the game with runners on base in twenty-two of thirty-six appearances.

Then again, this was the All-Star Game, so it was hardly a normal scene.

Up stepped Julio Franco of the Texas Rangers, who could handle just about any pitcher's fastball.

Dibble knew this, but when he got the count to no balls and two strikes, his ego got in the way, and he tried to blow some hot pepper cheese by Franco.

"I wanted to throw him a fastball up and in. I threw it over the middle of the plate," Dibble said. "Right down the heart. My wife could have gotten a hit off that pitch."

Franco *did* hit that pitch, a two-run double to right field, giving the American League a 2–0 lead.

Sam Perlozzo called closer Randy Myers the Reds' "savior" on the mound.

After a ground out and a walk, Dibble finally got his wish: Canseco.

One out, runners on first and third. Canseco flew out to right fielder Darryl Strawberry, who made a perfect throw to home plate to nail Franco. It wasn't quite what Dibble had hoped for, but it got the job done.

Some criticized Dibble's performance, to which he responded, "It doesn't bother me because this stuff doesn't count," he said. "I'm not ashamed of it. How can you be when you're pitching in the All-Star Game and playing with the best players in baseball? I'm not going to second-guess myself."

Which was true. He was too busy second-guessing the media. For the most part, it was all an act, a performance for the fans and a bit for the opponent. But it worked. For five years, the man who Reds announcer Marty Brennaman once called "my least favorite Red of all-time" was one of the most dominant relievers the game has ever seen.

❖ ❖ ❖ ❖ ❖

Dibble may have created quite a persona for himself, but Randy Myers was a flake of a whole different sort.

His locker at Riverfront Stadium held two metal ammo boxes, three nightsticks, two defused hand grenades, and two large Bowie knives, one lodged between lockers and used as a hook for his hats.

Though Reds' fans initially didn't like the off-season trade of popular John Franco for Myers, Lou Piniella had wanted a left-hander to share the stopper role with Dibble, and he knew that Franco wouldn't be that guy. Myers, who had shared the role in New York, would be much more amenable to doing the same in Cincinnati.

It wasn't just the shared role that bonded Dibble and Myers, however. They were kindred weirdos, both a little off-center, both with carefully cultivated personas that they used to intimidate batters. And both claimed that the other was the one to truly fear.

"Left-handers have a different perspective off the field," Dibble said. "I'm flaky only on the field. Left-handers are flaky all the time."

"(Dibble's) the crazy one," Myers said. "I'm the sane one. I'm Mr. Mellow. I don't know how I got the reputation that I have."

As usual, Myers was being facetious. He knew exactly what he was doing. The grenades, the knives, the fatigues were all intended to build an image. And Myers' refusal to discuss the objects in his locker fed that image of a loner on the edge.

Years later, Jeff Brantley, a fellow closer and All-Star in 1990, said Myers used the image "to cover up insecurities." He explained: "For a lot of guys that get nervous on the inside, they don't want to show that on the outside. The only way to protect that is to not let somebody in. Don't let anybody in because if you get to know me then you'll know I'm kind of sensitive. It's bad for your mentality as a closer. You act like you're a psycho so nobody comes around."

If those insecurities were there, Myers did a good job of hiding them on the mound.

Third base coach Sam Perlozzo, who managed Myers between 1984 and 1986 in Double-A and Triple-A, had a different take. "To me, the man's calm," Perlozzo said. "That stuff feeds his ego, helps him psychologically. He should feel like the savior. That's what he is. When he comes in the game, the rest of us feel the same way. It's like, 'Come on, big man, get us out of here.'"

He was not, however, closing out the All-Star Game. By the time he entered in the top of the eighth, the National League had managed only two base runners, with a single and a walk. The two runs surrendered by Brantley and Dibble in the seventh inning gave the AL a 2–0 lead.

He was brought on to face the four-five-six hitters—George Bell, Ken Griffey Jr., and Cecil Fielder. Bell flied out to right field, but then Kirby Puckett pinch hit for Griffey and singled, advancing to third on an error by Darryl Strawberry. Myers walked Fielder, putting runners at first and third.

Alan Trammell popped out, but Myers walked Lance Parrish to load the bases. He then faced the same hitter who got to Dibble in the previous inning, Julio Franco, the eventual game MVP. Myers was able to escape the jam when Franco flied out to right field.

John Franco took over in the ninth, breezing through a trio of batters, but his team managed only four base runners for the entire game and were unable to overcome the 2–0 deficit.

❖ ❖ ❖ ❖ ❖

When asked if he considered his All-Star experience a success, Barry Larkin simply said, "I made it through the day without getting hurt, so I'm fine."

A year after partially tearing the medial collateral ligament in his right elbow during the now defunct All-Star Skills Challenge, Larkin simply wanted to avoid a repeat of the previous year.

Despite the general agreement among nearly every-

Barry Larkin went to the All-Star Game twelve times from 1988 to 2004.

one in baseball that Larkin was the NL's best shortstop, the fans had voted Ozzie Smith the starter by a 79,000-vote landslide. Larkin accepted that it's hard to displace a legend.

Two decades later, he recalls thinking how many of his teammates could have been at the game. "I distinctly remember being in Chicago and thinking, 'Man, our entire team could be here.'" Larkin said. "We were really playing that well. Mariano Duncan was having a great year; Billy Hatcher was having a great year."

He didn't get to do much in the game. He pinch ran for Tony Gwynn in the bottom of the third inning and stole a base. He also played the field for three innings, making a couple of plays before turning over the position to hometown favorite Shawon Dunston.

But Larkin's day would come. He'd go on to start in five All-Star Games and be elected twelve times during his career. As for the 1990 game, he has only one regret: "I remember thinking, I should enter the home-run contest. Ha! It was crazy, but I really had a lot of confidence in our team and myself because of the way things were going."

And he had no reason to think that the way things were going would change anytime soon. But, of course, they would change quite a bit.

9

Channeling Pete

On July 19, Peter Edward Rose, former Reds manager, was sentenced to prison. The next day, Norman Wood Charlton stirred things up as only Rose the player could have done.

The Reds received good news on the final day of the All-Star break: Eric Davis's wife, Sherrie, gave birth to their second child, Sacha Kiare, at Good Samaritan Hospital. The team then went on an 8–3 roll. All appeared well in Reds Land.

The only dark cloud concerned former skipper Pete Rose, who on July 19 was sentenced in federal court to five months in prison and three months in a halfway house for underreporting his income—and underpaying it by $162,000 from 1984 to 1987.

Those years were the early and middle ones of Rose's tenure as the Reds' player-manager, when so many of the stars of the '90 Reds began coming up to the big leagues, including Eric Davis in 1984.

July 19, Cincinnati

After being sentenced, Pete Rose went home and cried. In court, before Judge Arthur Spiegel, Rose had said, "I'm very sorry. I am very shameful to be here today in front of you. I think I'm perceived as a very aggressive,

Ron Oester hit .299 in 154 at-bats in 1990, and his fiery personality and desire to win made him the heart of the Reds clubhouse.

135

arrogant type of individual, but I want people to know that I do have emotion, I do have feelings, and I can be hurt like everybody else, and I hope no one has to go through what I went through the last year and a half. I lost my dignity. I lost my self-respect. I lost a lot of dear fans and almost lost some very dear friends."

Rose's voice cracked on the word "dignity." He paused briefly.

"I have to take this opportunity to thank my wife for giving me so much moral support during this ordeal," he said. "It has to be very tough on her when our five-year-old son would come home from school and tell her that his daddy is a jailbird."

July 20, Cincinnati

Norm Charlton was going to pay.

And he knew it.

Three months earlier at Riverfront Stadium, Charlton had branded the Phillies' Von Hayes with a fastball in the chest, leaving a welt that lasted for days. Charlton, true to the pitcher's code, denied intentionally throwing at Hayes, but he had good reason for doing so: The Phillies had drilled Barry Larkin earlier in that game, and there was no way Charlton was letting that go unpunished. Nobody ordered him to hit the Phillies' best hitter, but Charlton didn't need to be told. He kept his own score. He was more than happy to do what he saw as his duty.

On July 20, Hayes wasn't in the lineup. No matter. The Phillies' collective memory hadn't faded.

"You never know," Phillies manager Nick Leyva

Norm Charlton expected retaliation from the Phillies in July, but he never backed down.

would later say. "There might have been a mark made in the book."

Despite knowing he was going to pay—or maybe *because* he knew—Charlton sent leadoff batter Lenny Dykstra sprawling in the dirt with a high-and-tight fastball to start the game. It was Charlton's way of saying that he knew what was up. And that he was not going to be intimidated. He wanted the Phillies to know that the Reds took everything personally.

"We're in first place, and everybody's gunning for us," Ron Oester said. "Other teams are coming at us with some extra intensity."

Although Charlton was not a homegrown Red, he felt like one. He joined the family on March 31, 1986, when the Reds traded third baseman Wayne Krenchicki to the Montreal Expos. At the time, the twenty-three-year-old Charlton had had two so-so seasons in A-ball. But left-handers who throw ninety-five mph—even if they aren't throwing strikes—are special.

At Double-A Vermont in 1986 and Triple-A Nashville in 1987 and 1988, Charlton played with Joe Oliver, Chris Sabo, Rob Dibble, Jack Armstrong, and Scott Scudder. He had grown close to them.

He loved the tradition of this franchise, especially the way guys like Bench and Morgan came around on Opening Day. He loved the idea of playing for Pete Rose, and he loved knowing that Doggie Perez was in the first-base coach's box.

Charlton saw sports as a contest of wills. He was born in 1963 in Fort Polk, Louisiana, where his dad was an army officer, just after the base began its conversion into the country's primary training ground for Vietnam-bound soldiers. It was hot and humid and swampy, and the training regimen was intense, featuring nighttime patrols with booby traps and aggressors. The instructors were all Vietnam-hardened veterans. The very nature of Fort Polk seemed to seep into Charlton's marrow. His father had taught him the value of honesty and integrity, and while it wasn't always easy,

Norm Charlton grew up facing the music.

He had played football and baseball while growing up in Rockport, Texas. By his senior season in high school he was throwing ninety mph, and Rice University took a chance on him. By his sophomore year, he was throwing ninety-five.

In the minors, he was a starter, and his ten appearances for the Reds in his debut year of 1988 were starts. In spring training 1989, Pete Rose tabbed him as the team's fifth starter, but told Charlton that he wasn't needed for a couple of weeks. So, Rose said, you're headed back to Nashville for a couple of weeks. Unless…

"Can you pitch out of the bullpen?" Rose asked.

"I did a couple of times in college," Charlton answered.

"Do you want to try it?"

"Hell, yeah, if it means being there on Opening Day."

He made sixty-nine appearances that year, all in relief, striking out ninety-eight in ninety-five and a third innings, and was 9–3 with a 2.93 ERA. Coming into 1990, he hadn't sensed that this season had a chance to be *the one*, unlike Oester, Browning, and Davis. Those veterans had picked up on the vibe right away.

"I was too young to understand," remembers Charlton. He had made his big league debut only eighteen months earlier. But in Charlton, the Big Three had a brother. Nothing energized him more than being on a team of like-minded fighters. He had been looking for

July 20, 1990, Riverfront Stadium. Norm Charlton has already sent Phillies' leadoff hitter Lenny Dykstra sprawling in the dirt with a high-and-tight fastball to start the game (note 7:37 pm. time on scoreboard), and will soon run the count to 3–2 before striking him out. In the sixth inning, Phillies' reliever Dennis Cook intentionally hit Charlton with a pitch that precipitated a fifteen-minute brawl after which both were ejected. The 5–1 Reds' victory highlighted the team's fighting spirit that year.

a team like this since graduating from Rice with a triple major. He had loved that about playing in college, and he sensed the same *esprit de corps* among the other college guys on the Reds, like Larkin, Sabo, and Morris, who all played for the University of Michigan.

The idea of being turned loose on the rest of the league by this new man from New York appealed to Charlton. This was the way baseball was meant to be played. Of course, it was still a game, and Charlton was light at heart, one of the most enthusiastic pranksters on the club, but the game was more fun and meaningful when everybody was in it together.

"It didn't come along that often," Charlton remembers. "I was part of it in Seattle in '95 (the "Refuse to Lose" Mariners) and 2001 (116 victories in the regular season), both under Lou. We didn't have great individual stars, but we were a *team*. When you have that chemistry, guys playing for one another, you've got something special."

And that's the way Charlton viewed it when he collided with Mike Scioscia or branded Von Hayes with a fastball or sent Lenny Dykstra sprawling on the first pitch of the game.

This is how we *play the game.*

After decking Dykstra, he struck him out and got the next thirteen Phillies in a row. By the fifth inning, he'd given up only a single. Charlton walked to lead off the fifth inning, and when Barry Larkin belted a one-hopper past the second baseman, Charlton bolted for second. He glanced at Dykstra in center field, planning on at least forcing him to make a throw to third, but then he noticed that Dykstra—determined to throw out that jerk Charlton—had picked up his head too soon. The ball got by him!

The crowd of 39,394 roared. *Here comes Normie— again—around third!* But, this time, third-base coach Sam Perlozzo, who was watching the ball roll to the center-field wall, signaled to ease up and coast home. Meanwhile, Larkin sprinted all the way home and beat the relay. The Reds had Lou-balled their way to a 4–0 lead.

Oh, how the Phillies hated these Reds. And, oh how they loathed Charlton.

Of all the people in the ballpark, only the players and coaches and managers had any inkling of what Charlton's next at-bat was going to bring. Twenty years later, Charlton recalls his buddy, Darren Daulton, being behind the plate for the Phillies when he stepped up to bat in the bottom of the sixth inning. But actually Steve Lake was catching.

"I know what you've got to do," said Charlton to Lake.

"Yeah," said Lake. "We've got to hit you."

Home plate umpire Bob Davidson was listening. This was back in the days before umpires had been ordered to be preemptive. Nowadays, such a conversation would have brought the umpire between the combatants, threatening ejections.

The man on the mound, Dennis Cook, was Charlton's friend, who he had tried to recruit to Rice. Cook's first pitch was a thigh-fastball that caught Charlton flush on the leg.

Davidson immediately ejected Cook and warned Charlton, as players from both teams gathered in front of their dugouts, waiting to see what might happen. They all knew that Charlton wasn't likely to let it end there. Sure enough. He made a halfback's cut around Davidson and sprinted for the mound, where he and Cook collided. They both went down.

"He was doing what he had to do, but I was doing what I had to do," Charlton said. "I would have hit him instead of just tackling him if I'd had the chance."

Players rushed the field. Von Hayes stood out there pointing fingers, drawing scorn from Oester.

"If you're mad at somebody, go get him," said Oester. "If I thought somebody hit me on purpose, I'd go get him myself. It's between you and the pitcher, and I wouldn't want somebody else to hit him for me."

Phillies pitcher Don Carman said he was looking for Charlton in the pile when he was confronted by an agitated Oester and punched him, knocking him down. Carman was talking big afterward, but the Phillies couldn't match up with the Reds. The Reds beat them seven out of twelve in 1990, and Charlton backed up his attitude that night with a two-hit, one-run performance.

Davis spoke for all the Reds when he said: "We play with a lot of intensity and we have a lot of intense players. That might stir some things. But we don't provoke, and we don't go out of our way to show anybody up."

The Reds were playing a brand of baseball that nobody was accustomed to. It wasn't that they disrespected

Ron Oester was always ready to mix it up in defense of his teammates.

BREAKING UP THE NASTY BOYS

Norm Charlton began to suspect a move to the starting rotation when pitching coach Stan Williams started bringing up Charlton's past as a starter in early July. "I said to myself, 'I wonder where this is coming from,'" Charlton said. "I knew he wasn't pulling it out of the blue."

Sure enough, about five days before the All-Star Game, Lou Piniella told Charlton he would join Tom Browning, Danny Jackson, and Jack Armstrong in the rotation after the break. Charlton took it in stride.

"I like relieving," he said. "I like coming to the ballpark every day with a chance to get in the game and make a difference. As a starter, I know I'll have to come to the park every fifth day looking to make a big difference."

Moving Charlton was a tough decision for Piniella, who still had second thoughts on it during the All-Star break. During the 1990 season, a *Sporting News* panel of NL hitters ranked Charlton in a tie for third as the National League's toughest pitcher to hit. The only pitchers ranked ahead of him were Dwight Gooden and Sid Fernandez. That type of respect made him the obvious choice to move into the rotation, and Piniella felt confident Charlton could handle the new role.

"He has outstanding stuff, and this has been in the back of our minds a long time," Piniella said. With Jose Rijo on the disabled list, Ron Robinson traded, and Scott Scudder struggling, Piniella needed him.

Charlton started his first game on July 15 against the New York Mets. Piniella may have thought the move was only temporary until the rotation was healthy again, but by the time Rijo came off the disabled list, Jackson was back on it. Browning missed a start in August because of a minor injury, and Armstrong had lost his magic.

Charlton stayed in the rotation for the remainder of the season, posting a 6–5 record with a 2.60 ERA. The move was just another in a year when everything seemed to work.

---

their opponents, but rather that they were putting their manhood on the line and daring their opponents to match it.

The melee lasted fifteen minutes. Charlton was ejected. Dibble went the final three innings and earned the save. Before the game he had dumped a bucket of water on the head of *Enquirer* beat writer Michael Paolercio for quotes accurately attributed to Dibble, but taken from a Philadelphia newspaper and inserted into a Paolercio story. Typical Dibble: *Fire first, think later.* To Paolercio's credit, he had a good comeback: "I just consider the source of where it came from. It could have been gasoline like he pours on every game situation he appears in."

July 24, San Diego

The Reds began what is remembered as an historic near-collapse on the West Coast. The first loss was a 10–0 pounding, unremarkable except for the fact that the Reds knew they probably weren't going to be able to count on pitcher Jack Armstrong as they had in the first half. He gave up seven runs in four and two-thirds innings.

The Reds didn't know it then, but they were about to crack.

July 25, San Diego

Just as Armstrong was flaming out, Charlton was soaring. In his third straight start, he was again a rocket. But the Reds offense could score only one run, on an RBI single from Oester, from whom even bigger things were yet to come.

But not right away. First, the Reds were done in by what had been their strength during their amazing first half of the season: Aggressiveness. Paul O'Neill beat out an infield single, stole second, and scored on an Oester single. But when Joe Oliver swung and missed on a hit-and-run, Oester was easily thrown out at second.

Dibble pitched a scoreless seventh and eighth, but the bleeding had begun. It was the first time in a month the Reds had lost two games in a row. And in the second game of that day's doubleheader, they would make it three.

❖ ❖ ❖ ❖ ❖

Norm Charlton was Ron Oester's favorite Nasty Boy. The only real Nasty Boy, as far as Oester was concerned. During the '90 season, Oester had a confrontation with Rob Dibble that Randy Myers tried to quell, and both relievers wound up backing down.

Dibble had thrown a brushback pitch that led to retribution on Barry Larkin by an opposing pitcher. Oester connected the dots between the two incidents and followed Dibble into the clubhouse after Dibble was removed from the game.

"He and Randy Myers were at the other end of the clubhouse," remembers Oester. "I heard Dibble say, 'I guess they're going to blame that on me, Larkin getting hit.' I said, 'You stupid ass—you don't think you had anything to do with that?'"

Myers replied, "We don't want to hear it right now."

To which Oester bellowed: "Well, you're going to hear it! I'm tired of this Nasty Boy stuff. Let's see how blankin' nasty you are.'"

Myers wanted no piece of Oester.

"He looked like a little puppy," Oester recalls. "I'd always thought the act (Myers' commando-style garb and demeanor) was phony. Right then, I knew."

Dibble apologized the next day. Oester recalls, "He said, 'You were right. I let my emotions get the best of me.' That was Dibs. I just told him, 'We can't lose Larkin. We've got to have Larkin.' And that was the end of it."

July 29, San Francisco

The three straight losses in San Diego were just the beginning. The Reds traveled to San Francisco and were swept in four games by the Giants. The first three were one-run losses, the last of which particularly angered Lou Piniella. The game was filled with fielding errors, botched bunts, and bad base running. It was lost in the eleventh inning after Chris Sabo was doubled off first for inexplicably walking off the base after Larkin had bunted into an out. In the bottom of the inning, the Giants drove in the winning run on a 120-foot bloop single by Kevin Mitchell.

"We've come in here and done everything wrong," Piniella said. "To win in this game, you have to execute. That's how we got where we are. All of a sudden, it hasn't happened. This is the series we were pointing to and we've come in and turned this thing into a comedy of errors."

Piniella's words—and a ten-minute, closed-door meeting after the game—didn't turn things around when the Reds faced Scott Garrelts the following afternoon. The bats remained silent, and if it hadn't been for a first-pitch, line-drive single by Paul O'Neill with two outs in the ninth inning, the Reds would have been held hitless for the first time since 1971. The hit did not change the outcome of the 4–0 shutout as the Reds were swept for the second time that year in San Francisco, losing their eleventh straight game at Candlestick Park.

The Reds' lead, which had been eleven only a week earlier, was now just five and a half games over the second-place Giants.

"It's hard to swing a bat when one hand is around your throat," wrote Hal McCoy in the *Dayton Daily News*, quoting former major league pitcher Bill "Spaceman" Lee. In the four-game sweep, the Reds managed only eight runs on twenty-two hits.

"There's got to be some lingering thoughts to know that you got beat four straight by the (defending) National League champions and they (the Reds) have never won it," said Giants center fielder Brett Butler. "That's got to be tough."

"Hopefully, we've hit rock bottom," Piniella said. "We have to turn it around because nobody is going to turn it around for us." The Reds players tried to mask their feelings, but twenty years later, former pitcher Tom Browning admits to some concern.

"We were feeling it," Browning says. "Those of us especially who'd been around in 1987 remembered it."

In 1987, the Reds had led the NL West for more than eighty days when they arrived in San Francisco on August 7 with a five-game lead. A four-game sweep cut the lead to one, and the Giants went on to catch them and win the division.

"And they'd caught us in 1989, too," Browning recalls. "We'd had all those injuries, but still, they'd caught us."

Outside the ballpark, a bus waited for the trip to the airport to catch a flight for Los Angeles. As Lou Piniella headed toward it, throngs of Giants fans, behind a chain-link fence, jeered him.

"You're bums!" they yelled. "We're going to win the pennant again, just like last year, you piece of s---! Take your sorry ass to LA! By the time you get home, this thing'll be tied up!"

And those were some of the nicer things they yelled. The other insults concerned his clothes, Hispanic parentage, association with the Yankees, and anything the

WINNING THE WEST WITHOUT WINNING OUT WEST

TUES 24	WEDS 25	WEDS 25	THURS 26	FRI 27	SAT 28	SUN 29	SUN 30
San Diego	San Diego	San Diego	San Fran	San Fran	San Fran	San Fran	Los Angeles
L	L	L	L	L	L	L	L
0–10	1–2	0–10	4–10	3–4	3–4	2–3	1–4

It would be incorrect to say that the Reds have never been able to win in California. From 1970 through 1981, they had seven winning seasons on the West Coast. Since the dismantling of the Big Red Machine, however, success has been rare. From 1982 through 1991, the Reds were forty games under .500 (115–155) in California, trudging through ten straight losing seasons.

In 1990, the Reds made four trips to California and returned with a 12–15 record and some serious jet lag. The most painful trip came in July, when the Reds headed west with a ten-game lead and came home nursing banged-up bodies, bruised egos, and a lead cut nearly in half. The trip started in San Diego, where the Padres, who were thirteen games under .500, were in a free fall after losing twenty-one of twenty-five games. The Reds took the first game of the series but then lost three in a row, including both ends of a doubleheader on July 25.

Perhaps the greatest pain occurred between games during the doubleheader when comedienne Roseanne Barr, whose sitcom was produced by Padres Chairman and Managing Partner Tom Werner, sang "The Star-Spangled Banner" before the start of the second game. Barr gave one of the most embarrassing performances of the song ever presented, igniting boos throughout the stadium. She finished by grabbing her crotch and spitting on the ground, and as she walked off the field, all Reds announcer Marty Brennaman could say was that Barr "ought to be put in jail." Her stunt captured headlines and appeared again and again on TV news and sports channels. It was a disgrace for the teams and for baseball in general.

hecklers thought might get under his skin.

Already upset about the sweep and the hapless performance that day, Piniella snapped. With one foot inside the bus and the other on the top step, he turned to the hecklers, some of whom had climbed halfway up the fence.

He insulted San Francisco and then yelled: "You can s--- my d---!"

As soon as he stepped fully inside the bus and the door closed behind him, he saw Kathryn Quinn, the wife of Reds general manager Bob Quinn, seated in the front of the bus, next to her husband. He then saw his players, heads bowed, mouths covered by hands. They were trying not to laugh out loud.

Lou's face dropped like yesterday's soufflé. Gone was any sense of satisfaction he felt from having told off the hecklers.

"Oh, Kathryn, I forgot you were here," he said.

To which Mrs. Quinn replied, not missing a beat: "Oh, don't worry, Lou. I feel exactly the same way."

No Reds player can retell the story without busting up, not because what it said about Mrs. Quinn, but what it said about their manager. He was always "stepping in it." That was the part the players loved: Their skipper having to explain his actions. With Piniella, the antics were always followed by an accounting. It was what made him such a lovable lunatic. Not many lunatics have Lou's sense of shame, and the manners to try to make things right.

Kathryn Quinn recently passed away, but even her husband laughed when reminded of the bus incident twenty years later. "She was something," says Bob.

July 30–31, Los Angeles
August 1, San Diego

Ron Oester says he shaved his head after the team's eighth straight loss in Los Angeles on July 30 because he understood Lou Piniella's anger following the sweep in San Francisco and the opening loss in LA.

"Lou had kicked over a table, something like that, slammed his door," Oester remembers. "I looked around and everybody had their heads down, real quiet. I said, 'We should be (ticked) off because we lost, but we're still in the driver's seat! We're still five and a half games in first place! Loosen up! We'll win tomorrow!'"

Oester then called for seven guys to join him in shaving their heads. He would lead the way.

"I'll never forget Dibble saying, 'My wife won't like that. If we lose ten in a row, we'll shave our heads.' I said, 'Ten in a row? We're not gonna lose ten in a row! If you think that, shave my head right now. Eric. Get your clippers!'"

And Eric Davis, more than happy to oblige, cut off all of Oester's hair.

The next day, July 31, Oester came into the clubhouse and saw that Piniella had inserted Oester's name into the starting lineup.

"That was Lou," Oester recalls. "He did stuff like that all the time. It was, 'Okay, big guy, get in there and let's see what you can do.' He'd show his faith in you with stuff like that. I was so pumped."

Piniella did more than insert Oester into the lineup. Hal Morris batted leadoff for the first time in his major league career. Oester was second. Eric Davis batted third, instead of his customary cleanup spot, which went to Barry Larkin, batting there for the first time in his career. Paul O'Neill was fifth, Chris Sabo sixth, and Joe Oliver batted seventh. Piniella dropped Billy Hatcher to eighth—and thought seriously about putting pitcher Jose Rijo there. When Rijo heard that news, he marched into Piniella's office and said with a big smile, "Try it. I have a three-game hitting streak. Give me some respect!"

Rijo was loose. Rijo was always loose. He pitched

six and third innings of six-hit, two-run ball, hit two singles, and even stole a base.

"My first time up," recalls Oester twenty years later, "we had a man on third base (Morris had tripled), and here I was, with a chance to do something. I was so jacked up, I swung at the first pitch. Sinker down and away. (He lined out to second base.) I came into the dugout, and I remember Lou not saying a word. I was thinking, 'Man, he must think I'm a big blankin' idiot swinging at the first pitch.' I was fuming. Next at bat I came through (sacrifice fly, to give the Reds a 2–1 lead)."

The third time up, with Morris at second and two out and the Reds nursing a 3–2 lead, the Dodgers second basemen muffed Oester's ground ball, and Morris scored to give the Reds a 4–2 lead. The Reds went on to win 5–2 to break the losing streak.

And baldheaded Ron Oester, who hadn't played much that whole season, was right in the middle of it.

"Lou knew," concludes Oester.

The next night, the Reds went to San Diego for a make-up game and pounded out fourteen hits, winning 6–3. They flew home with a fresh outlook, ready to play twenty of their next twenty-eight games at Riverfront Stadium. "We're going home on a positive note, with a little momentum," Piniella said. "And you can emphasize this: I am looking forward to this homestand."

August 4, Cincinnati

The lead was down to four and a half games. The Reds had just played twenty-six games in twenty-four days and hadn't had a day off since the All-Star break. The grind was taking its toll.

The homestand brought no relief as the Reds dropped the first two games to the Padres. Hoping their success on Saturdays would continue, the Reds entered the game on August 4 with confidence. They trailed most of the way but were able to tie it in the bottom of the ninth on a pinch-hit home run by Luis Quinones. The Padres eventually won in the eleventh inning on Joe Carter's grand slam off Rick Mahler.

The lead was now three and a half. The Reds had lost ten of their last twelve. Check out the scorecard:

- They banged out fifteen hits but scored only three runs. (Right about on average for their output during the 2–10 streak: 2.7 runs)
- They were three-for-seventeen (.176) with runners in scoring position. (They were only .186 during the 2–10 streak.)
- They made four outs on the base paths. (During the 2–10 streak, they made fourteen outs on the paths, including a whopping five at home plate.).

"Everything we do is wrong," Piniella said. "It can't persist, that's for darn sure. This thing has been going on for two weeks now, and with the balance in baseball today, teams that stay away from mistakes win. We've made too many mistakes."

Twenty years later, though, Paul O'Neill recalls that the Reds had something to draw upon. He and his teammates kept it fixed in their minds.

"It wasn't like we'd started the season with a two-week hot streak," he said. "We had played exceedingly

PITCHING STAFF WAS BUOYED BY THE NASTY BOYS

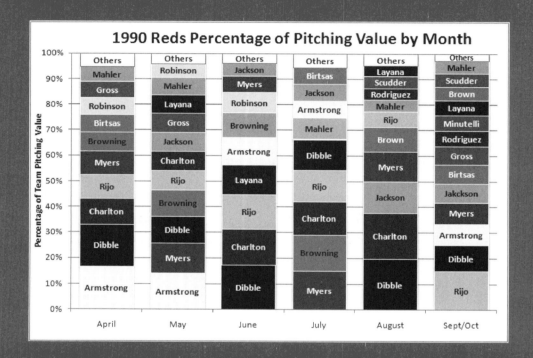

To say that the Nasty Boys carried the Reds pitching staff might be an understatement. Sure the Reds had good seasons from Jose Rijo, Jack Armstrong, and Tom Browning, but when you look at it at month by month, the Nasty Boys were among the most valuable pitchers for the Reds. Even after Norm Charlton was moved to the starting rotation in July, he continued to be one of the most valuable pitchers, if not more so. The "Boys" were a definite force for the Reds in 1990.

The Reds had to summon spring memories when summer ghosts arose.

well for two *months*. We knew we were good. We knew we'd come out of it."

But wasn't it possible that the Reds might blow it? Hadn't many of these same guys always blown it before? Had they ever been able to hold onto first place?

A start of 33–12 guarantees you nothing when you are 61–44. The guys chasing you don't know from 33–12. All they know is they're three and a half games back, there's a body in the water, and it's time for lunch.

FAST FACTS

- The 1990 Reds were the first team in MLB history to have three pitchers throw at least fifty innings out of the bullpen while striking out more than ten batters per nine innings.

10

Dog Days

After Joe Morgan was inducted into the National Baseball Hall of Fame on August 4, the Reds won their next two games, on August 5 and 7. But on the eighth, the bleeding began again (three losses in four games), as Pete Rose reported to prison in Marion, Illinois, birthplace and boyhood home of Ray Fosse, the catcher who Rose bowled over in the 1970 All-Star Game in Cincinnati. "Who," people asked themselves, "is writing this script?"

August 8, Marion, Illinois

On the first day of prison life, Pete Rose was given a hard time.

"On my way back to the mess hall," he wrote in his book, *My Prison Without Bars*, "I had to wait for several minutes for the electronic bars to open, which gave the lifers some time to stare at me and express their opinions.

"Since I had made the headlines just about every day during the previous year, all of the guys had read about me and had become 'experts' on my gambling case.

"One inmate raised his fist and called out, 'Hey, Charlie, you got hustled. Right on, man!' Another convict tried to put me in my place when he yelled out, 'Hey, Rose. You f----- up. Look at you now!'"

Todd Benzinger, a history buff, knew that August could turn wannabes into road kill.

151

August 8, Cincinnati

The Hit King wasn't the only one having a tough night.

Rose had just finished evening chow when Eric Davis stepped up in the first inning at Riverfront Stadium...and barely blooped a single over the infield.

When Davis got what *Enquirer* beat man Jack Brennan described as "an unusually slow start" out of the batter's box, many in the crowd of 30,700 let him have it. And it only got worse when Dodgers pitcher Fernando Valenzuela picked him off first. Davis later fouled out, popped out, and grounded out, completing the stink bomb.

Down went the Reds, 4–2, despite a decent start by Scott Scudder.

"I can't concern myself with what the fans are saying, or what somebody's saying about me on whatever radio show," said Davis after the game. "I'm trying to do as many little things as I can to keep guys up and motivated…. I think this has been my best year as far as leadership on this team."

Nobody in the Reds clubhouse could have disagreed. Davis was hitting a miserable .226, but he was still hustling in center field. He wasn't sulking or making excuses or ducking the media. He was showing what it meant to be a pro.

In his heart, Piniella felt it. But in his head, something else was happening.

Sweet Lou saw it all slipping away.

He called out Davis but not directly, saying "We need to get some production from some other guys in here." Piniella and GM Bob Quinn were already talking about who they could acquire to help light a fire. Piniella wouldn't let up. *Ya gotta get us somebody, Bob. We ain't got enough.* But who could they get? And how might they best clear a roster spot? And in clearing a spot, they had to at least consider the effect on clubhouse chemistry, which was still good despite the muddling on the field.

And when would the right moment come for Mount Ve-LOU-vius to erupt with some antics worthy of Billy and Earl, his two mentors who, for all their craziness, really knew how to galvanize a team?

Because I just can't sit here. I have to do something.

There was no doubt in Piniella's mind.

If the Reds were going to blow it, this would be the month.

They would win it or lose it in the dog days.

August 10, Cincinnati

Roger Craig, Giants manager and a noted pitching guru (especially of the split-fingered fastball), stopped the game five or six times—"More than it happened in the rest of my career, combined," starter Norm Charlton recalls—to have the umpire check him for foreign substances.

"He didn't throw many of them, (spitballs)," Craig said after the game. "He just threw it when he'd get two strikes."

Twenty years later, Charlton recalls that game—and others like it.

"Every time I pitched, it seems like Roger was accusing me of throwing a spitter," Charlton says. "It

By the middle of August, Hal Morris was batting nearly .400 and was getting serious consideration for the Rookie of the Year award.

wasn't helping their guys, either. I remember going out (for a beer) with Will Clark, and Will telling me that it (Craig's accusations) was putting it in their hitters' heads that I was somehow doctoring the ball and making it even tougher to hit me."

Whatever Charlton was doing, it was working. He shut out the Giants, 7–0.

And he denies ever throwing a spitter.

August 11, Cincinnati

Will Clark slid hard into Barry Larkin on a double play, practically body-blocking him. The Reds shortstop took exception. Jose Rijo, the losing pitcher, countered that the Giants—who had beaten the Reds nine times in their twelve meetings—played harder than the Reds, which is why the Reds had lost fourteen of their last nineteen games, including this one, 4–2.

August 12, Cincinnati

Hal Morris was sizzling, even receiving "Rookie of Year" mention. He went two-for-two with two RBI, one on a solo home run that that turned a tense 4–3 affair into an easy-breathing job for Browning and the Nasty Boys.

Since becoming the regular starter at first base on July 5, Morris hit .420 through August 15. His overall average was .391.

"I keep reading how we're playing scared," Morris said. "I don't think there's any pressure at all. There's excitement, big crowds (40,134 this night). This is a lot of fun."

The Reds won 6–4.

Piniella had batted Eric Davis leadoff and said he was going to leave him there. Davis had singled sharply to open the bottom of the first inning, igniting a four-run rally. After the game, Piniella predicted, "We're going to come out and beat them tomorrow. It's just that plain and simple." And then, taking Roger Craig's pet phrase and turning it on him, Piniella added, "No 'Humm-Baby,' no nothing."

Lou had been waiting for just the right time to use that one.

August 13, Cincinnati

The Reds delivered on their manager's promise. They won, 6–5. The lead was back up to six and a half games. Craig felt Piniella had showed him up by what he had said about "No Humm-Baby." Craig also was upset that Piniella had gone onto the field to question one of Craig's double switches,

"(He acted) like I didn't know what I was doing," Craig said.

When Piniella heard about Craig's pique, he bellowed, "He's the one who says everyone in the league is scuffing the ball. Take it like a man, Roger!"

When Piniella "finished his tirade," wrote the *Enquirer*'s John Fay, "he stepped into his office and said with a smile, 'I lit into him pretty good, didn't I?'"

Sweet Lou knew exactly what he was doing.

Well, *most* of the time.

August 15, St. Louis

Fifth outfielder Herm Winningham was about to get a start, only his second one since June 1. He had made only twenty-five plate appearances in the previous sixty-one games, during which he batted just .167. This would be only his fifth start since Eric Davis came off the DL on May 21. Since that day, Winningham had a mere forty-two plate appearances in eighty games, batting .205.

"I wasn't even getting in to pinch hit," recalls

The Reds were at their best when players like Luis Quinones and Jeff Reed were contributing at critical junctures in games.

Winningham twenty years later. "I was prepared. I was ready to hit. Lou just chose not to use me in situations that he normally would. I went to him and asked why. And he said, 'Herm, I don't know.'"

All the Reds remember Piniella for one trait above all others: He was honest. But Winningham could draw only one conclusion. His manager had lost confidence in him. And so, when Winningham saw his name in the lineup that night, he was determined to jog Piniella's memory on why Lou had kept him on the team in the first place.

After striking out to lead off the game, he tripled into the left-field corner in the third, lined out to left in the fifth, doubled to left in the eighth, tripled to left-center in the tenth, and knocked in the go-ahead run in the twelfth with a triple to right-center.

Three triples, one double, eleven total bases.

"Really, it should have been four," Winningham recalls. "On the (double to center), I just turned around and went back to second. I was tired."

Piniella couldn't recall ever seeing someone hit three triples in the same game.

"This is the type of game a division-leading club is supposed to win," said Piniella.

Glenn Braggs had started the twelfth-inning rally with a one-out single, and Luis Quinones, filling in for Chris Sabo at third base, had a terrific day in the field. ("You looked like Brooks Robinson out there," pitching coach Stan Williams told him.)

"We are starting to get team play like we did at the beginning of the season," Charlton said. "Back then, we didn't have to wait for our big guns to win games. It was a different guy every day, and now we're seeing that again."

Charlton had sat out a two-hour-and-twenty-one-minute rain delay and still come back to pitch. He didn't even go back to the clubhouse during the break.

"I knew it was cold in there, so I just sat on the bench in the dugout with my heaviest jacket on," he said. "I felt my arm stiffen a little but not enough to where I couldn't pitch."

What had he done in the dugout to pass the time?

"I just watched what they were showing on the big screen," he said. "It was some old baseball stuff. Those guys were driving some pretty nice old cars up to the ballpark."

August 17–19, Cincinnati

The Reds knew they were "in for it" if they met the Pirates in the NLCS in October. In the four-game series in August, the Reds scored a total of eight runs.

On Friday night they lost both ends of a twi-night doubleheader, and then they lost on Saturday and Sunday, too.

To make matters worse, after the Sunday loss the players were required to attend, in suits and ties, a charity benefit at Marge Schott's Indian Hill estate. Elephants would give rides to kids in the searing heat.

"I had a date with me," pitcher Scott Scudder recalls. "We wandered over to where the elephants were, and we watched the kids. I felt somebody come up behind me, and I looked around, and it was Marge. She says, 'Why don't you take a ride on that elephant?' And I say, 'Uh, no thank you.' Because I've got a nice suit on. And the next thing she says is, 'Do you want to go back to Triple-A?' I remember taking my jacket off, handing it to my date, and saying, 'I'll be back.' Let me tell you, I got on that elephant."

When Triple-A is only as far away as the owner's whim, you do what you're told.

Just as he had done a month earlier when he came onto the field at Riverfont Stadium right before the national anthem, eating a peanut butter sandwich. "You're on," he was told. "Danny (Jackson) just 'went down' in the 'pen. He can't go. You're on the mound. Right now."

Gulp—peanut butter sandwich gone, no time for butterflies. "Get a move on, young man," home plate umpire Country Joe West told him, handing him the game ball. To the mound Scudder scurried.

Second batter, Dave Martinez, went deep: 1–0. But

NASTY BOYS GAVE REDS CACHET FROM THE START

For many fans, memories of the 1990 Reds center mostly on the Nasty Boys—Norm Charlton, Rob Dibble, and Randy Myers coming out of the bullpen. Nobody wanted to face them because if they were in the game and the Reds had the lead, the game was over.

Charlton says that, even twenty years later, people tell him they still remember the Nasty Boys. "They forget, though, that the name 'Nasty Boys' started out as a name for the whole bullpen," he adds. "Everybody down there threw nasty stuff."

Opponents recognized in spring training how devastating the Reds bullpen would be. "The strongest part of their club is what they can do from the seventh inning on," said Phil Niekro, the pitching coach for the Atlanta Braves. "I don't think I've ever seen a bullpen that strong."

The Nasty Boys were intimidating, fearless, overpowering, and a little bit crazy. And Reds fans loved them. The bullpen made the Reds legitimate contenders from the start. The shortened spring training meant that starting pitchers would need the early part of the season to get stretched out and pitch deep into games. This situation favored teams with deep bullpens.

Charlton, Dibble, and Myers dominated from the get-go. During the Reds' nine-game winning streak, the trio pitched twenty-two combined innings, posting a 1–0 record with five saves and a 1.64 ERA while striking out thirty-six batters. By mid-season, all three had earned run averages under 3.00 while

striking out more than ten batters per nine innings. It wasn't long before the "Nasty Boys," a name coined by Randy Myers at the start of the season, were local celebrities with their own t-shirts, both authorized and unauthorized, popping up in stores all around the Cincinnati area.

The trio's success pushed their bullpen-mates to step up as well. "I fed off them," Scott Scudder remembers. "It allowed me to play my role more comfortably. If I could go out and get two innings and give the ball to the Nasty Boys, I knew we had a shot. And they appreciated the role the rest of us played to get the game to them."

The Nasty Boys brought a swagger to the team. To a man, everyone believed that if they could win the first six innings, the game was in the bag, and that's why from day one, the Reds knew they were going to do something special.

the Reds scored three in the bottom of the inning, and Scudder started dealing until Andres Galarraga ripped one out in the fourth. But that's all Scudder gave them, chalking up nine punchouts in six and a third innings. He got the leadoff man in the seventh, but then gave up a line-drive single, and out came Lou, and then Nasty Boy Dibble: *K-K*, good night, Irene, and Randy Myers finished it off in the ninth. Ballgame.

"The mentality of that bullpen in '90 was you could be in the game *right now*," recalls Scudder, snapping his fingers. "Knowing I had to have that mentality—everybody knew they had to have that mentality if they were going to play for Lou—helped me go straight to that mound that night and be successful."

It was the edge that Lou kept you on.

That's what it felt like to play for the Cincinnati Reds in 1990, even when five minutes earlier you were holding a peanut butter sandwich in your pitching hand.

Scott Scudder came up big several times in 1990, both as a starter and a reliever.

August 21, Cincinnati

Lou had been thinking about this for a while now. He couldn't recall exactly when he'd first heard the story of the Tortoise and the Hare (or, as Lou later referred to it with Dayton writer Hal McCoy, "The Taurus and the Turtle"), but he knew it.

Lou hadn't been a great student at Tampa Jesuit High. The priest who ran the "Precinct of Discipline," Father Lashley, had grown so exasperated with young Piniella that he made Lou draw the outlines of one hundred donkeys, scissor them from the pages, and write

on each one, *My name is Lou Piniella. I am a jackass.*

The team had lost five in a row—four to those damn Pirates, and last night 3–1 to the Cubs, when Terry Tata had called it at one in the morning due to rain. It was time to tell the story.

"Fellas, you've all heard the story of the taurus, er, tortoise, and the hare, right? The hare" (Lou assumes a hare-like position, squatting on his heels, paws dangling out front) *"gets off to a really fast start, but then goes for a siesta in the weeds."* (Lou hops to a vacant locker.) *"He's got this big lead on the tortoise, see? But the tortoise keeps*

on grinding." (Lou morphs into the tortoise—curled up and hunched over—and crawls across the clubhouse floor.) "*He doesn't stop moving. The hare is on still on siesta, but the tortoise is starting to catch up, slowly but surely, because he's grinding. We gotta become the tortoise. If we grind, the hare can't catch us. The hare is too far back. There aren't enough games left! If we grind, the hare...can...not...catch...us!!!*

It was pretty funny watching a grown man act out the story. ("And Lou was no actor," Norm Charlton recalls.) But nobody laughed. The point was clear. When Lou made a point, you listened.

As he told them at his first meeting: *Listen to everything I say.*

❖ ❖ ❖ ❖ ❖

The game began with a leadoff double down the left-field line by Billy Hatcher, who had been MIA since the All-Star break and was hitting leadoff for the first time in three weeks. The Reds didn't get Hatcher all the way around, but they did in the third when he lashed another leadoff double, this one into the right-field corner, and Larkin singled him home with a line drive between the second and first baseman to tie the game at one.

Hatcher's third double came in the fifth inning, a shot to the right of the center fielder. Then, with two outs and Paul O'Neill intentionally walked—*watch it now, here comes the tortoise*—Cubs pitcher Mike Larkey uncorked a wild pitch, moving O'Neill to second,

which is when Glenn Braggs grounded a pitch between short and third to score Hatcher and O'Neill, putting the Reds up 4–1.

And this is where we become the tortoise, fellas. If we grind, the hare can't catch us.

The bases were loaded with one out when out came the hare.

Herm Winningham was on third, Rick Mahler on second, Hatcher on first. Larkin grounded sharply to shortstop, forcing Hatcher at second and making for a bang-bang play at first. Larkin appeared to beat the relay to first, but umpire Dutch Rennert called him out to end the inning.

Lou was out of the dugout before Rennert's right arm had returned to his side.

Whaaaaaaaaaaaaaaaaaaaaaaaaaaaaaaaaaat?

That dugout-rattling whoop rocketed Lou all the way to first base where he greeted Rennert with a choice expletive and simultaneously ripped off his cap and fired it at Rennert's feet. ("For some reason I notice he likes to throw his cap," Rennert would later note, quite calmly.) Rennert's right hand shot back up to indicate that Piniella was ejected.

But Lou wasn't ready to go gently into *that* good night. Having thrown his hat, he looked for something else, which is when he saw first base. He reached down, wrenched it free, and hurled it just beyond the dirt portion of the infield and onto the Astroturf. Looking at the base with disgust—apparently incredulous that it hadn't flown far—he thundered toward it, picked it up, and threw it again, this time with some English that sent it rolling. It came to rest in short right field.

"Comical," Glenn Braggs would say later.

"Best base toss I ever saw," Rick Mahler would add.

"It was frustration," Piniella explained after the game. "It just happened. I came in here (to my office) afterward and thought, 'A forty-six-year-old man shouldn't be doing that.'"

The Reds scored two more times in the seventh and two more in the eighth (another leadoff double by Hatcher, four doubles in all, tying a major league record); eight runs total, no home runs, a throwback to the 33–12 start. A well-pitched start by Mahler, then two-innings of lockdown relief by Randy Myers.

The next day's headline in the *Cincinnati Post* declared "Piniella Uses Tale To Help Bring Club Out Of Its Shell."

The day after that, under a headline of "Summer's Last Fling," the *Enquirer* invited people to Fountain Square for a base-tossing contest. Mayor Charlie Luken won it with a launch of forty-three feet and one-quarter inch, but even more impressively, Mary Krutko of WKRC-TV won the ladies' division with a heave of forty feet—in high heels.

Take *that*, Sweet Lou.

❖ ❖ ❖ ❖ ❖

August 21 was an event-filled day. So much happened, in fact, that something almost got lost to history, overshadowed by Hatcher's four doubles and Lou's base toss, not to mention the telling of "the taurus and the hare."

When asked at Redsfest '09 why he threw the base, Piniella responded simply, "I think I was P.O.'d at the umpire."

REDS PLAYED WITH THEIR MANAGER'S PASSION

No team in recent Reds history embodied their manager more than the 1990 Reds. Lou Piniella ate, drank, slept, and showered baseball. He rarely put the game away during the season, and he wanted a team that felt the same way.

That's what he was trying to say when he threw first base: I've just begun to fight, and I need twenty-five guys fighting with me. And those guys fought for Lou from day one. It's hard to look at this team and not appreciate the passion. It sometimes teetered on the brink of chaos, as evidenced by their fourteen ejections, but it kept them going when the season got tough. "I want my players to know that getting thrown out doesn't help themselves or the team," Piniella said, "but if you ask me if I'd rather have players who automatically accept things or players who are aggressive, want to do well, have some fight in them, I'll take the latter."

Their attitude frustrated many opponents, who called them thugs, headhunters, and whiners. (And much worse.) The Reds were hit by pitches more than any other team in the league.

"The fact that we're aggressive on the base paths—not dirty, just aggressive—certainly plays a part in how we're perceived," Piniella said. "And the fact we've been so successful plays a part."

Surprisingly, there wasn't much fighting among the players that year, rare for close quarters and a 162-game season. Those guys loved each other, stood by each other, fought for each other. That's what their manager wanted and that's why they won.

1990 REDS EJECTIONS

1. **May 10, Pittsburgh:** Chris Sabo argued a called third strike with umpire Charlie Williams and was ejected in the second inning.

2. **May 10, Pittsburgh:** Mariano Duncan was thrown out trying to steal third base in the third inning. When he questioned the call, he was ejected by umpire Mark Hirschbeck. Duncan tossed his helmet and may have bumped Hirschbeck, earning himself a one-game suspension.

3. **May 24, Montreal:** Umpire Steve Rippley opened the game by calling Chris Sabo out on strikes. Piniella was ejected before he even left the dugout.

4. **May 27, Montreal:** Rob Dibble walked off the mound after completing the eighth inning and had a few words for umpire Frank Pulli. Dibble was told to hit the showers.

5. **June 22, Cincinnati:** Plate umpire Terry Tata called Eric Davis safe but reversed his decision, erasing the Reds' winning run and sending Piniella into a rage. He was ejected as the game headed into extra innings.

6. **June 26, Cincinnati:** Chris Sabo struck out in the bottom of the tenth, and on his way out to the field in the eleventh he had an exchange with plate umpire Bob Davidson. "I was just running to my position, and he was looking at me funny," Sabo said. "I looked at him and said, 'I didn't say anything,' and he threw me out."

7. **June 26, Cincinnati:** Also ejected from this game was pitching coach Stan Williams, who was trying to hold Sabo back during the argument. Williams wasn't completely sure what got him tossed but admitted, "I may have mentioned something to him about heredity."

8. **June 30, New York:** Umpire Dana DeMuth ejected Mariano Duncan, who tossed his helmet to the ground after a called third strike.

9. **July 12, Cincinnati:** Norm Charlton was ejected after complaining to umpire Steve Rippley about his strike zone.

10. **July 18, Cincinnati:** Lou Piniella was ejected for arguing that Dennis Martinez intentionally hit Glenn Braggs and Eric Davis. Piniella rushed out to umpire Jerry Crawford, who had warned both benches about beanballs prior to the game, and said, "We've had two guys hit now. You mean we can't retaliate without me and my pitcher getting ejected?"

    Crawford said, "Don't worry about it because you're gone right now."

11. **July 20, Cincinnati:** Charlton charged the mound in the bottom of the sixth inning after being drilled by Dennis Cook. Both Charlton and Cook were ejected.

12. **August 21, Cincinnati:** Dutch Rennert called Barry Larkin out at first on a close play. Piniella was sent to the clubhouse but not before tossing first base into the outfield.

13. **September 5, San Francisco:** Umpire Jim Quick called a strike on Barry Larkin and immediately tossed Lou Piniella for arguing from the dugout. "All I said was, 'That ball was low,'" Piniella said. "I had a little adjective before low, but it wasn't a bad adjective."

14. **September 6, San Francisco:** After striking out on a called third strike, Mariano Duncan put his helmet, bat, and gloves down at the feet of umpire Rennert and said, "You go ahead and try to hit those pitches for me." He was immediately ejected.

Before the game, Reds pitching coach Stan Williams called aside the Reds starting pitchers. He said, "Guys, we're thinking about maybe going to a four-man rotation."

"That's awesome!' Jose Rijo said.

"Well, good, Jose, because you're not one of them," Williams replied.

It is one of the great stories of 1990, but few people know it. Recalling it twenty years later, Tom Browning thought the meeting had taken place in late July or early August, but his recollection of the conversation between Williams and Rijo squares exactly with a sidebar written by the *Enquirer*'s John Fay:

"Before Tuesday's game with the Cubs, Piniella mentioned (the possibility of) switching to a four-man rotation, when starters Tom Browning (sprained ankle in the previous Friday's game) and Danny Jackson (coming off the DL August 29) are healthy. The rotation would also include Norm Charlton and either Jose Rijo or Jack Armstrong—'whoever is pitching well,' Piniella said."

Williams and Piniella were challenging Rijo.

"And that's when Jose kind of picked it up," Browning recalls.

Did he ever.

August 22, Cincinnati

Starting with this game—and over his next eight starts—Rijo went 6–2 with a 1.27 ERA. He threw five complete games and pitched nine innings in a game that went into extra innings, tied 1–1. He allowed more than two runs in a start only once. Three times in those nine starts he had double-digit strikeouts. Opponents batted .185 off him.

He was a workhorse—too much of one, in retrospect. In the course of a four-game span, he threw over 130 pitches three times. But at the time, he was putting the Reds on his back and carrying them to the finish line.

Piniella, again, had known which buttons to push. The experiment of "four-man rotation" didn't last long, but the mere threat of it lasted just long enough. After the game on August 21, the Reds won six of the next seven, and nine of the next twelve.

Somebody knew what he was doing.

This game marked the beginning of Jose Rijo's incredible nine-start stretch that helped the Reds win a division, a pennant, and a World Series.

Time of the game: 1:57.

A masterpiece—and a precursor: A five-hit, complete-game, 4–1 victory. It included a green-seat home run from Eric Davis, who had been moved to left field to put less stress on his bad knee, giving the fresh-wheeled Billy Hatcher the opportunity to roam center.

There'd been no controversy, no uproar, no sulking. The veteran Davis knew what was best for the club and agreed to Piniella's request. He had responded with class and grace.

In the sixth inning, he rocketed a blast over the 375-foot mark in left-center. At the time he was waiting for new contacts to arrive from his ophthalmologist. He wore sleek, black-rimmed glasses during batting prac-

When the going got toughest in August and September, Jose Rijo and Eric Davis carried the team.

tice but shelved them for the game.

"I'll keep trying (the eye glasses) in batting practice, and then when the contacts arrive, I'll try them," Davis said.

The homer was his first since August 10 and only his second since July 22.

In the eighth inning, he had played a carom perfectly off the left-field wall and pegged out Hector Villanueva at second trying to stretch a single into a double.

August 24, Cincinnati

Five days earlier, Ken Griffey Sr. had said he'd rather retire than "fake an injury" and go on the DL to clear a roster spot, and so the Reds released him.

"Ron Oester went ballistic," Herm Winningham recalls. "We had to calm him down. They (the management) didn't know what (Griffey) meant to us. Oester went running out the door and we had to go catch him."

Griffey "was granddaddy," Winningham remembers. "What he said went. You could talk to him about whatever, and boon-yah! (Boon-yah is South Carolinian for 'Griffey spoke with wisdom of the ages.') Grandfather had been there, done that. But when he was under the gun and being ordered to go on the DL, there was nobody there to help him."

Much of the season had been a struggle for playing time for Griffey, and the pinch-hitting opportunities often demanded a power bat he no longer possessed. He was forty years old. When he was young, he had more power than the "beat-the-ball-and-run-like-hell" philosophy manager Sparky Anderon demanded of him.

Griffey had sacrificed for the Big Red Machine, both power and stolen bases. Joe Morgan didn't want the kid trying to steal bases when Joe was batting, and so Anderson ordered Griffey to stay put, probably costing Griffey at least thirty or more bags a year. And now he was being asked to do something he no longer could do.

"They put him in situations where we needed a two-run (home run)," Winningham recalls. "That wasn't his thing. It was killing him, but he had nobody to talk to. But when I would pinch-hit and strike out or pop up or hit it hard and make an out and go sit on the end of bench, that man would come and talk to me. But there was nobody for Ken Griffey."

Winningham remembers Eric Davis calling on Griffey after the release.

"Eric said, 'Mister Griffey, come talk to us.' And what Senior said to us was, 'Don't worry about me. I've done played. I've got me a World Series. Yeah, I would like another one, but don't worry about me. Go on out there and get you one.' He was very reassuring about it, and it was good to hear."

Griffey had no hard feelings about the way things were handled at the end. It was just baseball. And it allowed him to play side-by-side with his son, Junior, in Seattle, the highlight of his career. In the end, Griffey was able to "take it like a man," to use Piniella's favorite phrase.

Griffey's teammates later voted him a full World Series share.

It was the ultimate sign of respect, and he was moved by it.

August 31, Chicago

Piniella and Quinn got the man they wanted.

Not a bopper but somebody they felt would get the fire burning again.

Bill Doran tells the story, many years later...

"When I came over here, the one thing that hit me was their pace. The Astros were a last-place team and our games just dragged. I got over here and suddenly—Snap! Snap! Snap!—things were moving. On and off the field. Get the ball, throw it. Catch the ball, throw it. Snap! Snap! Snap! Everything was moving. They were in such a rhythm.

"I think it had a lot to do with Lou—his impatience, his desire. He was so demanding, so on top of things all of the time. There was no time to breathe. Right from the get-go, he knew what had to be done with that club. He knew they had a lot of talent, and he wasn't going to settle for anything less than their best. He wasn't going to let them waste it.

"When they opened up (the season) in Houston, they jumped out of the gate like nothing I'd ever seen before. I think that carried over and lasted the entire season. Boy, they had a lot of fuel in that tank. Geesh."

FAST FACTS

- Only nine times in the previous thirty-five seasons had a player hit three triples in one game. Only twelve times had a player hit four doubles in one game. Within one week in August, the Reds had a player accomplish each feat.
- Hal Morris's .340 batting average in 1990 was the highest by a Reds' rookie (minimum three hundred plate appearances) since Cuckoo Christensen batted .350 in 1926.
- The 1990 Reds had five players who at least once during their career hit twenty home runs and stole twenty stolen bases in a season. Those players were Ken Griffey Sr., Eric Davis, Barry Larkin, Chris Sabo, and Paul O'Neill.
- Tom Browning, who led the 1990 squad with fifteen victories, had seven straight seasons of ten or more victories with the Reds, tied for the longest streak in club history since Bucky Walters had nine such seasons from 1938 to 1946.

11

Best in the West

With one month left in the season, Lou Piniella refused to let his team coast into the playoffs.

When Bill Doran entered the game as a pinch hitter in the seventh inning, the Reds were up 7–1 on the Cubs. If you could have heard the Mt. Healthy native's heart, you never would have guessed he was a nine-year veteran hitting in a game that was all but decided.

"As soon as I got my legs to stop shaking, I was okay," he said, smiling. Maybe it was the excitement of playing for the team he grew up following. He was twelve when the Big Red Machine of Rose, Morgan, Bench, and Perez began its run of four World Series in seven years. Now, here he was with a chance to go to the World Series as a Red, too. He was on sensory overload.

Doran lined out to first base in his first at-bat as a Red, but a single in the ninth capped off an enjoyable day.

"It's nice to be involved in the atmosphere of a pennant race," he said. "I've been playing for the last three months knowing the team had no chance. It's tough to play under those conditions."

Eric Davis and Marge celebrate the wire-to-wire division title.

Doran was regaining his fire. He'd need it to fit in with this clubhouse.

"I saw a lot of hungry people in that dugout today," he said. "I spent the first seven innings just observing, and there are a lot of hungry faces."

He made his first start as a Red at third base the next day. It was the first time he'd played third since becoming a pro. He wasn't immediately comfortable there, but he was so excited that it didn't matter.

"I'm just thrilled to be here at this time," he said. "I'm ready to do whatever they ask."

Lou Piniella was confident that Doran could handle whatever he threw at him. "This kid is an athlete," Piniella said. "I knew that when we got him. One of the reasons we got him is to spell Sabo. We feel he can definitely help us down the stretch."

The Reds won the final two games of the four-game series against the Cubs. They piled up twenty-four hits and fourteen runs while surrendering just three runs in the field. It was the Reds' seventh win in their last nine games.

The players attributed their recent success to returning to the easygoing attitude of the first month of the season.

"We've turned it down a notch," said first baseman Todd Benzinger. "We're more relaxed and going out there and having fun. We tried to turn it up a notch last month, and it caused tension and pressure when we didn't need it. It sounds like a cliché, but it's true: When you go out there and have fun, everything takes care of itself."

The laughter in the winning clubhouse suited Doran just fine.

"It puts a charge in my personality," he said. "I feel like a kid with a new toy right now."

September 6, San Francisco
Magic Number: 20

One constant throughout the season was that when things got rocky on the field, a player or coach would have a meltdown, often in reaction to the umpires.

The team was on its way to its fifth loss in nine games when Mariano Duncan had had enough. When umpire Dutch Rennert rang up Duncan for the second time in the game in the ninth inning, the Reds second baseman laid his bat, helmet, and gloves at the Duchman's feet.

"You go ahead and try to hit those pitches for me," Duncan told Rennert. Great line, great theatrics, but guaranteed to get you the boot. When Duncan got back to the dugout, he threw a shinguard off the dugout wall and then hurled three batting helmets onto the field. That's when Ron Oester stepped in. Not only did Oester restrain Duncan, he actually walked him to the clubhouse.

"I knew how important he was to us," Oester recalls, twenty years later. "My role was to settle him down and make sure he stayed in the lineup. We couldn't afford any suspensions. We had to have him."

What made Oester's gesture particularly important was that Duncan had taken Oester's job at the beginning of the year—even before spring training. A selfish player would have let Duncan get suspended and get himself back on the field. But if Piniella was the master field general, Oester was the platoon sergeant, helping keep the ranks in order. He knew he didn't have many chances at a championship left, and he was going to do everything to reach that goal. But he said that his role as a clubhouse leader on the '90 team was not contrived.

"I had always been about winning," he said. "Now I was going to have to do it coming off the bench and whatever support and watchdog stuff I could do in the clubhouse. It was the same mindset. You go out there and do all you can to help the ballclub win."

Oester had only 154 at bats in 1990, but he hit .299 (best in his career), and his on-base plus slugging percentage (.716) was second-best in his career. His role in the clubhouse was better than both combined.

"We wouldn't have won it without him," Billy Hatcher remembers.

September 11, Cincinnati
Magic Number: 15

The Reds took a seven-game lead in the West in a fine seven-inning performance by starter Norm Charlton. To some observers, it appeared the Reds should be waltzing home with the NL West flag, but anybody who had been watching the team since June knew better. To quote Tina Turner in "Rollin' on the River," the 1990 Reds never did anything "nice and easy." They did it "nice and rough."

Billy Doran went one-for-one against his old mates,

Legs-a-shaking, new Red Bill Doran went to bat.

knocking in an insurance run in the ninth inning of the 5–3 victory. Doran said that watching the Reds play reminded him of watching the Astros play in 1986, as they strove in September to make the postseason.

"There's a sense of trying to get (the race) over too soon," Doran said. "There's still a ways to go, but they can smell it. They know that all they have to do is go out and get it. I remember in 1986, the days

BORN TO RUN

This chart maps a team's offensive contribution against its pitching/defensive contribution. The farther to the right a team is on the chart, the better performance by the team's offense. The higher up on the chart a team appears, the better the performance by the pitching and defense. A team appearing in the upper-right quadrant was above league average in both offense and defense.

The Reds' success was built around pitching and defense. They were slightly above average offensively, but they were the best run-prevention team in the league. The Oakland A's weren't far behind in run-prevention and were a much better offensive team, which is why they won 103 games compared to the Reds' ninety-one wins. The Pittsburgh Pirates were much more of an offense-based team, posting one of the top offenses in the majors, but they were only slightly above average at preventing runs. Perhaps the biggest surprise on the chart might be the New York Mets, who were better than the Pirates both offensively and defensively but finished four games back in the National League East. Just goes to show that it's not always the better team that wins, even over the course of 162 games.

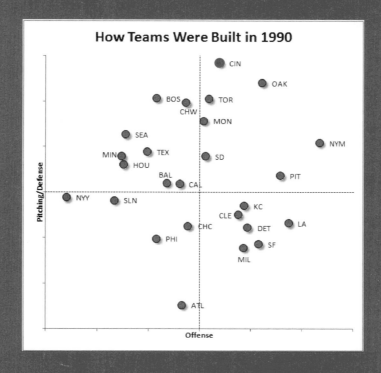

never came around fast enough. As soon as the game was over, it seemed liked it took forever for the next day to get there. I sense that here. It's great. That's the way it should be."

"Are the Reds loose enough?" somebody asked Doran.

"Yes, and I was a little surprised at that," he said. "There are a lot of young players here, players who've struggled in years past, finished second a lot and never gotten over the hump. But I don't see that affecting them."

September 13, Cincinnati
Magic Number: 14

Barry Larkin was frustrated. The Reds had lost six of their last nine games, including a thirteen-inning affair the previous night. He had hit into two double plays, one coming in the eleventh inning with men on first and third and one out. His eighteen-game hitting streak ended, but he didn't care. Right now, winning games was all that mattered.

Larkin was frustrated because he failed to do his job in the fifth inning. With no outs and runners on first and second, Piniella had called upon him to lay down a sacrifice bunt, but Larkin had popped out to third base.

The Reds went on to squander that opportunity despite loading the bases. Trailing the Astros 5–2 in the bottom of the seventh inning, Larkin came up again with a man on base—Doran with his third single of the game—but Jim Clancy wouldn't give him a

thing to hit, and Larkin walked on five pitches.

A deep fly ball by Hal Morris almost tied the game, but Eric Yelding snagged it.

As frustrated as Larkin was, at least he wasn't being booed. The same couldn't be said for Eric Davis, who had been up three times in the game with men on base, and all three times he had eliminated the lead runner.

Boooooo. The fans were frustrated. They seemed to be always frustrated with Davis, but somehow he didn't let it affect his game.

Then: *Crack!* Davis blasted a ball to deep left-center field. It landed 424 feet away. The fans loved him again.

With the game tied, Larkin found himself with another shot to help his team in the ninth. Doran led off with his fourth single of the game and was now batting .593 since coming to the Reds on his way to being named NL Player of the Week.

Larkin was once again asked to bunt and move the runner up, but after two pitches he managed only two foul bunts. "I was frustrated," Larkin said. "I'm the second hitter in the lineup and I'm asked to bunt. I should get it down."

He was surprised to see the bunt taken off by Piniella. The next pitch was a good one, but Larkin fouled it off. On the fourth pitch, though...

Crack!

He hit it hard, but it was hooking down the line. Would it stay fair?

"I couldn't tell," said Larkin. "I don't hit too many, not even in batting practice. It started off good, then it

Paul O'Neill didn't strive to be a power hitter but still could knock the ball out of the park.

started hooking. I couldn't tell until I heard the fans."

They erupted. Larkin had hit the first walk-off home run of his career, giving the Reds a 7–5 win and pushing their lead back to six and a half games.

"We've had a lot of big wins this year," Lou Piniella said, "but this one has to go at the top of the list."

September 17, Cincinnati
Magic Number: 11

"I don't think anyone can feel better than me right now," Jose Rijo exclaimed.

He was probably right. He had spent two hours and twelve minutes slicing up the third-place Giants on his way to a two-hit shutout. Dave Parker had home run trots that took longer. It was Rijo's fifth complete game of the season, all coming in his last eleven starts.

"Once he's in a groove, I don't think there's anyone better than Jose," said catcher Jeff Reed.

Rijo hit ninety-seven on the radar gun several times throughout the game, retiring twenty-four of the last twenty-six batters he faced.

"Every time I go out there I feel so strong," he said. "I feel almost unbeatable."

In the third inning, Paul O'Neill hit a two-run homer off Scott Garrelts that made the score 4–0 and gave Rijo all the breathing room he needed. It was O'Neill's sixteenth home run on the season.

Only sixteen?

"To me, Paul's a thirty to thirty-five guy," Piniella said. "But at times, he lets little things affect him that

shouldn't. A lot of young players are like that."

Piniella hadn't given up on the kid. He was still prodding, but he was also praising.

"The ball jumps off his bat," Piniella said. "He's a big kid. Once he gets all that honed and channeled in the right direction, he'll be a great player. Sooner or later, he's going to put it all together and light up the scoreboard."

The Reds were one game closer to clinching their first division since 1979, when O'Neill was sixteen and tearing it up at Brookhaven High in Columbus.

The 4–0 victory by the Reds pretty much sealed the fate of the Giants, putting them eight and a half games out of first place with fifteen to play. Somewhere Pete Rose was smiling. The Giants had twice finished first to Rose's second-place Reds.

September 20, Houston
Magic Number: 10

Things weren't going so well for the Reds lately. They were up-and-down more often than the Philadelphia Toboggan Company, makers of the roller-coaster trains for "The Beast" at Kings Island. They had managed only six wins in their previous sixteen contests. Starters Tom Browning and Danny Jackson were slumping, and Norm Charlton hadn't looked so warm in his last outing, going just two innings against the Dodgers four days ago.

"I hadn't been throwing as hard lately, and I hadn't been throwing as many fastballs," Charlton explained. "My stuff hadn't been that good, and in that situation, I'm not going to puff out my chest and say, 'I'll throw it by them anyway.'"

Thankfully, Charlton had his fastball working on this night. He went seven and a third innings, allowing only three hits and one run to the Astros. Unfortunately, it wasn't enough.

The offense managed only two runs, all on the bat and legs of Eric Davis. In the second inning, he singled, stole second, advanced to third on a throwing error, and scored on a passed ball. In the fifth, he homered to give the Reds a 2–0 lead.

The lead was 2–1 in the bottom of the ninth when Randy Myers loaded the bases on a single, hit batsman, and an intentional walk. Then with two outs, light-hitting catcher Carl Nichols punched a two-out fastball to left-center, driving in two runners and giving the Astros a 3–2 victory.

The loss, coupled with a Dodgers win, dropped the Reds' lead to three and a half games. And though the Reds were still in the driver's seat with only thirteen games to play, Charlton wasn't having any of it. "If we just sort of win the division by default, that sends us into the playoffs on a bad note," he said. "I'd like to see everyone get going and head into the playoffs with a positive feeling."

September 21, San Diego
Magic Number: 9

Enough was enough. Eventually the Reds were going to have to stop waiting for the games to run out and step up and take the division title. It was going to take the big guys coming through to make it happen.

Eric Davis was first in line. With two out and Billy Hatcher on third base in the first inning, Davis stepped up. He battled Padres starter Dennis Rasmussen, fouling off five pitches before hitting a hard grounder up the middle and into center field. Given his achy knee, Davis could have settled for a single and an RBI, but he was running hard out of the box, capitalizing on a lackadaisical effort by Joe Carter in center, and Davis slid feet-first safely into second.

The aggressive play was an unexpected uppercut that caught the Padres square on the chin. An error by shortstop Gary Templeton and a walk to Glenn Braggs loaded the bases. A single (Hal Morris) and double (Joe Oliver) later, and the Reds had a 5–0 lead with Mr. Rijo on the mound.

"Right now, Jose Rijo is the best pitcher in the National League," his manager said. And he would have a hard time finding a contrary opinion.

But Rijo struggled out of the gate. A dandy play up the middle by Larkin kept leadoff hitter Bip Roberts off the bases, but Rijo gave up a single and a walk to the next two hitters and one out later an error by Larkin loaded the bases.

Benito Santiago hit a shot to the hole between short and third, but Larkin pounced on the ball with a stabbing backhand, turned and threw in one motion to nab Fred Lynn at second base, ending the threat.

It was going to take *all* of the big guys to wrap up the division. An inning later, Larkin and Davis made sure the game was out reach with back-to-back home runs in the second inning.

Rijo, as he had done so often over the last two months, put the game on cruise control and mowed down Padres like a Toro, facing the minimum number of batters over the next seven innings.

Up 10–0, Rijo went out to pitch the ninth inning. A couple of singles and a walk later, the shutout was gone. And Rijo was angry.

"I wanted the shutout real bad," Rijo said. "Joe Carter got the hit for the run, and I thought I had him struck out before the hit, but the umpire (Bruce Froemming) wasn't giving me the corners all night. Then I walked the next guy."

Piniella came to the mound but left Rijo in the game, much to the chagrin of Mark Parent, who was standing in the on-deck circle.

"I was mad that Piniella left him in," Parent said. "He threw me three of the nastiest sliders I've ever seen."

Parent struck out on three pitches, and Mike Pagliarulo popped out to left field, leaving the bases loaded and giving Rijo his thirteenth win on the season against seven losses. It was the sixth time he had pitched nine innings in his last seven starts. Rijo needed the Nasty Boys about as much as Mark Parent did.

The victory marked the first time the Reds offense had put double-digit runs on the board since June 24. It also triggered a streak of six wins in seven games that saw the magic number drop to two with six games to play.

Jose Rijo roared into the ace's role with a month of dominating performances.

September 29, Cincinnati
Magic Number: 0

The Reds were trailing 3–1 in the middle of the seventh inning when the game was delayed by rain. Forty minutes later, word spread through the stands of the Giants' 4–3 victory over the Dodgers as chants of "We're number one!" and "We want the Reds!" echoed throughout the park.

The game the fans were watching no longer mattered. The Dodgers' loss meant a division title for the hometown Reds.

Minutes later the team emerged from the clubhouse onto the field wearing their commemorative division-champion hats and shirts ready to party.

"Call this (game)," Eric Davis pleaded to the umpires. "Let's go get drunk!"

The game wasn't called right away, but the players celebrated on the field with twenty thousand of their closest friends.

Paul O'Neill dove head first across the rain-soaked tarp. Jose Rijo splashed down right behind him.

"Maybe I'm not a wild guy usually, but I am today," said O'Neill. "I just saw the tarp and went."

"It wasn't my idea," said Rijo. "O'Neill told me to do it, and when he's doing stuff like that, you know it's a celebration."

When the game was finally called, the celebration moved to the clubhouse. Davis, covered in what the *Enquirer*'s Jack Brennan described as a mixture of "chocolate milk, beer, and shaving cream," sprayed his teammates with whatever he could get his hands on, including a squeeze-bottle of ketchup.

"You try to imagine what this feeling will be like from talking with friends who have been there," Davis said, "but it's better than what they conveyed to me. I guess you have to feel it yourself. It's more intense than I imagined."

Shortstop Barry Larkin was happy to finally quiet the critics. "I think we proved that we are the best team in the division," he said. "We went by the motto 'U Can't Touch This,' and nobody did the whole season."

Piniella's reaction was much more reserved. "It's

a wonderful feeling," he said, sharing a moment with his coaches. "I've experienced this as a player but not to this degree. This is really something special."

Nothing could ruin the joy Lou felt at this moment. Well, except for maybe somebody suggesting that the Reds had backed their way into the playoffs.

Dayton Daily News writer Hal McCoy recalls how often Piniella was asked toward the end of the '90 season if his team was "backing into the playoffs." In 2003, McCoy told the following story for the book *Opening Day*. Over the years it's become part of the Lou Piniella lore.

"After the Reds got off to that great start in '90, they barely played over .500 the rest of the year, and Lou was constantly being asked, 'Are you backing into the pennant?' He managed to keep his cool.

"But then, just before the playoffs started, I was sitting in his office at Riverfront, and a young fella came in carrying one of those big oversized tape recorders. He introduced himself to Lou: 'I'm so-and-so from the Christian radio station.' Lou nods. The young man holds the mike right in front of Lou's face and says, 'Lou, there's a lot of talk that your team may be backing into the championship, because of that fast start and slow finish.'

"Lou starts his answer with, 'My good man...' Well, you always knew you were in trouble when Lou addresses you as 'My good man.' Lou says, 'My good man, have you ever (expletive deleted) a (expletive deleted) from behind?' The young man just stood there, frozen, holding the mike. And Lou said, 'Well (exple-

The players partied on and off the field with thirty thousand of their closest friends. They would later describe it as a load-lightening experience that rekindled an April–May state of mind.

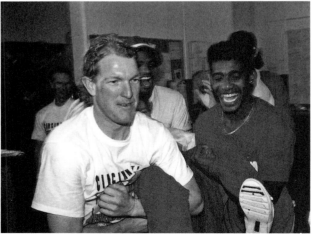

tive deleted) is still (expletive deleted)' All the fellow could say in response was, 'Thank you, Mr. Piniella,' and turned around and walked out. Interview over.

"After the guy left, I said, 'Lou, didn't you hear him say he is with the Christian radio station?' Lou said, 'I don't give a damn who he's with! He ought to know better than to ask a question like that!'"

September 30, Cincinnati
This is the game, it's really not hard,
Stay in school and you'll go far.
Don't do drugs, don't be a user,
Listen to us and don't be a loser.
We're the Reds. Red Hot!

Toward the end of the season the Reds players went into the recording studio to record the rap song "Reds Hot," written by Barry Larkin and a couple of his friends. It was a celebratory track with a message encouraging kids to stay in school and stay away from drugs. The proceeds from the sales of the song and accompanying video of the recording session benefited the Caring Program for Children in Cincinnati.

"It was all in fun and we had a ball doing it," Herm Winningham recalls. "Man, we laughed so hard. It should have taken us forty-five minutes, but it took us four or five hours."

Larkin remembers the recording session bringing the team even closer and solidifying the feeling that they were going to do something special that season.

"It seems as though we made that audio in late August or early September, but I can't remember for sure," Larkin says. "We were talking about going into the World Series and winning the whole thing. That was our feeling—it was our year, and that's what we were going to do. Lou set the standard when he said in the spring, 'I don't accept losing.' I fed off of that; I believed in it.

"During the season, despite all the trials and tribulations, we relied on what Lou had said. Doing that (rap song) helped solidify it. 'We are here to win this thing, and that's what we're going to do—we're going to win it.'"

❖ ❖ ❖ ❖ ❖

If the Reds were confident going into the postseason, they weren't showing it on September 30. It was a makeshift group—Todd Benzinger and Billy Hatcher were the only Opening Day starters in the lineup. Things were a little more relaxed after the celebration the day before, but the team looked flat and were shut out 3–0 by the Padres.

"I think some of the guys might have come here with a hangover," Piniella said. "We've lost three in a row now, and I certainly don't want to go into the playoffs in a losing posture.

"Today a few guys we haven't been playing were given a chance, and we expected more than we got. I have to rest Larkin and I'm gonna get Sabo out for a few days, but we have to swing the bats a lot better, whether it's after the fact or whatever."

Piniella was a little bit forgiving of the day's effort, but not much. "I can see today," Piniella said. "We clinched yesterday, and I understand that. But it can't continue."

The Reds had a few more regulars in the lineup on Monday and squeaked out a win over the Astros in the ninth inning on a throwing error. They followed that win with another on Tuesday, topping the Astros 3–2.

Despite losing the final game of the season on a ninth-inning triple by Ken Caminiti, Piniella still felt confident about his team going into the playoffs. "I think we'll beat Pittsburgh, I really do," Piniella said. "I feel good about the playoffs."

Rob Dibble shared his confidence. "I know we have a better team," Dibble said. "I'm happy for the Pirates. They've had a great year. It's going to be a shame to end their year in the playoffs."

Lou Piniella had won several divisions as a player, but his first as a manager scratched an itch that had long been lingering. Now, he wanted more.

FAST FACTS

- With his twenty-four home runs and twenty-one stolen bases, Eric Davis became the first Reds player to post five consecutive twenty-twenty seasons
- As of 2009, the 1990 Reds were the last World Series-winning team to not have a single batter with at least ninety RBI for the season.

12

The NLCS

The experts favored the Pirates over the Reds to win the National League Championship Series. The Pirates roster, after all, boasted the league's MVP and Cy Young Award winners, and such stars as Bobby Bonilla, Andy Van Slyke, and Jose Lind. But the Reds' re-invocation of their April–May "don't-let-'em-breathe" strategy proved decisive.

The Pittsburgh Pirates and Cincinnati Reds were the only National League teams during the 1980s to not go to the playoffs at least once. It was fitting that they would kick off the 1990s by facing each other in the National League Championship Series.

The Reds and the Pirates were two very evenly matched teams with different styles. The Reds relied on pitching and defense while the Pirates could hit with the best of them. They split their season series with six wins each, winning four games at their opponent's home.

When you look at the teams position by position, their balance becomes more evident. The Pirates were superior across the outfield, with the top two MVP vote-getters in Barry Bonds and Bobby Bonilla. The Reds held the advantage in the infield and on the bench, while the pitching staffs were a close match. When you break it all down, it's **Pirates 6, Reds 5**. Even before it started, it was clear this would be an exciting series.

Eric Davis' amazing throw to nail Bobby Bonilla at third base was one of several outstanding defensive plays by the Reds in the NLCS.

Catcher

Reds	PA	AVG	OBP	SLG	Off Runs	CS%	Def Runs	Net Runs
Joe Oliver	409	.231	.304	.360	-16	40%	7	-9
Jeff Reed	205	.251	.340	.360	-3	18%	-5	-8
Pirates								
Mike LaValliere	330	.258	.362	.344	5	35%	5	10
Don Slaught	267	.300	.375	.457	1	31%	1	2

Off Runs = Runs Above/Below league average generated on offense; Def Runs = Runs Above/Below league average saved on defense; Net Runs = the sum of offense and defense

Both the Reds and Pirates split their time behind the plate between two differing catchers. Joe Oliver and Mike LaValliere were more defensive minded, while Jeff Reed and Don Slaught were more offensively adept than their partner. The problem is that LaValliere was actually better offensively than Reed and was close to Oliver on defense. **Advantage: Pirates**

First Base

Reds	PA	AVG	OBP	SLG	Off Runs	Def Runs	Net Runs
Todd Benzinger	408	.253	.291	.340	-15	-4	-19
Hal Morris	336	.340	.381	.498	12	-1	11
Pirates							
Sid Bream	448	.270	.349	.455	8	10	18
Gary Redus	268	.247	.341	.419	4	3	7

First base is a tight comparison. On the one hand, the Pirates were much better defensively at first, but Hal Morris was much better offensively than either of the Pirates duo and in much less playing time. Given the Pirates twenty-five net runs at first base, it would be hard not to give them the advantage at the position,

but because of the emergence of Morris as the season went on, this position is a lot closer than it appears in the numbers. **Advantage: Pirates**

Second Base

Reds	PA	AVG	OBP	SLG	Off Runs	Def Runs	Net Runs
Mariano Duncan	471	.306	.345	.476	15	-13	2
Pirates							
Jose Lind	561	.261	.305	.340	-19	6	-13

These were two very different players playing the same position. Mariano Duncan was an all-hit, no-glove player while Jose Lind provided all of his value in the field. Duncan's offense was miles ahead of Lind, and despite the fact that his glove lagged considerably behind Lind's, it was enough to make up for the offensive difference. **Advantage: Reds**

Third Base

Reds	PA	AVG	OBP	SLG	Off Runs	Def Runs	Net Runs
Chris Sabo	676	.270	.343	.476	17	-1	16
Pirates							
Jeff King	402	.245	.283	.410	-9	-2	-11
Wally Backman	361	.292	.374	.397	8	-8	0

In 1990, Chris Sabo was one of the three best third basemen in the National League. Jeff King, who would go on to have some good years with the Pirates, was still developing. Wally Backman erased most of his offensive value with poor defense at third. **Advantage: Reds**

Shortstop

Reds	PA	AVG	OBP	SLG	Off Runs	Def Runs	Net Runs
Barry Larkin	681	.301	.358	.396	10	10	20
Pirates							
Jay Bell	696	.254	.329	.362	4	-11	-7

Jay Bell was a very good shortstop and usually didn't rate as poorly on defensive as he did in 1990, but much like offense, defense can slump, and Bell had an off season. It probably doesn't matter, however, as Barry Larkin was coming into his own as the best shortstop in the National League both offensively and defensively. **Advantage: Reds**

Left Field

Reds	PA	AVG	OBP	SLG	Off Runs	Def Runs	Net Runs
Eric Davis	581	.260	.347	.486	17	-2	15
Pirates							
Barry Bonds	621	.301	.406	.565	54	28	82

Eric Davis played more games in center field in 1990, but by the playoffs, he was playing left field to help save his ailing knee, which had also taken away some of his defensive prowess. It does not matter much, though, as whoever the Reds put in left field was going to pale in comparison to Barry Bonds, who won his first MVP in 1990, and deservedly so. Bonds was close to the best in the league at everything in left field. **Advantage: Pirates**

Center Field

Reds	PA	AVG	OBP	SLG	Off Runs	Def Runs	Net Runs
Billy Hatcher	545	.276	.327	.381	0	-2	-2
Pirates							
Andy Van Slyke	567	.284	.367	.465	24	-3	21

Billy Hatcher brought a spark to the Reds when he was acquired from the Pirates in early April, but offensively he tailed off in the second half of the season, and while he capably held down center field in Davis's absence, his season was far behind Andy Van Slyke's. Van Slyke provided the Pirates with offensive production like a left fielder while still playing pretty good defense at one of the hardest positions on the field. **Advantage: Pirates**

Right Field

Reds	PA	AVG	OBP	SLG	Off Runs	Def Runs	Net Runs
Paul O'Neill	564	.270	.339	.421	-8	0	-8
Pirates							
Bobby Bonilla	686	.280	.322	.518	25	-3	22

Paul O'Neill was a very good hitter during his career, but in 1990 he lacked the power you expect from a right fielder, and he wasn't a particularly good base runner. Those were both attributes that Bobby Bonilla held over O'Neill, and while O'Neill was the better defender, Bonilla held too big of an advantage on offense for the comparison to be close. **Advantage: Pirates**

Bench

Reds	PA	AVG	OBP	SLG	Off Runs	Def Runs	Net Runs
Glenn Braggs	362	.280	.365	.417	6	10	16
Herm Winningham	177	.256	.317	.425	-1	-3	-4
Ron Oester	171	.299	.339	.377	-3	-5	-8
Luis Quinones	164	.241	.301	.331	-6	1	-5
Billy Bates	40	.088	.179	.118	-4	0	-4
Pirates							
Carmelo Martinez	247	.240	.332	.419	1	-2	-1
R.J. Reynolds	240	.288	.354	.344	-2	-5	-7
Rafael Belliard	61	.204	.283	.259	-5	-3	-8

The Pirates bench wasn't as weak as it looks by these numbers mainly because of the platoons they had at first and third base. However, unless Sid Bream was on the bench, the Pirates didn't have a player to match Glenn Braggs, and in a short series, your bench is really as good as your top two players. Give the Reds a slight advantage here. **Advantage: Reds**

Starting Pitching

Reds	PA	AVG	OBP	SLG	Off Runs	Def Runs	Net Runs
Jose Rijo	197.0	2.70	6.9	3.6	0.5		15
Tom Browning	227.2	3.80	3.9	2.1	0.9		-7
Danny Jackson	117.1	3.61	5.8	3.1	0.8		0
Pirates							
Doug Drabek	231.1	2.76	5.1	2.2	0.6		13
Bob Walk	129.2	3.75	5.1	2.5	1.2		-7
Zane Smith	215.1	2.55	5.4	2.1	0.6		13

K/9 = Strikeouts per 9 IP; BB/9 = Walks per 9 IP; HR/9 = Home Runs per 9 IP; Net Runs = Total Runs saved by the pitcher based on the things he has most control over (K, BB, HR).

This is not how they matched up during the series,

but Jose Rijo and Doug Drabek were two of the best starting pitchers in the National League in 1990. Tom Browning and Bob Walk both depended on their control and their defense to get the job done. The wild cards were Danny Jackson and Zane Smith. Jackson had a good year despite battling injuries, but Smith, who came over to the Pirates mid-season, is the difference maker and gives the Pirates a very small upperhand at starting pitcher. **Advantage: Pirates**

Relief Pitching

Reds	PA	AVG	OBP	SLG	Off Runs	Def Runs	Net Runs
Randy Myers	86.2	2.08	10.2	3.9	0.6		9
Rob Dibble	98.0	1.74	12.5	3.1	0.3		26
Norm Charlton	154.1	2.74	6.8	4.1	0.6		4
Others	372.1	4.01	5.3	3.1	0.9		-10
Pirates							
Bill Landrum	71.2	2.13	4.9	2.6	0.5		4
Bob Patterson	94.2	2.95	6.7	2.0	0.9		5
Stan Belinda	58.1	3.55	8.5	4.5	0.6		3
Ted Power	51.2	3.66	7.3	3.0	0.9		2
Others	435.2	3.64	4.8	2.3	0.9		-4

The Pirates had a solid, though not outstanding bullpen. The didn't have a clear closer during the year (nine pitchers recorded a save and none had more than thirteen), but they had five reliable arms that could get the job done. They didn't have the Nasty Boys, though. In a short playoff series, a bullpen is better off with quality than quantity, and the Reds definitely had the quality. Norm Charlton would likely have been the best reliever out of the Pirates' pen, and he was third in Cincinnati—though his numbers were somewhat depressed because of the time he spent as a starter. **Advantage: Reds**

Game One, Cincinnati

"Our magic number is eight."

That's what the sign said that Lou Piniella put in the Reds' clubhouse. The Reds manager wanted to keep his message simple. Win eight games, and you're the champs. Don't worry about anything else.

"Our job is only one-third done," Piniella said. "We don't plan to stop now. We want it all."

❖ ❖ ❖ ❖ ❖

Former Reds outfielder Ken Griffey was in town to cover the series for Cincinnati's WCPO-TV. He was still missed by his former teammates, who had voted before the playoffs to give him a full share of the playoff money, and many of the players had written Griffey's number "30" on their hats, socks, and shoes.

"I was very emotional about that," Griffey said. "It feels real good that that they think that much of me, but then those guys have made me feel good all year."

Several Reds players also wrote Tim Layana's number "43" on their uniform, in honor of the role the rookie played during the season. Piniella had left Layana off the postseason roster in place of Jack Armstrong, Scott Scudder, and Rick Mahler, all of whom were more prepared to go several innings if needed. Layana was frustrated by the decision, but the gesture from his teammates let him

know that he was still part of the team.

Game One of the National League Championship Series started off in grand style. After Jose Rijo breezed through a nine-pitch top of the first, Barry Larkin led off with a walk from Pirates' starter Bob Walk. Then Piniella had the Reds do something they'd done only once the entire season: He had the two-hole hitter lay down a sacrifice bunt with no outs in the first inning at home. Billy Hatcher dropped down a beauty right in front of home plate, and Larkin advanced to second. Piniella wasn't going to manage this game like any other game. This was the playoffs.

Hal Morris then slapped a single the other way, scoring Larkin. Eric Davis followed with a run-scoring double. Paul O'Neill closed out the scoring with a double of his own, giving the Reds a 3–0 lead.

It looked like those runs might be more than enough for Rijo, who breezed through the middle of the Pirates' order in the second. The third inning, however, did not go as easily. It started with a leadoff walk to Mike LaValliere. Second baseman Jose Lind followed with a shot into right field. O'Neill fell down trying to get to the ball, and LaValliere scored from first while Lind coasted into third base with a triple.

The fourth inning found Rijo in more trouble. After he retired Andy Van Slyke and Bobby Bonilla, another walk—this time to Barry Bonds—did him in. With Bonds on first, Sid Bream slugged a homer to tie the game at three. The Pirates were 15–0 during the season in games in which Bream homered.

Jose Rijo's day ended in the sixth inning after back-

Barry Larkin scored five runs in the NLCS. Left fielder Eric Davis rooted for the Pirates batters to hit the ball to either side of his buddy at shortstop so the national TV audience could see "the new Ozzie."

to-back, one-out singles by Bonilla and Bonds. Piniella brought in lefty Norm Charlton to face Bream, who promptly walked to load the bases. Charlton got LaValliere to hit into a double play and end the Pirates' threat.

With one out in the seventh, Gary Redus batted for Walk, who had faced just sixteen batters in his final five innings, and blooped a single to right field. After Redus stole second, Jeff King flied out, and Jay Bell walked to put runners at first and second for Van Slyke.

The Pirates' center fielder sliced an 0-1 pitch to left field. Davis back-pedaled but quickly realized that he had no shot at catching the ball.

"I misjudged it," Davis explained. "He hit it harder than I thought. It was an inside-out swing, so I didn't think he hit it that good." The ball sailed over his head and bounded off the turf and over the wall for an automatic double, scoring Redus from second and giving the Pirates a 4–3 lead.

"Ten out of ten, hundred out of a hundred, I make that play," Davis said. As Hal McCoy wrote in the *Dayton Daily News* the next day, "This was (number) eleven or 101."

Charlton recovered to strike out Bonilla on three pitches, but the Reds had only one hit since the first inning, a single by Chris Sabo in the fourth that he tried—and failed—to stretch into a double. Their only other base runner was Larkin, who walked and stole a base in the fifth but was left on second.

By the ninth inning, things were looking bleak for the home team. However, a pinch-hit single by Todd Benzinger to start the inning was followed by a walk to Davis, and the Reds had men at first and second with no outs. The situation called for a bunt, so Piniella replaced O'Neill with Ron Oester, who had been six-for-six on the season in sacrifice bunt attempts. Oester pushed it down the third-base line, but pitcher Bob Patterson pounced on it and made the throw to get Benzinger at third base.

"The shortstop held me close, and the last thing I want there is to get picked off," said Benzinger afterward. "And I had to make sure Oester got the bunt down. If he pops it up, I get doubled off."

Even with the delay, the play was close.

"I could have made it with one extra step, no question about it," Benzinger said.

Oester reached first on the fielder's choice, and speedy Billy Bates came in to run for him. When Davis stole third and put himself in position to score on a sacrifice fly, Bates aggressively tried to take second base behind him and was thrown out.

"Davis was on his own to steal third," Piniella said. "(First-base coach) Perez told his runner (Bates) that if he didn't get a good jump when Davis ran for third, stay on first. The kid thought he had a good jump and got thrown out."

Bates admitted after the game that his jump wasn't good.

"I shouldn't have been going," he said. "If you don't get a better jump than I got, you definitely stay."

Former Red Ted Power struck out Sabo on the next pitch, and the Reds found themselves down one game to none.

"We gave that game away," said second baseman Mariano Duncan. "In a short series, you have to take the win no matter what."

Their magic number still stood at eight.

Game Two, Cincinnati

The Reds destroyed left-handed pitching in 1990. Their .282 batting average against lefties was tops in the National League, and only the Oakland A's and Atlanta Braves had a higher OPS against southpaws.

Against right-handed pitching they were league average. In Game Two they faced another right-hander, twenty-two-game-winner Doug Drabek, the National League Cy Young winner.

If the Reds were going to have any success in the series, they needed left-handed Paul O'Neill to start hitting. He struggled during September, batting only .195 for the month, but he showed signs of improvement

Paul O'Neill was a one-man wrecking crew in Game Two, and led both teams with a .471 NLCS batting average.

during the last week of the season, finishing on a seven-game hitting streak. He also had a double and an RBI in Game One of the series.

His improvements were due in part to work he had put in with Piniella. "We lowered his hands about six inches to see if we can get him to drive the ball," Piniella said.

The Reds would take whatever they could get from O'Neill. This series would be nearly impossible to win without him.

❖ ❖ ❖ ❖ ❖

In Game Two, they practically didn't need anybody *besides* O'Neill.

The late-afternoon game meant there was a melange of sun and shade sprinkled throughout the park.

"It was tough, what with the shadows and everything," O'Neill said. "It was one of those cases where you forget about your fundamentals and just try to get a piece of the ball."

When O'Neill came up to bat in the first, a walk by Larkin and a single by Herm Winningham had already put runners at first and third. Battling the shadows, O'Neill got a piece of a belt-high fastball on the end of his bat, sending a stinger through his hands. It hurt so much he thought he had broken his thumb, but he got enough wood on the ball to loop it over the leaping Lind at second base and into right field. Larkin came home to score, and the Reds had a 1–0 lead.

Drabek rallied to escape the inning without anymore damage, but he had thrown thirty-four pitches by the end of the first.

The Pirates' hitters were making Reds' starter Tom Browning work too, as they put on two runners in each of the first three innings. He managed to avoid any damage to the scoreboard with some quality pitches and by picking off Jeff King at second base. Gary Redus was caught stealing in the third.

The score remained 1–0 until the fifth inning when light-hitting Jose Lind, who had hit only one home run during the regular season, hit a line drive into the green seats in left to tie the score at one.

In the bottom of the fifth, with Winningham on second after a fielder's choice and a stolen base, O'Neill came to bat with another RBI opportunity. The shadows were worse now than they were in the first inning, but he was able to smack the ball into left field, where it banged off the wall for an RBI double, and the Reds took a 2–1 lead.

O'Neill traded lumber for leather in the sixth inning. After back-to-back singles put runners at first and second with no out, Bonds hit a fly ball to right field. As O'Neill lined up under the ball, Van Slyke, the runner on second, made plans to tag up.

"I was thinking, 'I'm going to be on third base. All R.J. (teammate R.J. Reynolds) has to do is get it in the outfield, hit a high chopper or something,'" Van Slyke said. "Then Gene (third base coach Gene Lamont) told me to get down. I said, 'Oh-oh.' Then I heard the ball whiz by my ear and I said 'Oh-oh' again. Then when Jerry (third base umpire Jerry Crawford) rung me up, I said 'Oh-oh' again. So three oh-ohs and two outs is not a very good situation."

O'Neill had thrown a laser to third base to get Van Slyke and stifle the Pirates' rally. It was his second kill from the outfield in two games; in Game One he threw out Sid Bream trying to stretch a single into a double.

The Nasty Boys put the game to bed, with Rob Dibble pitching one and a third innings, striking out two batters, before turning it over to Randy Myers.

Myers closed out the game with some help from Larkin at shortstop, who turned in two outstanding defensive plays to keep the Pirates off the bases, including

PINIELLA'S FIDDLING MADE SWEET MUSIC

Lou Piniella liked to fiddle so much he could have played in the Charlie Daniels Band. He fiddled with his bullpen and his starting rotation, but most of all he fiddled with his starting lineup.

Despite few injuries during the season, the Reds played with 125 batting orders, more than any other team in the National League and nearly sixty more than the Pittsburgh Pirates, who used a league-low sixty-seven batting orders. Their most frequent lineup took the field forty-four times compared to the Reds most frequent of six.

During the NLCS, Piniella used five lineups in six games. But he knew what he was doing.

"I don't do things helter-skelter, by the seat of my pants or on hunches," he explained. "I like the percentages on my side. Every day when I make out the lineup card, my first consideration is defense. Twice this year I did it by considering offense first, and both times I got burned. After the second time, I told my coaches, 'That's it, I've learned my lesson.'" For those who thought Piniella was fiddling too much he had one word: tough.

"I don't have to give a reason, that's why I'm paid to manage," he said. "It's easy and safe to make out the same lineup every day. But I know my team. I've done it this way all year and...well...we're here, aren't we?"

a wide-ranging stop on a ball smashed up the middle by Barry Bonds.

"It was a tough situation," Larkin said, "especially with Barry Bonds coming up there. Before the pitch, I took two steps toward the middle. Thank God, I did."

The plays had Larkin's teammates singing his praises after the game.

Eric Davis said, "Not to demean Ozzie Smith, but he's got to realize there's a new kid on the block."

The star of the day, though, was O'Neill, who said, "All the way from Little League you fantasize about doing well in the playoffs or World Series." He'd made his dream come true.

Game Three, Pittsburgh

The Reds came into Pittsburgh much looser than they had been in the regular season.

"Staying in first place all season is a burden in itself," Braggs said. "Once we clinched the division, it seemed like the weight was off our shoulders. All we had to do was worry about one team."

Billy Hatcher was one of the loosest of the bunch. His ten-minute clubhouse preacher performance on the day off had his teammates passing around the collection hat and the sports writers grabbing their sides.

Amen!

These weren't the same Reds who appeared burdened throughout the second half. They had regained

The Reds were not intimidated by Oakland before the World Series, and they were confident they could win.

(Above) Two old teammates from Tampa faced off in the World Series thirty years later. (Right) Owner Marge Schott rolled out the red carpet for the World Series, putting her grounds crew in tuxedos and bringing First Lady Barbara Bush in to throw the first pitch.

A good series by Rickey Henderson wasn't enough to fight the relentless attack of the Reds at the plate and on the bases.

Oakland's Bash Brothers, Jose Canseco (left) and Mark McGwire (below) wilted in the World Series, combining to go 4-for-26 with seven strikeouts. (Below, left) Eric Davis (right, with Joe Oliver and Paul O'Neill) led the charge in Game One of the World Series with two hits, including a first-inning home run, and three RBI in the Reds 7–0 win in the opener.

Ron Oester called Billy Bates the team mascot because of his small stature, but he scored perhaps the biggest run of the season when he crossed the plate with the winning run in Game Two of the World Series.

*The celebration of the Reds'
championship lasted for months
and went from Oakland to
Cincinnati's Fountain Square all
the way to the White House with
President George Bush.*

One year earlier, when Marge Schott assembled her team of Lou Piniella and Bob Quinn, her only goal was to bring the World Series trophy back to Cincinnati once again.

the spring in their step. And they came out with some fire in the first game in Pittsburgh.

❖ ❖ ❖ ❖ ❖

Piniella shook up the lineup for Game Three, flopping Hatcher and Mariano Duncan in the order and sticking Glenn Braggs in right field against lefty Zane Smith. The moves paid dividends in the second inning when Hatcher hit a two-run homer to left field, giving the Reds an early lead.

The Pirates tied the game in the fourth after getting to starter Danny Jackson for three hits and two walks. Hatcher led off the top of the fifth.

"Lou told me to get on and try to make something happen," Hatcher said. "Any time you jump back out in front after a team has just caught you, it gives you momentum."

Hatcher ripped a 2–1 pitch to left-center for a double. Jackson bunted him to third base. A Larkin infield single forced Hatcher to hold his ground, but the Reds still had runners at first and third with one out.

That's when Mariano Duncan went to work. He started off the season white hot but cooled as the year continued. He batted just .252 over the last forty-seven games, and by early September he was surrendering a lot of playing time to Bill Doran at second base.

And he wasn't happy about it.

"When they got Bill, they told me they just did it to give an off day to all the (infield) guys," Duncan said. "Then I was the only one getting off days. But

there was nothing I could do about it. I didn't want to get lazy, and I didn't want to start any problems on the team. I decided I better stay ready every day."

When Doran went down with an injured back and was forced to miss the playoffs, Duncan became the man again at second, and he had something to prove. He went hitless in the first two games of the NLCS, striking out three times, perhaps because he was pressing.

He was also facing a lot of right-handed pitching. He batted only .226 off righties, compared to .412 against left-handers. When he faced lefty Smith in the fifth, with men on base, he wasn't trying to hit a home run, just to hit the ball hard.

"When I start to overswing, bad things happen," Duncan said. "I'm sure he was looking to jam me. The first pitch was a fastball high. I thought he might come back with the same pitch, and he did, and that was what I was looking for."

The ball sailed over the wall in left-center and slammed into the Pirates' 1909 World Series championship banner as Duncan leaped into the air and pumped his fist.

The Reds now had a 5–2 lead as they moved into Nasty Boys territory. Piniella didn't waste any time going to the bullpen early in the sixth inning. Jackson had squeaked through a bases-loaded jam in the fifth, and after Jose Lind doubled with one out in the sixth, Piniella brought in Rob Dibble, who pitched a perfect one and two-thirds innings, striking out three of the five batters he faced.

Norm Charlton came on to pitch the eighth. With two on and one out, he got what should have been an inning-ending ground ball, but Duncan lost the handle on the throw after getting the first out at second and allowed Barry Bonds to score from second base.

Duncan got the run back in the ninth when he singled home pinch-runner Billy Bates to give the Reds a 6–3 lead.

Randy Myers pitched the bottom of the ninth, striking out the side on eleven pitches. The bullpen that had carried the Reds all season was becoming an even bigger asset in the playoffs.

"Rob, Norm, and Randy all threw a lot of balls, and I think (the Pirates are) overanxious," Todd Benzinger noted. "They're swinging at balls in the dirt, balls that are high. They know we have a good bullpen, and I think it's working to our advantage."

It was the fifteenth time that all three Nasty Boys had pitched in the same game that season. The Reds were 13–2 in those games.

More importantly, they were just two wins away from their first World Series in fourteen years.

Game Four, Pittsburgh

Throughout the season, Lou Piniella liked to say his team was, "nothing spectacular, just a well-rounded team. We play well defensively, that's our one constant, and when we get good pitching we always have a chance to win a ballgame."

They weren't going to wow you, but they were very hard to beat because they didn't make many mistakes.

Every once in while, though, they would wow you.

The Pirates got on the scoreboard first for the first time in the series after a leadoff double by Wally Backman to start the game was followed by two ground outs that pushed him around to score.

The Reds' bats were quiet for the first three innings, managing a lone single by Paul O'Neill in the first off starter Bob Walk. O'Neill would face Walk again in the fourth inning, this time going deep to right field for his first home run of the playoffs, a solo shot that evened the score at one.

Two singles later, Chris Sabo gave the Reds the lead with a sacrifice fly that plated Eric Davis, making it 2–1. Sabo had been working with Piniella and hitting coach Tony Perez before the game, trying to get the rhythm back in his swing.

Said Piniella, "He needed to get some movement in his hands. He wasn't getting cocked. The reason I know is because I went through that bullcrap as a player for seventeen years."

The work paid off for Sabo in the seventh inning when he blasted a two-run home run to give the Reds a 4–2 lead.

The Pirates had tied the game at 2–2 in the fourth inning when Sid Bream doubled to score Andy Van Slyke from second base. Two batters later, the Pirates thought they had the lead after a Jose Lind single to center looked like it would score Bream from second.

Billy Hatcher, however, had other ideas. Charging the ball all the way, Hatcher came up throwing toward home. The throw beat Bream to the plate, and catcher Jeff Reed applied the tag to end the rally.

"I didn't really have a good grip on it; it slipped out of my hand," Hatcher said. "But I had enough on it to get it home."

"It was a perfect throw," Reed said. "In that situation, he's going to try to knock the ball out of my glove. The ball was up the line a little bit, and I couldn't brace myself. I caught the ball and put the tag on him."

The Pirates could do little other than tip their caps to the Reds. For the third time in the series the Reds had erased a Pirate base runner with an excellent throw from the outfield.

"They've been making some perfect throws," Bream said. "You've got to credit their outfielders for the way they're throwing."

The best was yet to come.

❖ ❖ ❖ ❖ ❖

A home run by shortstop Jay Bell to lead off the Pirates' eighth inning tightened the score and forced starter Jose Rijo to the dugout. Piniella went to the bullpen for Randy Myers, who came on to face the heart of the order.

After a flyout by Andy Van Slyke, Bobby Bonilla hit what Piniella called a "one-iron shot" off the center field wall. Hatcher leaped to catch the ball but just missed, and it bounded back toward center field. Bonilla raced toward second base and assumed that once he saw Hatcher fall to the ground, he could take third base easily.

What he didn't realize was that Eric Davis had picked up the ball in center field with his back to the play, spun and fired a laser to third base that reached Sabo on one hop, just in time to nab Bonilla, who was sliding head first into the base.

"I knew after I threw it and it bounced ahead of him, I had a chance to get him," Davis said.

"I'm a very aggressive base runner," Bonilla said. "You know it's going to take two perfect throws to get you. That wasn't the case. It was one. That's why I'm calling that the defensive play of the year."

Sabo was surprised when the ball got to him.

"Eric made an unbelievable play," Sabo said. "It came out of nowhere. I didn't even see the ball and all of a sudden it just appeared to me at the very last second, and at just the right place."

Piniella was at a loss for words to describe the play.

"That's baseball, isn't it?" he said. "That's winning baseball." And later: "Eric Davis has the greatest baseball instincts of any player I've ever seen."

The Reds tacked on another run in the ninth inning to make it 5–3, and Rob Dibble came in to record his first postseason save, giving the Reds a 3–1 series lead.

Game Five, Pittsburgh

The Pirates' Game Five starter, Doug Drabek, came up through the Yankees' organization, and his first manager in the big leagues was Lou Piniella.

"He gave me a chance when my Triple-A statistics were terrible," Drabek said.

"I brought him up when he was 0–5 in Triple-A and

1990 REDS FIELDING, BY THE NUMBERS
by Justin Merry

The 1990 Reds were a run-prevention team: they led the league in ERA and runs allowed. What is less straightforward, however, is how they accomplished this feat. Defense is generated by both pitching and fielding, and they are not easy to disentangle. As a result, a major focus in recent sabermetric research has been how to directly assess the impact of fielding.

We don't have a perfect solution yet, but we have a number of tools that, used together, give us a pretty good idea that if all the measures rate a player or team as above average, we feel confident that he was, in fact, above average!

Let's look at the individual positions and then the team as a whole.

CATCHING

The Reds' catching platoon of Joe Oliver and Jeff Reed were a pair of opposites. The left-handed-batting Reed was the better hitter, whereas the right-handed Oliver—at least based on his ability to control the running game and prevent passed balls, wild pitches, and errors, which is the basis for his fielding numbers—was the better defensive player (+7 runs saved above average compared to his position for Oliver, -5 runs for Reed). In 1990, Oliver got the lion's share of playing time, for good reason: he gunned down 40 percent of would-be base stealers, tops in the league among starting catchers.

OUTFIELD

Eric Davis was officially the starting center fielder but often played left field to help spare his ailing knee. Billy Hatcher, who had played both positions throughout his career, performed well in both spots in 1990 (+3 runs-saved). Davis, perhaps because of his knee, rated as below-average (-4 runs-saved), despite spending almost half his innings in left, where he should have excelled.

One aspect of Davis's game that remained strong was his throwing arm, which, by itself, rated as three runs above average in 1990. Davis, along with fellow gunslinger Paul O'Neill (+4 run arm rating) made running on the Reds' outfield a dangerous proposition. The Pirates discovered this several times during the NLCS. The Reds proved throughout the series that fielding is important, and it was part of what pushed them over the top.

INFIELD

Barry Larkin was clearly the best fielder on the team. His +17 runs-saved ranked second in the league among shortstops only to Ozzie Smith. In fact, if the Reds had replaced Larkin with an average-fielding shortstop, they would drop from above-average to below-average overall.

Chris Sabo also ranked as above-average (+3 runs-saved). However, even in just his third year, Sabo's range had declined compared to his rookie season. Many have implicated his hard-nosed style of play—which probably is part of what got him to the big leagues—as a reason for the rapid decline in both his fielding and base-running skills.

The right side of the infield didn't look as

good. Mariano Duncan, a converted shortstop, sometimes struggled defensively at second base (-8 runs-saved). Bill Doran and Ron Oester were slight improvements, but both saw limited action at second base.

Todd Benzinger had a reputation as a good glove at first base. The numbers don't entirely bear this out, rating him as having below-average range but above-average ability to prevent infield errors in throws, putting him at average overall (+0 runs-saved). Hal Morris rated as slightly below-average in the field (-3 runs-saved).

TEAM DEFENSE

Using four different measures, the 1990 Reds' fielding performance was estimated as a combined fourteen runs above average. It ranks the Reds ninth among the twenty-six 1990 MLB teams. Their eventual playoff opponents, the Pirates (+32 runs) and the Athletics (+88 runs) ranked third and first, respectively: it's hard to build a successful team that doesn't have good fielding. The Reds probably weren't exceptionally good in the field, but, like most aspects of their game, they were better than average.

Tom Browning's Game Two victory was the first playoff win by the Reds since 1976.

game. Barry Larkin had doubled to leadoff the first, and when Drabek threw the ball into center field trying to pick off Larkin, the Reds' shortstop moved to third and scored on a sacrifice fly by Herm Winningham.

The Pirates came back in the bottom of the inning and took the lead right back. Reds' starter Tom Browning ran into trouble right away.

"I knew we had a chance to win this thing," Browning said. "I just started working too fast instead of relaxing."

On an 0-2 pitch, he hit the second batter of the game, Jay Bell, and was forced to face the Pirates' bangers with runners on base. Andy Van Slyke followed with a line drive to right-center field that took a big hop off the Astroturf and bounced over Paul O'Neill's head, allowing Van Slyke to take a triple and score Bell from first.

After a walk to Bobby Bonilla, Barry Bonds hit into a fielder's choice that plated Van Slyke with the go-ahead run.

The score stayed 2–1 until the fourth inning, when the Pirates tacked on a run on a sacrifice fly by catcher Don Slaught. The Reds put together a brief rally in the eighth inning when Larkin doubled in Luis Quinones to make it 3–2, but a Winningham pop out ended the threat.

Drabek started the ninth inning, but Paul O'Neill and Eric Davis hit back-to-back singles, and Hal Morris bunted both runners into scoring position. Manager Jim Leyland brought on lefty Bob Patterson, who intentionally walked Chris Sabo so that he could face

no one wanted to bring him up," Piniella said. "I said I want him here. (Yankees owner) George (Steinbrenner) said it will be your fault if he doesn't pitch. I said it's going to be my fault anyway, so don't worry about it."

Piniella liked what he saw from the young right-hander, but the higher ups in the organization thought differently and they shipped Drabek off to the Pirates.

Now four years later, Drabek faced his former manager in a do-or-die game.

His teammates picked him up after an errant pick-off throw in the first led to the Reds' first run of the

the left-handed Jeff Reed. Reed had been brought in to catch in the eighth inning after Ron Oester had pinch hit for Joe Oliver in the top of the inning. Now, with no other catchers left on the roster, Piniella was forced to let the lefty face the lefty.

Reed hit a weak ground ball that ended in a double play and the Reds were finished. Game Six would be played in Cincinnati two nights later. Despite the tough loss, manager Lou Piniella was still confident.

"I think we are in much better shape than Pittsburgh is," said Piniella. "We only have to win one game and they have to win two. I'd rather be us."

Game Six, Cincinnati

For two days, Pirates' manager Jim Leyland had told the media that left-hander Zane Smith would be his starter, but just hours before the game, Leyland decided to start right-hander, and former Red, Ted Power.

"Everybody thinks I'm nuts and I probably am," Leyland said before the game. "My coaches are still passed out on the floor from when I told them. Power's reaction? He was on the floor with them."

It was all part of the chess match that had been going on throughout the series. It was a series that *The New Yorker*'s Roger Angell called "pure entertainment" as the teams "went at each other with a ferocious tenacity."

Leyland called the series "baseball at its best." Two evenly matched teams played well-fought games, both sides fighting for every last scrap on the field, like two pit bulls over a steak.

It was what postseason baseball was meant to be.

The Power move by Leyland was meant to unbalance the Reds, but Piniella didn't take the bait.

"I don't think trickery wins playoff games," Piniella said. "It is done on the field by the players. I figured he'd want to turn our lineup around some."

Piniella stuck to the same personnel that he would have used with lefty Smith on the mound, knowing full well that Power wasn't likely to go more than a couple of innings. So when Smith did come in, as Piniella expected, his lineup was ready for him.

❖ ❖ ❖ ❖ ❖

The players were enjoying the intensity of the series. The close games had been exciting and tiring at the same time. Even for role players like Herm Winningham, who spent a large portion of the series on the bench, the games were mentally exhausting.

"Doggie (Tony Perez) told us before the first game, 'This is going to be the hardest game you will ever play in your whole life,'" Winningham recalls twenty years later. "And doggone it if he wasn't right. Every pitch in the LCS you'd stop breathing and watch the play. I didn't even play in a game and afterward I thought, 'Man, I'm so tired!' But you were into the game, ready to do it again tomorrow."

Shortstop Barry Larkin wouldn't trade the experience for anything. "This has been fun; this has been great," Larkin said of the playoffs. "Too bad it has to end today."

And Larkin came out of the gate ready to do everything he could to make sure that Game Six was the last one of the series. He led off the bottom of the first with a ground-ball single, the fourth time in the series that he reached base to lead off the game. In the previous three instances the Reds scored at least one run in the inning. After a stolen base and an errant throw allowed Larkin to move to third, another first-inning run looked promising.

When Piniella said, "You can't walk your way to a pennant," he was talking about remaining aggressive at the plate, but it also applied in the field and on the bases. As Roger Angell put it, the Reds "kept leaning on their opponents all through these games, shouldering and hip-shoving, in other guys' faces."

They didn't let up. They knew that the only way to win was to keep taking it to their opponents until they collapsed. It was the way Lou pushed them to play.

With Larkin now on third and Paul O'Neill on first after a walk, Eric Davis grounded into a fielder's choice that brought Larkin home with the first run of the game. In true Reds' form, Davis tried to steal second base, but he was thrown out, ending the inning.

There are risks when you play an aggressive style of ball, but it's always fun to watch.

❖ ❖ ❖ ❖ ❖

Danny Jackson was built for October. As a relentless battler, the pressure of the postseason drove him to a new level of focus and intensity.

"I just seem to concentrate better in these postseason games," said Jackson, the winner in Game Three. "I'm just really intense, and the big crowds get you excited. I just block the noise out and bear down."

Jackson had the most experience in the postseason of any of the Reds' pitchers, having pitched in four games for the Kansas City Royals in the 1985 playoffs and World Series, including three starts. He was outstanding in those games, pitching twenty-six innings and allowing only three runs. In Game Five of the World Series with the Royals on the brink of elimination, Jackson threw a five-hitter and held the Cardinals to just one run in the 6–1 victory that forced a Game Six.

The Reds would need Jackson to step up with a similar performance in tonight's game.

And he delivered.

The lefty rolled through the first thirteen batters, striking out three and not allowing a base runner. His only mistake in the game came in the fifth inning with one out. He walked Barry Bonds and then Carmelo Martinez hit a solid double off the right-field wall.

"It was just an outside fastball," Jackson said, "and he hits it to the wall. I felt I had lost a little bit as far as mechanics go, but I calmed down after that."

That ended up being the only hit that Jackson would allow, but it was enough to tie the score.

As expected, Zane Smith had relieved Ted Power back in the third inning for the Pirates. The Reds put together a threat and had the bases loaded with two outs, but a deep fly out by Chris Sabo to center field fizzled the run-scoring opportunity.

Danny Jackson channeled his Kansas City days, coming up huge at crunch time, stymieing the Pirates in Games Three and Six.

Smith retired seven in a row until the bottom of the sixth inning, when O'Neill, the only left-handed bat in the Reds lineup, singled to lead off the inning. Davis followed with a single of his own, taking second base on an error by right fielder R.J. Reynolds as O'Neill advanced to third base.

One out later, Smith intentionally walked Todd Benzinger to load the bases for Mariano Duncan. It was a surprising move since Duncan batted .412 against left-handers in 1990, but Smith struck him out.

He then got Joe Oliver to pop out to second base on the first pitch, killing the rally.

Jackson ran into trouble in the seventh inning, walking the first two batters—Bonilla and Bonds—on ten pitches. Piniella went to the bullpen.

With right-handers Martinez, Don Slaught, and Jose Lind due up to bat, the entire stadium figured it was Rob Dibble's turn to come into the game. But to everyone's amazement, the call to the bullpen was for lefty Norm Charlton.

"I was very surprised," Charlton said. "We were both warming up in the bullpen. I said, 'Rob, this is you, right here. They've got three righties coming up.' When they said left-hander, I thought, no, they messed up."

Manager Lou Piniella was thinking three steps ahead in this chess match. He knew that by bringing in Charlton, he'd maintain the Reds' upper hand in the situation.

"Carmelo Martinez was the first guy up, and I know he hasn't bunted much," Piniella said. "A left-hander can field a bunt and throw to third quicker. And if I brought in (right-hander) Rob Dibble, they'd bring in Sid Bream, which I didn't want."

Leyland left the bunt on with Martinez, and he hit a weak pop up to Sabo at third, forcing the runners to hold their bases.

Piniella let Charlton face Slaught, liking his chances against the right-hander as opposed to Dibble versus the lefty Mike LaValliere. Slaught lifted the first pitch to center fielder Billy Hatcher. It was deep enough to move Bonilla to third, but now there were two outs.

Lind hit Charlton's second pitch to right field where O'Neill camped under it for the third out of the inning. Charlton had thrown five pitches to get three outs.

Check.

Piniella was obviously pretty good at this game of chess.

❖ ❖ ❖ ❖ ❖

Ron Oester was itching to get into this game. He could see his opportunity might be coming, so he did what he could to ensure it.

"I knew Lou was thinking about a double switch," Oester said. "I walked by him a couple of times just to try to remind him about it a little more."

The reminder worked, and Oester went into the game as part of a double switch when Charlton came on in the top of the seventh. Oester was going to have a chance to help his team, and that helped ease the frustration he had felt all season. The fire still burned in him to play everyday, but he accepted his bench role and did what he could to help his team win.

"He wasn't very happy," Piniella said. "But he never complained. A couple of times, I've called him into my office and thanked him for the leadership he's provided."

That leadership was also appreciated by his teammates.

"He's the heart and soul of this team," said pitcher Tom Browning. "He lives and dies with the Cincinnati Reds. I'm happy for him. He's the one guy everybody looks up to because of all he's been through."

When Oester led off the bottom of the seventh, he knew this was the moment he had been waiting for his whole career.

"I just wanted to get on base any way I could," Oester said. "If the ball was close to me, I would have let it hit me. I just wanted to try to get something going. I worked him to three-and-two. I was trying to hit the ball to right field. I hit it to the spot I wanted, and it fell in."

The single, Oester's first career playoff hit, was the Reds' seventh hit of the game, and it brought up the top of the order with no outs. Uncharacteristically, Barry Larkin popped a bunt foul down the first-base line that was caught by Martinez and left Oester at first.

Hatcher then lined a single to center that moved Oester all the way to third.

That's when Piniella made his next move in the chess match.

Despite being the hottest hitter in the Reds' lineup, O'Neill was pulled in favor of Luis Quinones to face the left-hander Smith. Quinones had been incredible as a pinch hitter in '90. In forty-one plate appearances, he batted .361 off the bench. Piniella was hoping for just a little more magic.

Fans thought the manager was certifiable (whether he was certifiably a genius or insane would depend on what Quinones did at the plate). Consider: Going back to the regular season, O'Neill was riding a twelve-game hitting streak; he was batting .415/.467/.585 during the streak, including .471/.500/.824 during the playoffs; he had hit a line-drive single off of Smith in the previous inning; he was two-for-ten against Smith in his career, but the two hits had come in his previous four at-bats; Quinones was a very good pinch hitter in 1990 (.361/.390/.500), but his career numbers as a pinch hitter were .224/.282/.302; Quinones was hitless in seven at-bats in his career against Smith; also on the bench at that time was Glenn Braggs, who had batted .385/.467/.615 against Smith in fifteen plate appearances that season, including one for two in the NLCS.

Quinones didn't give in to Smith, and after being down 1-2, he got the count to 3-2.

"I was nervous," Quinones said. "You have to be. But after those first three pitches, I was more relaxed. I was looking for a high fast ball, something I could drive."

Quinones got the fastball and hit a looping liner between first and second. He knew it was a hit and clapped his hands all the way down the first-base line.

Oester scored from third, yelling and pumping his fists all the way to home plate. The Reds had taken a 2–1 lead. Piniella's move worked. No nuthouse for Lou.

Baseball fans in Cincinnati had to ask the poetic question: *How Big Were Lou's Cajones To Have Pinch-hit Quinones for O'Neill?*

The Reds' rally ended quickly after Quinones' hit, and Piniella went to Randy Myers to close it out. Myers walked Reynolds with one out in the eighth, but then he got a ground out and a strikeout. The ninth inning posed a much more daunting task. Myers would be up against the top two vote-getters for the NL MVP award in Bobby Bonilla and Barry Bonds. Bonilla popped up to shortstop for the first out, but Bonds walked for the sixth time in the series. With the speedy Bonds and his fifty-two stolen bases standing at first, Myers faced Carmelo Martinez, who had the Pirates' only hit so far.

Martinez waited…and waited…and waited for his pitch. The count was 2-2 before he even swung

Randy Myers closed out victories for the Reds in Games Two, Three, and Six.

the bat. He fouled off the next pitch and then took a ball. Myers was having to work to get this out. Finally, Martinez got a pitch he could drive.

"I wanted it to be a fast ball down," Myers said. "It was a straight pitch up and away. If it's any further inside, he probably takes it out."

Glenn Braggs, who was playing in right field for O'Neill, felt his heart stop for a second when he saw the ball coming his way. Luckily, Piniella had the outfielders playing deep to cut off the extra base hit.

"We were playing very deep in the outfield," said Braggs. "If it was going over my head, it was going over the fence."

The ball did go over his head, and it would have gone over the fence if it hadn't been for a perfectly timed leap and snag, right in the web of the glove. The burly right fielder's back slammed into the wall with the force of a dump truck, rattling the wall all the way to center field.

In a series full of remarkable defensive plays by the Reds, this was perhaps the best of them all.

Don Slaught struck out swinging in the next at-bat, and the game was over. Another move by Piniella worked perfectly.

Checkmate.

The Reds won the pennant! For the first time since 1976, they were champions of the National League!

❖ ❖ ❖ ❖ ❖

Myers and Dibble shared the series Most Valuable

Glenn Braggs' homer-robbing grab in Game Six may have damaged the wall as much as the Pirates' chances.

Player honors. They combined for ten and two-thirds innings of shutout ball, striking out seventeen, walking four, and allowing only two hits during the series. It was the first time the award had been shared, and it is the only time a reliever has won the award in the NLCS.

Myers said, "I consider it a bullpen MVP. Dibble and I are co-closers, but we're a group down there and that's what made us so good. You guys know what Norm Charlton did, and Tim Layana, who was with us all season but isn't eligible for the playoffs, should also share in this. They were all part of it."

Dibble, who had spent most of the series complaining about his contract to whomever would listen, was much more magnanimous after the victory.

"This is a great team, no big egos," he said. "I may

have a big mouth, but I've tried to back it up all year. There's been a lot of doubters in this team, but there's been some believers, too."

The biggest believers were the players themselves.

"All year we said we were a team—that's twenty-five players," Eric Davis said. "That means respecting all twenty-five. And tonight that respect, that belief, paid off."

Piniella was proud of his squad for continuing to fight all series. "Tonight's game was like so many this season, especially when we struggled a bit in the second half," Piniella said. "Every time you looked up we seemed to be in a one-run game in the ninth inning, and our guys nearly always found the strength and desire to win."

Ron Oester, the dean of the squad, summed up the victory this way: "It's just a great, great feeling."

❖ ❖ ❖ ❖ ❖

At the end of the 1990 season, WLWT-TV asked Thom Brennaman, who was an announcer for the Chicago Cubs at the time, to cover the playoffs for their nightly newscasts. After the Reds won the pennant, Brennaman happened to be sitting in Piniella's office as he flipped through the scouting report on Oakland put together by scout Jimmy Stewart. Piniella flipped through it for about ten minutes while the celebration was going on in the clubhouse and then tossed it on his desk.

As Brennaman recounts it, Piniella told him, "We're about to put an ass-kicking on Oakland. Jimmy Stew-

Randy Myers and Rob Dibble shared the spotlight in the bullpen and the NLCS MVP award.

art says it's all right there. We've got their number."

Piniella wasn't just blowing smoke. He knew the Reds' power pitching gave them an advantage over the Oakland hitters. He didn't tell anybody that—they wouldn't have believed him anyway—but he knew in his heart that the Reds had more than just a fighting chance in the World Series. He knew that they were going to win.

While the Reds celebrated winning one of the most exciting, best-played NLCS games ever, Barry Bonds had nowhere to go but home. The Reds were headed to their ninth World Series.

The season had begun with a movie and was heading for an even bigger climax: Oakland and the World Series. Reds fans couldn't wait.

13

World Champions

The Reds dominated Oakland in the World Series, but injuries to two key players in Game Four put the team in a much more dangerous position than most people realized.

The Oakland A's came into the 1990 World Series as *heavy* favorites. Their power bats as well as their strong defense and pitching made them the obvious pick for the experts over the Reds, who hovered around .500 for most of the second half.

The experts, however, missed some things. On a position-by-position basis, the Reds matched up bet-

ter than expected against Oakland. The A's had big advantages at a few positions, but the Reds had no true weak spot in the lineup. Our analysis has the position breakdown at **A's 6, Reds 5**. The A's definitely deserved to be favorites, but the difference between the two teams was not as vast as many had assumed.

Jose Rijo's dominance of his former team in 1990 was legendary.

Catcher

Reds	PA	AVG	OBP	SLG	Off Runs	CS%	Def Runs	Net Runs
Joe Oliver	409	.231	.304	.360	-16	40%	7	-9
Jeff Reed	205	.251	.340	.360	-3	18%	-5	-8
A's								
Terry Steinbach	410	.251	.291	.372	-11	32%	-1	-12
Ron Hassey	286	.213	.288	.299	-12	38%	5	-7
Jamie Quirk	144	.281	.353	.413	2	52%	-1	-1

Off Runs = Runs Above/Below league average generated on offense; Def Runs = Runs Above/Below league average saved on defense; Net Runs = the sum of offense and defense

Joe Oliver's offense was a real weakness for the team, but his defense improved his value greatly. Terry Steinbach had been an All-Star in previous years but was not so valuable in 1990. Ron Hassey and Jamie Quirk were both past their primes and played limited roles. This is a close position comparison. **Advantage: Reds**

First Base

Reds	PA	AVG	OBP	SLG	Off Runs	Def Runs	Net Runs
Todd Benzinger	408	.253	.291	.340	-15	-4	-19
Hal Morris	336	.340	.381	.498	12	-1	11
A's							
Mark McGwire	650	.235	.370	.489	31	12	43

Mark McGwire wasn't what he had been in his rookie season or what he'd, ahem, become in St. Louis, but he still had a very good year both offensively and defensively, and neither of the Reds options could come close to replicating his success. **Advantage: A's**

Second Base

Reds	PA	AVG	OBP	SLG	Off Runs	Def Runs	Net Runs
Mariano Duncan	471	.306	.345	.476	15	-13	2
A's							
Willie Randolph	446	.260	.339	.325	-2	6	4

This position was very even and could go either way, but Duncan's defense could not be overlooked and while Randolph wasn't very good offensively, he wasn't bad either. **Advantage: A's**

Third Base

Reds	PA	AVG	OBP	SLG	Off Runs	Def Runs	Net Runs
Chris Sabo	676	.270	.343	.476	17	-1	16
A's							
Carney Lansford	564	.268	.333	.320	-7	-5	-12

Carney Lansford won a batting title in 1981 and nearly won a second one in 1989, but he had absolutely no power at a traditionally power-hitting position, and Chris Sabo was one of the tops at the position in the league. **Advantage: Reds**

Shortstop

Reds	PA	AVG	OBP	SLG	Off Runs	Def Runs	Net Runs
Barry Larkin	681	.301	.358	.396	10	10	20
A's							
Mike Gallego	447	.207	.277	.272	-26	9	-17

Regular Oakland starter Walt Weiss injured his knee during the ALCS and missed the World Series. It would have made the position closer, but Larkin was still better. **Advantage: Reds**

Left Field

Reds	PA	AVG	OBP	SLG	Off Runs	Def Runs	Net Runs
Eric Davis	581	.260	.347	.486	17	-2	15
A's							
Rickey Henderson	594	.325	.439	.577	67	19	86

For the second series in a row, Eric Davis was matched up against a league MVP. Rickey Henderson was unquestionably the best non-pitcher in the AL in '90. He ended up being the only real threat to the Reds during the entire series. **Advantage: A's**

Center Field

Reds	PA	AVG	OBP	SLG	Off Runs	Def Runs	Net Runs
Billy Hatcher	545	.276	.327	.381	0	-2	-2
A's							
Dave Henderson	594	.271	.331	.467	17	8	25

Billy Hatcher was a good option in center field, but Dave Henderson had an excellent season across the board in 1990. He topped Hatcher both offensively and defensively. **Advantage: A's**

Right Field

Reds	PA	AVG	OBP	SLG	Off Runs	Def Runs	Net Runs
Paul O'Neill	564	.270	.339	.421	-8	0	-8
A's							
Jose Canseco	563	.274	.371	.543	38	-1	37

For all of his attitude problems, Jose Canseco was still a heckuva player, even if he was chemically enhanced. The gap between Canseco and O'Neill was too big in 1990 to write it all off to steroids. **Advantage: A's**

Bench

Reds	PA	AVG	OBP	SLG	Off Runs	Def Runs	Net Runs
Glenn Braggs	362	.280	.365	.417	6	10	16
Herm Winningham	177	.256	.317	.425	-1	-3	-4
Ron Oester	171	.299	.339	.377	-3	-5	-8
Luis Quinones	164	.241	.301	.331	-6	1	-5
Billy Bates	40	.088	.179	.118	-4	0	-4
A's							
Harold Baines	489	.284	.378	.441	10	-2	8
Willie McGee	665	.324	.373	.419	22	2	24
Doug Jennings	180	.192	.275	.301	-6	1	-5
Lance Blankenship	162	.191	.295	.213	-8	4	-4
Mike Bordick	15	.07	.133	.071	-3	1	-2

The Reds had a pretty good bench, but two mid-season trades gave this one to the A's. The acquisition of Harold Baines gave them an excellent left-handed designated hitter. Adding Willie McGee gave them a former NL batting champion as well as some defensive insurance in the outfield. There was no way the Reds were going to be able to match that on their bench. **Advantage: A's**

Starting Pitching

Reds	PA	AVG	OBP	SLG	Off Runs	Def Runs	Net Runs
Jose Rijo	197.0	2.70	6.9	3.6	0.5	15	
Tom Browning	227.2	3.80	3.9	2.1	0.9	-7	
Danny Jackson	117.1	3.61	5.8	3.1	0.8	0	
A's							
Dave Stewart	267.0	2.56	5.6	2.8	0.5	17	
Bob Welch	238.0	2.95	4.8	2.9	1.0	-7	
Mike Moore	199.1	4.65	3.3	3.8	0.6	-9	

K/9 = Strikeouts per 9 IP; BB/9 = Walks per 9 IP; HR/9 = Home Runs per 9 IP; Net Runs = Total Runs saved by the pitcher based on the things he has most control over (K, BB, HR).

The A's had two Cy Young contenders, but Bob Welch was a bit overrated by his win total in 1990 and actually was much more comparable to Tom Browning than his luck-induced ERA and twenty-seven wins would imply. Danny Jackson gave the Reds a solid and experienced third option at starter, while Mike Moore was a weak link for the A's. **Advantage: Reds**

Relief Pitching

Reds	PA	AVG	OBP	SLG	Off Runs	Def Runs	Net Runs
Randy Myers	86.2	2.08	10.2	3.9	0.6	9	
Rob Dibble	98.0	1.74	12.5	3.1	0.3	26	
Norm Charlton	154.1	2.74	6.8	4.1	0.6	4	
Others	372.1	4.01	5.3	3.1	0.9	-10	
A's							
Dennis Eckersley	73.1	0.61	9.0	0.5	0.2	21	
Todd Burns	78.2	2.97	4.9	3.7	0.9	-3	
Gene Nelson	74.2	1.57	4.6	2.0	0.6	4	
Rick Honeycutt	63.1	2.70	5.4	3.1	0.3	6	
Joe Klink	39.2	2.04	4.3	4.1	0.2	2	
Others	330.2	4.25	5.0	3.2	1.2	-24	

The A's had the best closer in the game. The Reds had the next two best closers plus one of the toughest lefties in the league to face in late innings. The A's bullpen was very good, but the Reds' pen was better. **Advantage: Reds**

The 1990 World Series was supposed to be a blowout. In fact it was a blowout, but not in the way people

Oakland's fans were as cocky as the team they followed, but the Reds had the last laugh.

expected. The Reds beat the Oakland A's in every way possible through the first three games.

In Game One, they pounded the A's for seven runs, led by Eric Davis's first-inning home run off Dave Stewart, while Jose Rijo and the Nasty Boys shut out the A's for a 7–0 victory.

In Game Two, the Reds came from behind and won 5–4 in the tenth inning on a single down the line off the bat of Joe Oliver.

A seven-run third inning in Game Three, fueled by Chris Sabo's second home run of the game, gave the Reds another dominating win by a score of 8–3.

Despite being up three games to none, the Reds faced a fight to the finish. A World Championship was anything but a lock. The A's were still a strong, confident team as reliever Gene Nelson reminded the media before Game Four when he said, "This team is capable of doing anything. If we get rolling, we can win a lot of ball games."

Reading that today, Reds fans might laugh. What they might not remember, however, is how close their team was to blowing the series, even with a 3–0 lead.

Before the start of Game Four, Dave Stewart, the ace of the A's, said, "No one has ever come back from a three-to-none deficit, but if there is a team that can do it, this team can."

And he could have been right.

Game Four: Top of the first inning

Dave Stewart stared down Reds leadoff hitter Billy Hatcher as he walked to the plate to start the game. Hatcher was hitting .750 for the Series. In fourteen at-bats, he'd made only three outs. On an 0-2 count, Stewart came in hard, the fastball catching Hatcher on the left hand, crumbling him to the ground. Hatcher, true to the code, didn't rub it. But the pain shot all the way down his arm, as though he'd stuck

The only thing that could stop Billy Hatcher in the series was a fastball off the wrist.

out his hand to stop a passing truck.

Did Stewart drill Hatcher intentionally? The A's ace traded on his reputation as an intimidator and was well known for busting hitters inside. His manager, Tony LaRussa, also has a well-documented history of calling for message pitches.

"That was a horses--- thing to do, hit a guy because he's hot," Reds reliever Rob Dibble barked.

"(Stewart's) lucky he isn't in the National League where he has to bat. If he would have ruined Billy's career, I guarantee somebody would (get) him."

Stewart denied any intention of hitting him. What did Hatcher think?

"He threw me inside, and I wasn't going to back down," Hatcher recalled twenty years later at the 1990 team reunion at RedsFest. "I think he did kind of throw me in tight, but I don't think he threw at me."

Reds announcer Marty Brennaman, who was emceeing the reunion, could not believe what he was hearing.

"You don't think he was throwing at you? C'mon, Billy!"

No matter what was true, the Reds needed a Plan B. Game Four was barely under way. With Herm Winningham stretching his legs outside the dugout, Hatcher convinced Piniella to leave him in the game. "Hatch" tried to steal second base on the first pitch—just something to get the blood flowing and take his mind off the pain—but the ball beat him to the bag. *Out!*

Hatcher played the field in the bottom half of the inning, but the swelling got to be too much and Piniella was forced remove him and call for X-rays.

"I was mad; I didn't want to come out," Hatcher remembers. "I couldn't swing; I couldn't hold the bat. But I didn't want to take a chance on not being able to contribute with the bat. (But) I knew we had guys on the bench like Herm and Glenn (Braggs)."

Hatcher's .750 batting average set a new World Series single-season record, as did his on-base percentage (.800). His on-base plus slugging average of 2.050 was second only to Lou Gehrig's 1928 Series total of 2.433. Hatcher also set a new World Series standard when he reached base successfully in his first nine plate appearances—including his seventh straight hit, a triple, to start a game-tying rally in Game Two.

"I don't really care about records," Hatcher said after Game Two. "I just want to win two more games; I just want a World Series championship ring."

Hatcher may not have been excited by the record, but his hometown of Williams, Arizona, was particularly proud of him.

"I think almost everyone in the town has sent me something—telegrams, cards, whatever," Hatcher said. "All three thousand of them."

Game 4: Bottom of the first inning

With one out, Willie McGee slapped a looping liner to left field. Eric Davis charged it, eyes locked on its trajectory. Even though he'd been banged up all season, Davis still ran with such grace. On his final step before lunging to snatch the ball out of the air, Davis slapped his glove on his left thigh. Joe Oliver loved that glove slap.

"Standing at home plate, nothing's better than when you see that glove hit his thigh," Oliver recalls years later. "It meant don't worry, Eric's got this."

Eric did have this one, but only for a moment. His glove closed around the ball an instant before he slammed violently into the turf. He had positioned his right arm to brace his fall, and that arm boomeranged into his rib cage and sent a piercing pain throughout his right side. The intensity of that reaction loosened the ball from his grip, and the ball fell to the turf. Davis summoned just enough strength to flip the ball backhanded from his knees toward the infield as McGee raced into second.

"E.D." crumbled. Reds trainer Larry Starr rushed toward him. As Starr searched for the source of the pain, Davis laid on the field for a full five minutes. Finally, he was able to stand on his own power, and he convinced Starr and Piniella he could stay in despite the pain. *Can't play with pain, huh?* With every step, he winced.

❖ ❖ ❖ ❖ ❖

Other than his thunderbolt of a home run in Game One, Davis wasn't having a monster series. But his five RBI were tied for most on the team, and his heart and soul during the season had no equal.

"He was the guy that got us there," remembers Winningham. "He was one of the mainstays, one of the pillars."

He was also the guy who took the most heat from the fans. Before Game One, many fans were upset with him, calling him selfish for refusing to bat lead-off when Piniella asked him to. Davis knew how to change their attitude, if only temporarily.

After Jose Rijo breezed through the top of the first inning of Game One, striking out Rickey Henderson

and Jose Canseco, Davis strode to the plate. Two were out; Hatcher was on first.

"The year before—in the All-Star Game—I had faced Stewart, and he threw me a first-pitch fastball for a strike that I took," recalls Davis, twenty years later. "And then he threw me four splits (split-finger fastballs) in the dirt and walked me. I had that in the back of my mind, that he was going to try to get ahead with a fastball. I wasn't going to take it."

Sure enough, here came Stewart's fastball, thigh-high, outer-half. Davis ripped at it, nailing it, screaming it toward the concourse in center, a roar rocking the house that grew into a tumult as the ball bounced around the concrete, 429 feet away. Stewart could only shake his head.

And the invincible A's?

"Sort of put a dent in the steel," said Braggs.

It is what leaders do. *Don't worry, Eric's got this.* His teammates followed.

❖ ❖ ❖ ❖ ❖

Oakland's Carney Lansford singled home McGee in the bottom of the first inning of Game Four. Davis was having trouble breathing after his dive in left field. Rijo got a strikeout to end the inning, and Davis jogged gingerly to the dugout and grasped for Starr's shoulder to hold him up. The pain was too much, and he was feeling weak in the legs.

It took two men to help Davis back to the clubhouse. If the cameras hadn't been on him, he'd have let them carry him. He was rushed to Merritt Hospital in Oakland where X-rays showed a severely bruised right kidney. He spent the next week in the intensive care unit and was unaware of the outcome of the game or the series until three days later.

Billy Hatcher had ridden with Davis to the hospital to get X-rays on his hand. Even in his agony, Davis was still trying to be the leader. Hatcher: "The final words he said to me (in the hospital) were, 'Hatch, tell the guys I'm with them.' This guy is sitting in the hospital with a bruised kidney, spitting up blood, and he's telling me, 'Hatch, let the guys know I'm with them.'"

Back at the Coliseum, Lou Piniella was in a tight spot. Two of his three starting outfielders were gone, probably done for the series. Braggs and Winningham were able replacements, but there were no more outfielders on the bench. *We'd better win this game.*

Game Four: Top of the second inning

In one of the most memorable moments in the series—maybe even in Reds history—Glenn Braggs led off the second inning. It wasn't a moment that determined the outcome of the game in any way, but fans witnessed something that they'd never seen before and would always remember.

Braggs swung at a high fastball and missed, taking the bat all the way around to his back. When the bat hit the back of his front shoulder, it snapped in two at the handle, and the barrel of the bat clunked down onto home plate. He'd broken the bat across his back with the sheer force of his swing!

Braggs already was known as one of the strongest players in the game, a true physical specimen, but breaking a bat across his back with a swing demonstrated to any doubters that this guy was a beast. No discussion of the series among Reds fans ever leaves out the story of the broken bat. If the A's weren't already a bit intimidated by the physical Reds, this display surely would have clinched it.

Game Four: Bottom of the second inning

Jose Rijo hadn't looked all that good in the bullpen before the game. Pitching coach Stan Williams was particularly nervous.

"His fastball didn't look as good as usual," Williams said. "We talked about it on the way in (from the bullpen)."

Two outs into the second inning, Rijo started nibbling. He walked weak-hitting Mike Gallego on a two-strike count. With American League MVP Rickey Henderson at bat, Gallego stole second and moved to third on the errant throw by Joe Oliver. Rijo went 3-2 on Henderson, walked him, and Piniella moved toward the mound.

Rijo's previous start in Game One had been no picnic. Staked to a 2–0 lead by Davis's bomb, Rijo surrendered seven hits and two walks over seven innings, but he had gotten the big outs when he needed them—Mark McGwire twice, stranding five runners. The big Dominican followed Jimmy Stewart's scouting report like sheet music, hitting his spots and pounding the power hitters with high heat. Piniella had pulled Rijo with a 7–0 lead in that one, wanting to keep him fresh on three days' rest for Game Four.

But now, Piniella felt the momentum starting to shift. Two runners on, two outfielders gone. He reminded the group gathered around him that if Henderson tried to steal second (he did), Rijo should focus on the batter (he did, getting Willie McGee with a nasty slider).

Game Four: Top of the fifth inning

Chris Sabo led off the fifth with his second single of the game and his eighth hit of the series. Sabo and Joe Oliver were the only two Reds to have hits in all four games. Sabo had owned Game Three, lining a 3-2 pitch from Mike Moore over the wall in left-center to lead off the second inning, his twenty-seventh home run in 1990. Lou had predicted that Sabo would hit fifteen home runs "by accident" that year; Sabes had almost doubled it. In the Reds' seven-run third inning in Game Three, he lashed number twenty-eight.

"Nobody wanted to make the last out," said Davis of that third inning. "We just kept rolling and rolling and rolling."

Shades of April and May, when the Reds were scoring at will and beating everybody in sight, and Sabes was in the middle of it then, like he was in the middle of it now.

"I don't want them to think I'm an easy out," Sabo would say of the A's.

Really, Sabes? You're batting .500 on the series with two home runs and five RBI and you're afraid they might think you're an easy out?

Tom Browning had cruised in Game Three. Only the inimitable Rickey H had touched him up with a homer to lead off the third inning.

"Nobody knew what kind of team was going to show up for us this World Series," Benzinger said. "We were supposed to finish fourth or fifth (in the division), and we win it. Then we're supposed to lose to the Pirates (in the NLCS); we win it. Then we're supposed to lose to the A's and we're up three to none. It's like, you say I can't do it, I'll say I can."

Barry Larkin, however, added some perspective: "Until we can put those rings on our fingers, we haven't accomplished anything."

Now, down a run with only four innings left in Game Four, the Reds had reason to fret.

"We were a little bit worried," admits Oliver twenty years later, noting the absence of Hatcher and Davis. "It was critical for us to win Game Four and not give the A's any shot at getting back into the series."

❖ ❖ ❖ ❖ ❖

Marge Schott may have been the one person in the organization—well, the only person besides Piniella—who had no doubt the Reds were going to win it all. She had actually suggested to Sweet Lou back at the hotel before Game Four that maybe the Reds should lose a couple of games here so they could go back to Cincinnati and clinch on their home field and celebrate with their home fans. Marge hadn't used the phrase, "tank it," but she might as well have.

"What?" he exclaimed. "Marge, you can't be serious."

"It would be for the fans, honey," Schott replied.

"We're not going to try to lose—forget it," said Piniella, walking away, shaking his head.

Game Four: Bottom of the fifth inning

Rickey Henderson was a good hitter. Actually, he was a *great* hitter. He had led the league in on-base percentage, stolen bases, and runs, and finished second in batting average and slugging percentage.

He made pitchers work. You don't get to be second all-time in career walks without having a good eye and the patience of a whale rider. High fastball. *Nah, Rickey don't like that.* Ball one. Slider on the outside corner. *Rickey'll give you that one—but just this once.* Strike one. Fastball at the knees. *That ain't a strike to Rickey.* Ball two. Two-and-one count, here came a slider that didn't snap. Henderson, fouled it off. Next, a wild slider, high, a foot over Henderson's head. And then came a slider that did snap, barely clipping the outside corner.

Not this time, Rickey. *Ka-ching!* The umpire rang him up.

And that's when the A's really began to realize how much trouble they were in.

❖ ❖ ❖ ❖ ❖

Sitting in the bullpen at the Coliseum, Scott Scudder knew it, too. The A's were getting a lesson in r-e-s-p-e-c-t: A lesson in how to earn it.

"I can remember very well, prior to Game One, we worked out first, and were about to clear the field," recalls Scudder twenty years later. "Oakland was coming onto the field. They had a whole different aura about them. I can remember Rickey Henderson using a cell phone. And I was thinking, 'You know, these guys really don't have a lot of respect for us. We ought to try to gain some respect in this series.'"

It was true. The A's were open in their disdain of the Reds.

"In 1993, I was playing with the Giants," recalls Todd Benzinger, "and Willie McGee was on that team. He said to me, 'I told them in the World Series. We had those meetings to talk about the other team, and nobody was paying attention. I said to them, 'Listen, Rijo can pitch. Browning can pitch. They've got speed….' He said nobody would listen to him. They were so cocky."

Scudder did his part to gain that respect in Game Two with some help from Jack Armstrong. The Reds were trailing 4–2 in the third inning of Game Two when Scudder came on to relieve starter Danny Jackson with two outs and two men on. He got Bob Welch to strike out to end the threat and then worked his way around a couple of walks in the fourth to keep the A's at arm's length, including a big whiff of the mighty Jose Canseco.

Armstrong took over in the fifth and shut down the A's for three innings. In the last of those innings, the seventh, he whiffed Canseco and Mark McGwire back to back, just like in the All-Star Game.

AL MVP Rickey Henderson was the only batter in the A's vaunted lineup to do any damage in the series.

"I have a new appreciation for adrenaline," Armstrong said.

"We played with a reckless abandon," Scudder recalls. "We were at the peak of our intensity at the time, and (the A's) couldn't match it."

Game Four: Top of the sixth inning

Barry Larkin walked, and with Herm Winningham at the plate, the Reds played a little hit and run. Winningham slapped a single to left field and Larkin—with the play right in front of him—never broke stride, hitting second base perfectly and digging to third.

After an O'Neill pop out and a Braggs walk, the bases were loaded for Hal Morris, who had managed just one base hit in the entire series. His struggles continued as he hit a weak grounder right to Randolph at second base who flipped it to Gallego who tossed it across to McGwire at first. Double play. Rally snuffed.

BULLPEN WAS NASTY IN THE POSTSEASON

Throughout the 1990 season, opponents felt they were playing a six-inning game against the Reds and were doing everything they could to not let the Reds have a lead to turn over to their bullpen.

"They try to score a run or two early with bunts," Norm Charlton said. "They know if they get a run or two behind, it enables us to come in and go right at them."

This mindset was even more obvious during the playoffs, when the Reds' bullpen was nearly unblemished. As a team, the relievers threw thirty-one innings in the ten postseason games and allowed just one earned run. That's an incredible 0.29 earned run average. Calling them dominant seems like an understatement.

Maybe the most impressive statistic is that they inherited eleven runners from previous pitchers, but not a single one scored. Even when they came into the middle of a mess, it got no messier.

And it wasn't only the three Nasty Boys getting it done. Scott Scudder, Jack Armstrong, and Rick Mahler each turned in shutdown performances during the playoffs. In fact, Norm Charlton was the only reliever to allow a run—an earned run in Game One of the NLCS and an unearned run in Game Three of the NLCS.

Ultimately it was the Nasty Boys who put the fear into the opposition.

"With three guys like that, you don't have to worry about going after your starter in the fifth or sixth inning," Piniella said.

And when they perform like they did in the playoffs, it's easy for the manager to look like a genius.

Reds Relievers' Postseason Performance

Pitchers	G	IP	W-L	Sv	ERA	H	R	ER	HR	BB	SO	WHIP
Rob Dibble	7	9.2	1–0	1	0.0	3	0	0	0	2	14	0.52
Randy Myers	7	8.2	0–0	4	0.0	4	0	0	0	3	10	0.81
Norm Charlton	5	6.0	1–1	0	1.5	5	2	1	0	3	3	1.33
Scott Scudder	2	2.1	0–0	0	0.0	1	0	0	0	2	3	1.29
Jack Armstrong	1	3.0	0–0	0	0.0	1	0	0	0	0	3	0.33
Rick Mahler	1	1.2	0–0	0	0.0	2	0	0	0	0	0	1.20
Total	23	31	2–1	5	.29	16	2	1	0	10	33	0.84

The Reds were finding out what the American League already knew. It's hard to come back on the A's; they don't blow leads.

During the regular season, the A's were an incredible 73–3 in games they led after five innings. That's right, *five* innings. Sure the Reds had come back in Game Two after trailing late, but to do it *twice in three games* against a team that had given away a lead only three times in seventy-six tries during the season?

A comeback was looking more improbable as each inning passed.

❖ ❖ ❖ ❖ ❖

Then again, the Game Two comeback had seemed just as improbable at the time.

Trailing 4–2 after three and a half innings, Ron Oester pinch hit for Scudder and singled to drive in Joe Oliver, who had doubled earlier in the inning. It was a huge hit for Oester in what would end up being the Cincinnati native's only at-bat in World Series play. It was also his first pinch-hit RBI since August 14, 1983.

As the bullpen kept the A's bats quiet, the offense kept biding its time, waiting for an opportunity.

That opportunity came in the eighth inning of Game Two when Billy Hatcher led off with a triple to right field. It was a play that many right fielders would make, but Canseco didn't. And his manager was none too happy about it.

"He got a horses--- jump," La Russa said. "If you're going to win the game, that (catch) has got to be made."

A walk to O'Neill and a short fly out by Eric Davis left runners at first and third with one out. When LaRussa decided to go to his bullpen for left-hander Rick Honeycutt to face Morris, Piniella called upon his bench one more time.

This time it was Glenn Braggs, celebrating his twenty-eighth birthday. He gave Reds fans a reason to join the party when he hit a ground ball up the middle that Gallego fielded at shortstop. But Gallego had to make an awkward tag on O'Neill, and by the time he made the throw to first base, Braggs dove in head-first and was called safe—while Hatcher was scooting home to score the tying run.

Only once during the entire 1990 season had the A's blown a lead in the eighth inning. But, for the Reds, once was enough. It was a whole new ballgame.

❖ ❖ ❖ ❖ ❖

Joe Oliver doesn't have to start many conversations when he comes to Cincinnati.

"Usually the first thing I learn about somebody when I meet them (is) where they were during Game Two," he says. "It's almost always the first thing they bring up to talk about."

The game was tied at four, bottom of the tenth, a crowd of 55,832 at Riverfront Stadium. Oakland A's ace reliever Dennis Eckersley was on the mound. His numbers in 1990 were unheard of: 0.61 ERA, forty-eight saves, and seventy-three strikeouts against only four walks in seventy-three and a third innings. He had allowed one—yes, o-n-e—run over the last two months of the season. The A's were 60–3 in his appearances in 1990.

The Reds were facing one of the best major league closers in history. And after Eric Davis led off the tenth inning with a groundout, they'd be doing it with one out.

Up stepped Billy Bates. Many Reds fans did not even know he was on the team. The smallish backup second baseman had been acquired with Braggs in June from Milwaukee, but Bates had only seen action in eight games with the Reds during the regular season. His claim to a sliver of fame was for racing against a cheetah in a promotion in late September.

Joe Oliver's naiveté kept him calm during the biggest at-bat of his career.

But now he was facing a different breed of cat. Nobody expected the career .125 hitter to go toe-to-toe with Eckersley with the game on the line. But the Reds' bench was thin, and Piniella had to put out an all points bulletin for Tom Browning, who had left midway through Game Two to rush his wife, who was in labor with their third child, to the hospital. Piniella hadn't even realized that Browning was gone.

"When I saw we were starting to eat up pitchers in the middle innings," said Piniella after the game, "I said, 'This game is close. Make sure Browning doesn't go anywhere.' And Stan said, 'He won't go anywhere.' About the eighth inning, I said, 'Where is he? I don't see him.'"

Piniella advised Reds radio broadcaster Marty Brennaman to put out an APB for Browning. Clubhouse attendant Rick Stowe called around to several hospitals until he found Browning and asked him to

Billy Bates' last appearance on the field in a Reds uniform was a memorable one.

head back to the park, but by then the game was almost finished.

But now it was the tenth inning of Game Two, and Piniella was forced to send up Bates to face Eckersley, who quickly got ahead, 0-2. Bates had yet to get the bat off his shoulder. He fouled off one pitch, then beat the next one into the carpet, racing destiny like a cheetah and again coming out on top, this time in front of third baseman Carney Lansford's throw.

What a way to get my first hit as a Red.

Sabo followed with a grounder through the hole between shortstop and third.

Two on, one out, welcome to prime time, Joe Oliver.

Was he nervous? He had never before faced Dennis Eckersley.

"I was too naive to be nervous," recalls Oliver, twenty years later. "Looking back, I should have been nervous, but the gravity of the situation never really struck me at the time. I guess it's a good thing I was so young then."

223

Oliver took the first pitch to see what Eckersley's stuff looked like. A slider right over the heart of the plate. The next pitch was a fastball that Oliver jerked down the line. It darted past Lansford at third, just inside the bag, and carried down into the visitors' bullpen. Bates sped home from second as the fans erupted.

Reds win! And now they had a two-to-none lead in the series.

"I have so many emotions running through me right now, I don't know how to react," Oliver said afterward. "You always dream about something like this, but there's a lot more excitement and fulfillment when you experience it. We're not in dreamland anymore."

❖ ❖ ❖ ❖ ❖

Through six innings of Game Four, the Reds hadn't been able to get into the A's bullpen. Dave Stewart was dealing, overcoming having runners on base in five of his six innings. During the season, Stewart had an ERA of 0.95 in the seventh, eighth, and ninth innings. The Reds were down to nine outs between them and a scenario they didn't want to contemplate: Game Five…in Oakland…with no Hatcher and no Davis.

Game Four: Top of the eighth inning

Barry Larkin singled. He'd had a great series, so far. To the untrained eye, his production lacked the layering of Hatcher's and Sabo's hits and the theatrics of Davis's and Oliver's, but as always, Larkin was in the middle of the action.

This was the fourth straight inning that the Reds had gotten the leadoff hitter on base. Piniella wanted to get that run home. The Reds had done it all season. Why not now? He signaled third-base coach Sam Perlozzo to have Winningham bunt.

But Winningam couldn't get one down on the first two strikes, and everybody assumed he'd be swinging away now. Rule Number One in Lou Ball: Never assume. Winningam laid down a perfect bunt between pitcher's mound and home plate; catcher Jamie Quirk's only play was to first base. His throw was right on target, but Winningham was hustling all the way and beat the ball. *Speed!*

"Who bunts on a oh-and-two pitch?" Benzinger later asked. "A team of destiny bunts on an oh-and-two pitch—and beats it out."

Up stepped Paul O'Neill. "Big" was second on the team in RBI. He'd been a big-time producer against right-handed pitchers in '90: .274 with 13 homers and 16 doubles. A big hit here against the right-handed Stewart could give the Reds a lead and perhaps the series. It was a situation that screamed for O'Neill, the guy who Piniella had predicted just a month ago would one day "be a great player."

Great players, however, can't be great without great moments.

Piniella sometimes said one thing and did another. In calm moments, he would formulate a plan or a way to treat a certain player, and he would stick to it. He would say the right things to the media or to the player, calculated to produce a certain result, and it would work. But, then, at other times, such as in the heat of battle, especially in the NLCS when every pitch is taut, Piniella's true feelings would come to the fore, and he would show everybody—including himself—what he thought of a player.

And that is when you knew.

In his heart of hearts, Piniella did not have faith in O'Neill. It had shone through first when Piniella insisted that Quinn acquire Braggs. It had shone through when Piniella would not let O'Neill play against tough left-handers like Tom Glavine, and it had shone through in Game Six of the NLCS, when Piniella replaced O'Neill with pinch hitter Luis Quinones in what O'Neill would years later refer to as "one of the four of five most disappointing things that happened in my career." Because, no matter what Piniella thought, O'Neill wanted to be up there when the game was on the line. He loved the feeling of the outcome of a game resting on his shoulders.

But when O'Neill came to bat in Game Four, Piniella walked over to Sabo and said, "Can O'Neill bunt? I guess we'll see if he can." And then Sweet Lou flashed the bunt to Perlozzo, who relayed it to O'Neill, who got the bunt down perfectly to move the runners up. With some help from first-base umpire Randy Marsh, the A's botched it. Marsh signaled that second baseman Willie Randolph had pulled his foot from the first-base bag; replays showed otherwise. The bunt turned out to be the right move.

"It's just what you do in that situation," O'Neill remembers twenty years later. "You don't sit back and wait for a bomb. You don't need a three- or four-run lead with that bullpen. You use the bunt, you get the run, and you turn it over to the bullpen. That's the way baseball is, and that's the way Lou played it."

Bases loaded and no outs. The Reds had been putting runners on base all game, but this inning felt different. Their aggressiveness had the A's against the ropes with the Reds in their face—just where they wanted to be.

Braggs, who was in the game only because Davis had gone down, came to the plate with the A's infield at double-play depth. He hit a chopper to short that Gallego had to charge. He made the throw to second to get the force play, but O'Neill was bearing down on Randolph, who couldn't get the ball out of his glove and had no chance to get Braggs at first; Larkin cruised across the plate with the Reds' first run.

The Reds had done something twice in the span of four days that only one other team had managed to do during the six-month regular season: Taken a lead away from the A's in the eighth inning.

That brought up Hal Morris, who had been to the plate six times in this series with runners in scoring position and did not have a hit. His lone RBI had come on a ground out. Prince Hal was frustrated; he felt as though he hadn't really contributed.

Jeff Brantley, who at the time was a Giants reliever and is now a Reds broadcaster, would remember this twenty years later: "(Morris) was the last guy you

Rickey Henderson didn't make Joe Oliver's life easy at the plate or on the base paths.

wanted to face at the end of the ballgame because he always kept the inning going."

Morris didn't need a hit. He just needed to get the ball into the outfield and the go-ahead run would score.

"I wanted to be disciplined," he said. "The first time, when (Stewart) got me to hit into that double play, he was smart. He knew I was overanxious on stuff away. (This time) I was just concentrating on getting something up in the strike zone so I could get it in the air."

Morris got what he wanted on the second pitch, launching it into deep right, far enough to score Winningham easily with the go-ahead run.

The Reds managed only one hit to the outfield in the inning but used aggressive base running and managing to move the runners around. They had pressed the potential winning runs across the plate.

The Reds did to the A's what the Reds had done to their opponents since Day One. They had stuck their hips into them and just kept coming.

Game Four: Bottom of the ninth inning

Jose Rijo's father-in-law, Juan Marichal, who was working as a broadcaster for Spanish radio during the series, pitched in only one World Series game in his career. In 1962, he started Game Four for the Giants against the Yankees but threw only four shutout innings before leaving the game. Rijo had already bettered Marichal's Game Four…and then some.

Coming into the ninth inning, Rijo had retired nineteen consecutive batters. He'd already thrown 110 pitches—ten or twenty more than Piniella had expected to get out of him, because of a blister on Rijo's finger.

Rijo blistered Dave Henderson with a 1-2 fastball on the outside corner. All Henderson could do was watch. Rijo's ninth strikeout. Twenty outs in a row. No base runners since the second inning. Two hits. And yet, it was a performance that couldn't have happened without the sheet music from the maestro—the scouting report from advance man Jimmy Stewart.

"When I came into Cincinnati before (Game One), I met with Lou behind closed doors for forty-five minutes," Stewart remembered.

"I said, 'Lou, we can beat this club. But it won't be easy.' I just thought we could beat them with our pitching. He thought so, too."

Stewart had talked with Mel Didier, who had scouted Oakland before the 1988 World Series for the Dodgers. "He said they threw hard, high stuff," Stewart said. "That's what we've done."

The A's batted only .207 during the series. Take out

Rickey Henderson's at-bats and that number drops to .192. They were dominated in every way by Reds pitching, and it was all rooted in Stewart's scouting report.

❖ ❖ ❖ ❖ ❖

As Randy Myers stalked to the mound, Tom Browning stood on the top step of the dugout, soaking it all in. It had been an eventful series for Browning both on and off the field. His third child was born thirty minutes after Oliver drove home Billy Bates in Game Two. Two days later, Papa Tom had pitched a fine six innings against Oakland in Game Three. It was a long way since that day in March when Sweet Lou had run into him and Pete Rose on the eighth tee at Walden Lakes Country Club.

Browning knew that somewhere Rose was watching his team in Game Four. *This one's for you, Skip.*

❖ ❖ ❖ ❖ ❖

Myers was brought in to face left-hander Harold Baines, but Tony LaRussa countered with right-handed Jose Canseco, who hadn't started Game Four because of a stiff back. His lone hit in the series was a solo shot in Game Two. Canseco could still tie things up, but Myers came right after him, getting a weak chopper to third, and Sabo threw him out easily at first. *Two gone.*

In the dugout, Hal Morris moved from sitting to standing and back to sitting. A lot of other guys were fidgeting, too. Some had been fidgeting for years. At shortstop, Barry Larkin thought of Marge Schott's line, "Always a bridesmaid, never a bride." Billy Hatcher, back from the hospital (the X-Rays were negative on his hand, no break), stood on the top step, ready to bolt for the mound. From the moment he had arrived in Plant City back in March, he had envisioned this moment. In his vision, he was in the outfield. But he could still hardly believe it.

Ronnie O was now, literally, shaking.

One more out, baby.

Todd Benzinger, one of three Cincinnatians on the team (the others were Oester and Larkin), thought of the Big Red Machine, who he had grown up watching.

Now it's our turn to bring one home.

Randall Kirk Myers, as Marty Brennaman liked to call him, was loaded with adrenaline. Closers dream of this moment from the day they are given the job. Myers had watched as New York Mets closer Jesse Orosco threw his glove in the air when the 1986 Mets knocked off the Red Sox. Myers was ready for his own Orosco moment. It was why Piniella and GM Bob Quinn had traded for him. They wanted a power lefty on the mound. And oh had he ever delivered this season.

But his first two pitches to Carney Lansford flew wildly out of the strike zone. *Too pumped up.* Oliver urged him to dial it back a notch, but Myers couldn't. This, too, is what he had envisioned when he had posted that calendar in his locker and counted down the victories to the ninety-nine he had predicted for the regular season. He had been slightly off, but now, here it was, number ninety-nine: Game Four of the World Series.

It was theirs, if he could nail it down.

Two pitches later, Lansford popped a 2-1 fastball into foul territory. Benzinger back-pedaled beneath it—calling off his teammates, the two umpires, and anyone else within earshot who might have an inclination to try to catch that ball—and got ready. When Benzinger finally closed his glove around the ball, it didn't feel real. A season's worth of struggle and battling had led to this moment. He and his teammates were overcome with excitement, piling up together behind the mound, embracing each other in joy.

In the dugout, Sweet Lou hung back, hugging his coaches and letting his players have their moment. He knew how much work they had put into it. He knew they deserved what they were feeling at that moment. They had earned it.

❖ ❖ ❖ ❖ ❖

As the players made their way back to the clubhouse, owner Marge Schott greeted each of them at the door with a giant smile.

"Great job, sweetie! Way to go, honey!"

She was proud of her boys. They'd set their goal at the start of the season and followed it all the way to the end.

The players were proud they won this championship as a team, with everybody contributing.

"We were very modest and humble in going about our jobs," Larkin said. "Our attitude was, 'Don't show people up. Don't talk trash. Don't hot-dog it.' But we were ready to play when the bell rang."

As Sabo said, "We didn't have an MVP or a Cy Young winner, but we're the champions."

In fact, they beat both the NL and AL MVP and Cy Young Award winners in the postseason.

"People who see us once or twice say, 'They're not that good,'" Norm Charlton added. "But day in and day out, we go out there and make the plays."

They won it as a team, and they played their best baseball when it mattered most. For ten games in the postseason, they managed to recapture that magic from April and May.

"We were on top of our game right down from the starting pitching to the scouts," Benzinger wrote in a daily diary he penned for Cincinnati's afternoon newspaper. "You name it, the Reds came through in the postseason. We were clicking on all cylinders. It was just very gratifying to know that what we were capable of doing, we actually did. That doesn't happen often."

❖ ❖ ❖ ❖ ❖

In the Oakland locker room, Rickey Henderson said, "Somebody forgot to tell us it was the Reds' year."

Dave Stewart was defiant.

"This doesn't make them a better ballclub than we are," he said. "They just played better for four games."

Hall of Fame second baseman Joe Morgan, who lived in Oakland and saw the A's play a lot, disagreed.

As Marty Brennaman related years later, "Joe said to me right in the middle of the Reds clubhouse, 'That team over there in the home clubhouse could play this team right here every day between now and Christmas and still not beat them.' And I said, 'Why?' He said, 'Because this team has a bunch of guys on the mound that throw ninety-four, ninety-five, or better.' And he said, to him, at that moment, that was the single biggest difference. That their hitters could not catch up to the fastballs."

It was an interesting observation, and right in line with the Reds scouting report. "High, hard stuff,' is what advance scout Jimmy Stewart had called for, and the Reds pitchers delivered it. The A's had more talent for the regular season, but not for a short series. The Reds were built to win a championship—and had done just that.

❖ ❖ ❖ ❖ ❖

There was plenty of joy in the Reds clubhouse, but there was also some emptiness.

"It was bittersweet," Herm Winningham remembers twenty years later. "Bittersweet because Eric wasn't there. We wanted to go (to his hospital room) and party with him, not knowing how bad it was. The champagne was flowing, sure, but it was a little bittersweet because he was the guy that got us there. And he was not there."

Before the season started, *there* was the only place that Davis dreamed of being. It had been his only wish.

"I'd like to drink champagne in October," he had said. "I dream of that kind of stuff. You see the guys run out on the field, you know the excitement and joy they're feeling. I always picture myself pouring champagne on people's heads and jumping for joy and everybody's watching. That's prime time. That's where I want to be."

Where he was, though, was in the intensive care unit at Merritt Hospital, where he would stay for the next seven days. A CAT scan showed three lacerations on the bottom portion of his kidney, and though his condition was stable, doctors were concerned he might have to lose that kidney.

"After everything he's gone through this year," said Barry Larkin, "we wish he could be here."

Rick Mahler agreed: "It's a sad feeling. He really has been the leader on this club all year."

Merritt Hospital is about eight miles from Oakland Coliseum, but to Davis's teammates, it felt a world away.

❖ ❖ ❖ ❖ ❖

Lou Piniella had a difficult time putting into words what this championship meant to him. It had been a marathon season. One in which Piniella never let up, not for a single day.

"He put in more hours than anybody I've ever seen," pitching coach Stan Williams said. "His mind has been in it every minute, every inning, every pitch. He was working mentally all the time."

Piniella did it because he had something to prove—to himself, to his doubters, to his previous boss. There would be no satisfaction without a championship. He got his players to buy into it, and they'd left it all out on the field. Reds broadcaster George Grande, who had worked for the Yankees when Piniella was there, told a story years later that captured the emotion Lou was feeling.

"I walked into Lou's office when it was all over," Grande recounted. "I went in with Dulio Constable, who was the cameraman for WPIX for thirty-some-odd years, and (*New York Times* writer) Dave Anderson. Lou walked in and said, 'Close the door.'

"He looked at us and he started crying. He said, 'Only you guys know what this means to me.'"

These three men had seen him struggle to learn how to manage in New York, knew the pain he had put up with there. They saw the beating he took from his owner and the press, and they knew what he had gone through to turn himself into a good manager.

It meant everything to him.

"We'll take eighty burgers to go."

After celebrating and showering in the clubhouse at Oakland Coliseum, the Reds headed back to their hotel, still riding high from their victory, but they were disappointed in what they found when they got there.

"We get to the hotel and there's no party, no open bar, nothing," Herm Winningham recalls. "All we heard was, 'Thank you for playing. The bus leaves for the airport at eight o'clock. See you all tomorrow morning.'"

After fighting and scrapping all season, the team wasn't just going to sit by without a party. So, Billy Hatcher and a few others walked across the street to Carl's Jr., a fast-food chain, and ordered some hamburgers for themselves and their teammates. It was perhaps the strangest World Series celebration meal in history.

"I don't know what a team usually does for a World Series," said Winningham, "but I know they don't go to no Carl's Jr."

The Champions Come Home

The city of Cincinnati didn't cut any corners on their Reds. Despite a steady drizzle all morning, a crowd of 15,000 gathered downtown for a ticker-tape parade—led by two street sweepers, symbolizing the Reds sweep—and celebration on Fountain Square.

Fans held up signs that said, "Go Reds!" and led chants of "Sweep! Sweep!" while the team made its way to Fountain Square. There were also signs that said, "Wish you were here, Eric!" as well as a giant get-well card with 10,000 signatures for the injured Reds outfielder.

Manager Lou Piniella was overwhelmed by the outpouring of love from the fans.

"This is fantastic," Piniella said with a huge grin. "I never expected anything like this, especially with the inclement weather. It shows how great the fans are here in Cincinnati. We are very appreciative. Without the fans, it certainly would not be as much fun and as rewarding as it is."

A Public Relations Nightmare

Eric Davis spent the week after the World Series in the intensive care unit at Merritt Hospital in Oakland. When he was finally given the "OK" by his doctors to fly home, they told him that he would need to fly in a prone position, so a commercial flight was not an option.

Davis had his agent, Eric Goldschmidt, call Reds General Manager Bob Quinn and ask him to set up a charter flight back to Cincinnati. According to Davis, the response he received was, "Eric Davis makes three million a year. He can set up his own flight." The response hurt Davis, so he called Marge Schott directly to see if there was any way to make this work. Davis was surprised to find that "with all the money and friends she had, Marge claims she didn't know a single person with a private jet. Can you believe that?"

Davis was forced to arrange his own flight back home, but he and the Reds still battled over the $15,000 bill. Schott eventually relented and reimbursed Davis for the flight, but the damage had already been done to her image as fans overwhelmingly supported Davis.

His teammates weren't particularly happy about it either.

Said Jose Rijo: "It's wrong. He deserves better, and not just because of who he is, but because he is a human being."

Davis and Schott eventually made up. The incident linked Schott's image permanently to Davis, who didn't hold a grudge against her. He even considered her a friend and truly appreciated that she brought him out of retirement and back to Cincinnati in 1996.

"Her comments live on because I still hear them today when people ask me about Marge," Davis wrote in a letter to *Sports Illustrated* in 2004 after Schott's death. "It's unfortunate because deep down inside she wasn't a bad person."

To this day, many fans do not understand Davis, but he has always been a much bigger man than most ever gave him credit for.

Off-season Complacency Sets Stage for Disappointing Defense

Two weeks after the World Series, the Reds faced the test of trying to repeat as World Champions, something that hadn't been done since the 1977–78 New York Yankees did it. The team faced the loss of five free agents—Tom Browning, Bill Doran, Danny Jackson, Rick Mahler, and Ron Oester—if they weren't able to work a deal with them.

The Reds' priority was to work on deals with the pitchers. They offered Browning a three-year deal, but he insisted on five years, claiming he had five-year offers from at least two other teams. The Reds held firm to their policy of no guaranteed deals for longer than three years; they had been burned by a five-year deal given to Mario Soto early in the 1980s.

After negotiating unhappily through the media for three weeks—at one point Browning called the Reds "complacent" in their success—he signed a four-year, $11.9 million deal. It was the largest total value

contract ever given out by the Reds. His contract bit the Reds in the behind, too, as Browning began to rack up injuries in 1992.

Danny Jackson signed a four-year deal with the Chicago Cubs on the same day, and Rick Mahler went on to sign with the Montreal Expos. Reds' management had decided that Scott Scudder was prepared to step into the rotation full time in 1991 along with Browning, Jose Rijo, Jack Armstrong, and Norm Charlton.

With Browning in the fold, the Reds focused on signing Bill Doran, reaching agreement with him in early December on a three-year, $7.4 million contract. Once Doran signed it became obvious the Reds wouldn't have a spot for Oester. As he contemplated retirement, he also looked for other offers around the league. When no intriguing ones arose, he decided to call it quits.

As the Reds lost three players to free agency, they got one back. Ted Power re-signed with the Reds in mid-December to help the bullpen that was somewhat depleted after the loss of Mahler, the move of Charlton, and the release of Tim Birtsas. Power had played with the Reds from 1983 to 1987 before being traded to the Kansas City Royals with Kurt Stillwell for Danny Jackson.

Although the return of most of the position players made fans think it was the same club, management placed undue confidence in Armstrong returning to first-half form and Scott Scudder having enough stuff to cut it as a full-time starter. Bob Quinn refers to '90

Tom Browning had dreamed of this moment since the first time he played baseball as an eight-year-old.

Barry Larkin was buoyed by the confidence of his friend and mentor, Eric Davis. Glenn Braggs listens and Paul O'Neill takes notes.

as "magical," but in '91, a series of misplaced assumptions were the equivalent of a tortoise being pulled out of a hat, the stage assistant really being sawed in half, and the volunteer from the audience (call him the starting pitching) actually disappearing.

They didn't make the same mistake in 1992. They added pitchers Tim Belcher and Greg Swindell to the rotation and reorganized the bullpen. Though they didn't match the success of the wire-to-wire

team, they did win ninety games, something they've done only once since. The magic between Piniella and Schott was lost, however. Lou, feeling unappreciated because he hadn't been offered a contract extension sooner, left for Seattle after the '92 season.

For the fans, though, the magic never left. The memories linger. The fondness goes on forever…

14

Reunion

December 12–13, 2009, Cincinnati

"Hey, Lou…Lou!" Joe Oliver yelled, catching Lou Piniella's attention on the middle of the main stage at the downtown convention center.

Eleven of the 1990 players—only two of them pitchers—were gathered around their former manager for a reunion photo.

Piniella, looking tanned and fit, turned toward his former catcher.

"Lou, you know that *everybody* was going to be here," said Oliver, his voice rising, so that everybody would hear, "but then they heard you were coming and none of the pitchers showed up!"

Everybody cackled at that, including Piniella, because everybody got the joke. Skip was notoriously hard on his pitchers.

"Yeah, but they all love me now!" said Piniella, grinning.

They laughed some more and then turned toward the photographer and smiled.

Click.

❖ ❖ ❖ ❖ ❖

Twenty years ago, they were here, then gone in an instant, a flash across the sky.

Ever the storyteller, Billy Hatcher entertains fans—and Lou Piniella—at the team's reunion at Reds Fest

237

The '90 Reds still laugh with each other like they've never been apart.

Now, they were back.

Suddenly, it was 1990 again.

"I can't believe it's been twenty years," said Marty Brennaman, speaking for everybody.

"It's like I never left," said Scott Scudder, one of the two pitchers (along with Tom Browning) who showed for the reunion. "You get back among these guys, and it's like you just pick up the conversation from 1990."

The beauty of being a World Champion is that, in a way, you never really leave. You are a breed apart, feted like a conquering hero upon your return. Every-body in town knows your name and what you did, and most of them can recite the names of the players, position-by-position (the batting order is harder be-cause Lou used a lot of batting orders). That doesn't happen with anybody except World Champions, and it goes on for five…ten…fifty years later. People al-ways remember.

"And everybody on that team really did contrib-ute," said Todd Benzinger. "It was a team, in the tru-est sense of the word."

In the twenty years since 1990, there has not been a World Champion like this, not even close, a group of just-now-blossoming players (or, in the case of Eric Davis, just barely beyond the blossom of his astounding prime years) who won a World Championship without a true Most Valuable candidate (Barry Larkin was the highest, at seventh) and no strong Cy Young candidate (Randy Myers was the highest at fifth).

These players have never gotten their due, partly because they won it all so soon after the Big Red Machine (fifteen years later, less than a generation), and partly because they've always been viewed as a bit of a one-shot wonder, just this side of a fluke, a sprinkled-by-magic-dust fairytale troupe.

None of those perceptions is true, except the Big Red Machine part. But there were no vestiges of the Big Red Machine at the convention center, not in the hall and not in the hallways. Not even on anybody's lips. It was refreshing. It really did feel like 1990 again.

"Feels pretty good," Benzinger admitted. "It feels like we're getting to tell our story a little more now. I haven't heard about 1975-76 yet this whole weekend."

Reds owner Bob Castellini has made it clear he wants to recapture the glory of the Big Red Machine years.

He would do well to recapture the spirit of '90.

There's hardly an ego in the group ("Well, hardly anybody, except Dibs," says somebody, laughing, because they all really did love one another, including Dibs). There were no superstars beyond the pale—even those who were bona fide stars, guys like Eric Davis and Barry Larkin, were and remain remarkably down to earth.

The Big Red Machine is revered, but as a group the '90 guys are more enjoyable, easier to approach, quicker with a laugh. Nobody from that team was anointed anything—not before, not since, not during. Simply put, it was a whale of a *team*. They became what Pete Rose was as a young player...but paradoxically they didn't become that until after he was banished.

Piniella, seeing the rocket fuel in those young legs, lit the fuse.

Well, actually, one guy has been anointed—Barry Larkin. He won the MVP in 1995, and three weeks after the twenty-year reunion in Cincinnati, received a very strong first-year vote for Cooperstown, which means he's a dead lock for immortality. And that means the 1990 team will now be remembered, too.

That was Larkin's team. No, that team made Larkin. He admits it.

"Of everything, it's the most special thing—the winning," says Larkin. "So many guys come up to me and say, 'Man, you got there. You won.' There's nothing like it."

Yes, at Redsfest it really was 1990 again.

Glenn Braggs, who had drawn the ooohs and ahhhs of teammates when he arrived in the Reds clubhouse on June 9, 1990—all buffed and muscled up with that big, wide, off-a-toothpaste-commercial smile—looks very much the same now. When he shed his shirt in the green room at the convention center to put on his Reds jersey for the autograph session, he was wearing a white muscle T-shirt on Friday and a black muscle T-shirt on Saturday. After that, nobody

FROM WAGNER TO QUINN: ASSEMBLING THE 1990 CHAMPS

by Greg Gajus

WORLD CHAMPIONSHIP TROPHY
PRESENTED BY THE COMMISSIONER OF BASEBALL

Just as the roots of the Big Red Machine of the 1970s sprouted a decade earlier under Bill DeWitt, the 1990 Reds can trace their beginnings to decisions made in the 1980s. Five general managers—Dick Wagner, Bob Howsam, Bill Bergesch, Murray Cook, and Bob Quinn—had a hand in developing the wire-to-wire champs.

The first three players of the 1990 team to join the Reds were Eric Davis (eighth round), Paul O'Neill (fourth) and Tom Browning (ninth), drafted by the Dick Wagner regime in 1980, 1981, and 1982. Wagner also drafted Barry Larkin in the second round in 1982, but Larkin opted for college. Bob Howsam replaced Wagner in 1983 and added two regulars and a key reliever in the 1983 draft: Joe Oliver (second round), Chris Sabo (second) and Rob Dibble (first). When Marge Schott bought the club in 1984, Howsam chose to retire and Bill Bergesch replaced him.

Bergesch—who had previously worked for the Yankees—redrafted Larkin in the first round and signed him in 1985. He also made the first significant trade that resulted in a contribution to the 1990 team. He dealt utility infielder Wayne Krenchicki to the Expos for prospect Norm Charlton. Charlton was hardly a success as a twenty-two-year-old in A ball (7–10, 4.57 ERA with seventy-nine walks in 128 innings), but Bergesch's assessment proved correct when Charlton developed into a competent starter and reliever.

After the Reds third consecutive second-place finish, Schott fired Bergesch in 1987 and hired

Murray Cook, who had been general manager of the Yankees and Expos. Cook made several moves that netted nine players on the 1990 Reds. His most successful deal was the trade for Jose Rijo, who Cook knew from his days in New York. Signed as a sixteen-year-old in 1981 by the Yankees, Rijo was traded to Oakland in 1984 as part of the package for Rickey Henderson. He struggled in his age twenty to twenty-two seasons with the A's (17–22, 4.74 ERA with poor control). After the 1987 season, Cook began shopping Dave Parker to American League teams because of the aging outfielder's potential as a DH. The A's were looking for a replacement for Reggie Jackson and offered Rijo and Tim Birtsas for Parker. It proved to be one of the best trades in club history as Rijo found his control in 1988 and developed into one of the best pitchers in Reds history.

Cook made another important deal in the fall of 1987, trading Kurt Stillwell and Ted Power to Kansas City for Danny Jackson. At the time, the twenty-two-year-old Stillwell was a highly regarded shortstop prospect (he had been the second overall pick in the 1983 draft), but the emergence of Larkin made him expendable. The Royals had an excess of pitching and a hole at shortstop, so the deal was obvious. Stillwell never developed into much more than a light-hitting shortstop, and when Jackson won twenty-three games in 1988 the deal looked like another Rijo bonanza. But Jackson developed arm problems and saw limited action in the next two seasons. In 1990, Jackson was 6–6 in twenty-one starts and was in the rotation for the postseason.

He started the pennant-clinching game against Pittsburgh and Game Two of the World Series.

Cook also acquired several role players on the 1990 team, adding backup catcher Jeff Reed, first baseman Todd Benzinger, outfielder Herm Winningham, and infielder Luis Quinones in exchange for Nick Esasky, Tracy Jones, Rob Murphy, Pat Pacillo, and Bill Landrum. In addition, Cook signed Rick Mahler, who started sixteen games in 1990 and drafted Jack Armstrong in the first round of the 1988 draft.

Cook's final contribution to the 1990 team was his 1989 midseason trade of Kal Daniels and Lenny Harris to the Dodgers for Tim Leary and Mariano Duncan. Daniels was a great young hitter and considered one of the crown jewels of the late '80's Reds youth movement. However, he was an indifferent fielder and injury prone. Leary did not last with the Reds, but Duncan strengthened second base, having arguably the best year of his career in 1990, hitting .306 with 55 RBI and murdering left-handed pitching (.412).

After the disappointing 1989 season, Cook was sacked and replaced by another ex-Yankee, Bob Quinn. Quinn finished the work of his four predecessors with a series of trades that rounded out the 1990 club.

The '90 Reds were a true "team," and fittingly, it took a team to assemble them—five general managers can claim credit for building the World Champions.

else dared shed their shirt publicly.

"Show-off!" somebody said, good-naturedly, and Braggsie beamed that Ultra Brite smile again.

Larkin looked as though he could still do the back flip he did after the World Series; his buddy, Eric Davis, looked as though he could reprise that catch-and-throw carom off the center field wall in Game Four of the NLCS, with that one-hop laser to Sabo at third. (*That,* you remind yourself, is the play he should be remembered for, even more than for the World Series Game One bomb off Dave Stewart.) Yes, right then is when you wish it really could be 1990 again, not for Davis's sake, but for yours. The last time, you had rubbed your eyes as though to say, "Did that really just happen?"

Billy Hatcher was his ebullient self, retelling that wonderful story about being in the delivery room on April 3, 1990, while his wife was giving birth to their daughter, Chelsea, and receiving a call from Pirates manager Jim Leyland telling him that he'd been traded to, to, to whom? Leyland had told him, but Hatcher didn't even recall the call, let alone the team, until he was driving home from the hospital and turned to his son, Derek, and said, "I remember I've been traded, but I can't remember to who!"

Tom Browning, loose and easy as ever, rattled off his stories at the drop of a hat, no wasted time, no wasted motion, boom-boom-boom, just like on the mound.

The famous Nasty Boys couldn't make it, but Piniella spoke for them.

"It's the first time I think a team has ever had three legitimate closers on one staff," Lou remembered. "A talented bunch."

Classy Hal Morris, erudite as ever, demonstrating what Piniella had taught Paul O'Neill back in the day about getting some rhythm in the batter's box, a tip Paul adopted—but not until he was a Yankee, so he wouldn't have to give any credit to his antagonist, Sweet Lou. We all laughed. Benzinger summed up the '90 team—as only Benzinger can—by saying he would much rather hear the story of the team that shouldn't have been able to but did (the '90 Reds) or the one that was supposed to and didn't (the Oakland A's) than the one that was supposed to and did (1975–76 Reds), We all assent; Benzoo has nailed it again.

At one point, somebody asked Oliver: "Is Herm (Winningham) around?" To which Joe responded: "He's here somewhere, but if he were around, you'd *hear* him."

Winningham was one of the '90 guys who kept things loose, along with Luis Quinones.

On stage, the '90 team gathered to tell their stories—baited and bantered and brought forth by Marty Brennaman. Chris Sabo stood just behind his teammates, seated in a row. Sabes declined the offer of a seat, still a part of the team but maybe still ever so slightly in his own world.

"Sabes" has never been comfortable with fame, and is completely, and will forevermore shall be, irrevocably unreconciled to the idea that he did anything deserving of this adulation, no matter the goggles and

Marty Brennaman called the '90 Reds his favorite team because of guys like Lou Piniella, Billy Hatcher, Tom Browning, Eric Davis, and Ron Oester.

the Spuds McKenizie nickname, and the run-till-you're-out reputation.

Off to the side, Piniella talked about spring training that year.

"When I first watched these guys in the spring, I recognized early on that, 'Boy, these guys can run, they're athletic, they can *play*,' and I asked Tony Perez, 'What the hell's the problem?' I talked to Tony at length. He said, 'They need to be pushed. You got to get after them a little bit. You got to step on their toes a little bit.'"

Lou, today, deflects the credit. Really, he has always deflected it.

"Pete Rose deserves a lot of credit," Piniella demurs. "He had these kids; he taught them how to play. Pete's coaches deserve credit, too."

Lou admired Pete. He still can't believe Pete had been a Tampa Tarpon when Lou was a senior in high school and was "still playing long after I was done."

Lou also made a point on stage to mention the

work that Ron Oester had done that season. Everybody felt "O" was a key guy, on the field and in the clubhouse. Oester, who Larkin praised as the quintessential "Cincinnati work-ethic guy" and whose drive Larkin credits for making him the player he became, nods appreciatively at the mention.

Piniella once said that the secret to managing is keeping happy "three or four" key guys on the club—the stars. But on the '90 Reds, the players all say that Lou's message shot directly into their main veins, un-

What made it all come together?

Was it talent, the right mix, health, luck?

"It's a combination of a lot of things," Piniella said. "Health, sure. But there's no substitute for talent. Talent is the most important ingredient. But you've got to stay healthy; you've got to be lucky. You know, I had some good teams in Seattle—reminded me a lot of this Cincinnati team—but we could never get by the Yankees. You know what, though? When it's all said and done, the players get it done."

Marge Schott's dog Schottzie didn't make it to the reunion, having long since passed away, but her commemorative dog collar is part of the Reds' Hall of Fame collection.

diluted. There were no middlemen.

"I was young," answers Piniella, breaking into a grin. "They were young. They probably would have enjoyed the journey a lot more at my age now. But, you know, we pushed them. *We pushed them.* Look, it's not easy to win. It's so much easier to lose than it is to win. Anybody can lose."

Sixteen years later, the statheads were able to quantify what only Piniella knew at the time—his Reds were perfectly built for the postseason. In *Baseball Between the Numbers*, Nate Silver and Dayn Perry argue that three factors more than any others correlate to playoff success: closer quality, defense, and pitcher's strikeout rate. Of the 180 teams to make the playoffs from 1972 to 2005, the

'90 Reds were the second-best-suited team for success in the playoffs, ranking high in all three categories. As Hal Morris would say at Redsfest, "We were a team more constructed to win a short series than not. Somebody did an excellent job of constructing that team."

The '90 Reds got off to such a hot start: 9–0, 33–12, and Piniella was strategic in how he rode his team to the finish.

"I knew that if we didn't get into any kind of sustained losing streak, and we played around .500, we'd be okay," Piniella said. "After the fast start, we played something like 51–50, but that's okay. We didn't push them during that stretch. We played everybody, rested guys When we got to the postseason, we were ready again."

Piniella, a horseplayer, used the term "hand-ride." That was the key. He didn't whip them through the second half. Too hard on the psyche. In New York, from whence he had come, his old boss, George Steinbrenner, would have demanded the whip. But that's where Lou won it. He didn't go to the whip again until after the Reds had clinched the division. He knew how to hand-ride a young team to the wire.

Somebody in the audience asked Lou about the famous "base toss." (You always know that is going to come up.) Lou, who normally shies away from talk of that episode, feeling embarrassed by his behavior (even though the team, which had been floundering, went 9–3 immediately after that), smiled easily and had a good time with it.

"I learned that from Earl Weaver and my manager Billy Martin," he said, grinning.

Brennaman asked Sabo about the two homers in Game Three of the World Series—the dagger in the heart of the Oakland A's—and Sabes harrumphed it…again. Hey, he's still just Walt the Plumber's son from Detroit, doing his job. His only unrequited sports dream is wondering what might have been had he stuck with hockey. Sabes was a goalie, you know. Beyond that, he does not wonder a thing, except why so many people still want his autograph. Happiest now in fatherhood, Sabes will nonetheless be forever remembered—like Heinie Groh in '19, Billy Werber in '40 and Rose in '75–'76—as a most unique third baseman. What's with Cincinnati and our third baseman, anyway?

"I enjoyed watching these guys play every day," Piniella interjected. "It was fun. They played with reckless abandon, and they played to win. It was a fun, fun year for me as a manager, coming to the ballpark and watching these kids play."

It is 1990.

Gone in an instant, and suddenly back again.

February 1, 2010. Goodyear, Arizona

Sitting by the fireplace on the patio outside the Hilton Garden Inn are Tom Browning, Joe Oliver, and Kent Mercker. They are surrounded by five or six Reds Fantasy Campers and are trading stories about their playing days. This is why the players come to these camps—for the chance to tell their stories.

Baseball players love to talk about the good old days. It is especially true when you get former teammates together. One guy starts recounting a story about a bus ride where he locked a superstar in the bathroom, and that spurs another story about the manager tossing the buffet table across the locker room.

And then Eric Davis shows up. Davis is used to having microphones and tape recorders in his face and eyes on him wherever he goes. He knows how to remain guarded and keep people at a distance when he's in public. But when he's around his former teammates, you can see his true personality shine. He's affable and warm. He's intelligent and reflective. He's witty and insightful.

What's most striking is how his former teammates regard him. He appears to be both friend and hero at the same time. He is just one of the guys, but it is clear that he is more than that. He is teased by his former teammates just like anyone else, but at the same time he is spoken of with a level of reverence that is reserved for the best of the best. They knew he was someone special, but appreciated the fact that he never held that over them. It is counter to the superstar image of many of today's athletes. It is enjoyable to watch.

For the next three hours, Davis, Oliver, and Browning answer questions from campers and tell some of the funniest stories you'll ever hear. Davis tells the stories of minor leaguer "Mississippi Mike" Smith, a man that had an interesting way with words. Oliver does his spot-on impression of Rickey Henderson at home plate ("Rickey don't like that pitch! Rickey's a Hall of Famer!"). Browning retells the story of how he ended up on the roof of the building across from Wrigley Field during a game.

The whole time this is going on, one thing becomes clear. The camaraderie shared between these guys when they were teammates on the World Championship team is still there. There is a mutual respect and friendship among them. They would go to battle together tomorrow, if the opportunity arose.

And as a matter of fact, a chance to go to battle shows itself this night in the person of Jack Billingham, who sat down with the group about two hours into the conversation. Billingham is an instigator, a quiet sort who only pops up to push buttons. This time he wonders aloud if the 1990 Reds could handle the Big Red Machine. When facing three members of that '90 squad, he knows what he's getting into.

Oliver and Browning remain modest and try to skirt the subject until Davis takes the bull by the horns. "You all couldn't handle our pitching," Davis says. "And we'd run you ragged."

Billingham counters with stories of sweeping the playoffs in 1976, but Davis isn't backing down. "We swept too, Jack," he says, "and the A's were a better team."

This goes back and forth for a few minutes in a fun, trash-talking manner. Davis loves this stuff, and he doesn't back-pedal. The only thing that can end the conversation is his cell phone, but he doesn't take the call without getting in one last argument.

"Three words, Jack: Wire-to-wire."

And that was it. The '90 Reds weren't the Big Red Machine. They were their own team, with their own identity. They did something no other National League team had done. They were the Wire-to-Wire Reds.

'90 Cincinnati Reds

Team Mascot: Schottzie

Front Row: Chris Sabo • Billy Hatcher • Ken Griffey • Coach Sam Perlozzo • Coach Tony Perez • Coach Jackie Moore • Manager Lou Piniella • Coach Stan Williams • Coach Larry Rothschild • Norm Charlton • Todd Benzinger • Glenn Braggs

Middle Row: Equipment Manager Bernie Stowe • Batboy Dave Reynolds • Danny Jackson • Jose Rijo • Hal Morris • Ron Oester • Rob Dibble • Jack Armstrong • Tim Birtsas • Paul O'Neill • Joe Oliver • Eric Davis • Traveling Secretary Joel Pieper • Trainer Larry Starr

Back Row: Scott Scudder • Luis Quinones • Chris Hammond • Tim Layana • Randy Myers • Rick Mahler • Tom Browning • Barry Larkin • Mariano Duncan • Jeff Reed • Herm Winningham • Assistant Trainer Dan Wright

Where Are They Now?

Jack Armstrong - Athletic trainer in Florida

Billy Bates - Retired, out of baseball

Todd Benzinger - Head coach, Class A Dayton Dragons

Glenn Braggs - Investment real estate, part-time coach, actor

Tom Browning - Pitching coach, Arizona League Reds

Norm Charlton - Hunting and fishing guide, Rockport, TX (Gulf Coast)

Eric Davis - Special Assistant to Reds General Manager Walt Jocketty, Cincinnati Reds

Rob Dibble - Analyst for the Washington Nationals, XM Radio Personality

Bill Doran - Assistant Field Coordinator of Instruction, Cincinnati Reds

Mariano Duncan - First base coach, Los Angeles Dodgers

Ken Griffey - Hitting coach, Class A Dayton Dragons

Billy Hatcher - First base coach, Cincinnati Reds

Danny Jackson - Manages bowling alleys in Kansas City

Barry Larkin - Analyst for MLB Network

Tim Layana – Deceased

Rick Mahler – Deceased

Hal Morris - Scout, Pittsburgh Pirates; Stanford University, MBA

Randy Myers - Retired, out of baseball; working to revive the baseball program at
Clark College in Vancouver, WA

Paul O'Neill - Analyst for YES Network

Ron Oester - Roving instructor, Chicago White Sox

Joe Oliver - High school baseball coach and real estate agent, Florida

Luis Quinones - Hitting coach, Class A Oneonta Tigers

Jeff Reed - Hitting coach, Rookie ball Elizabethtown Twins

Jose Rijo - Retired, was Special Assistant to General Manager, Washington Nationals

Chris Sabo - Retired, out of baseball; post-graduate studies

Scott Scudder - High school baseball coach in Texas

Herm Winningham - High school baseball coach in South Carolina

Acknowledgments

JOEL

We would like to thank the Cincinnati Reds for their support during this project. Specifically, thanks to Phil Castellini, Rob Butcher, Michael Anderson, Nick Krall, and Stephanie Ben. Special thanks to Ralph Mitchell and Jarrod Rollins in the Reds communications department for guiding us through the team photo archive and for putting up with our frequent visits. Without their help, we never would have had many of the excellent photographs you find in this book.

Thank you to all of the players and coaches from the 1990 team who took time out of their schedule to tell us their stories. We hope we've done them justice.

A special thanks to Rick Walls and Chris Eckes at the Reds Hall of Fame for their support of this project and for help with photographs and information.

This book would not have been nearly as easy to write without several excellent, and mostly free, online resources. The Cincinnati Public Library website gave us access to a wealth of newspaper archives and other research tools without which we'd still be digging through paper clippings.

Much of the historical game information originates from Retrosheet.org, an incredible resource of historical baseball information that has enabled an amazing amount of baseball research to be completed easily.

Several baseball statistical sites were also integral in our research. Baseball-Reference.com, BaseballProjection.com, BaseballProspectus.com, and FanGraphs.com all give even the novice baseball fan new ways to learn about and think about their favorite player and favorite team.

Thanks to Greg Rhodes, Greg Gajus, and Justin Merry, who all contributed much to this book.

Thanks to my brother, Andy, who was the source for many of the first-hand memories of the Reds' 1990 season.

Lastly, thanks to my co-author for taking a chance on a computer nerd to help write this book. It was an incredible experience that I'll never forget.

JOHN

To all the reporters and writers of 1990, who made our research a lot of fun, including past and present *Enquirer* colleagues: John Fay, Tom Groeschen, Rory Glynn, Tim Sullivan, Greg Hoard, Jack Brennan, Bill Koch, Paul Daugherty, Mike Paolercio, Howard Wilkinson, Cliff Radel, John Kiesewetter, Greg Noble, Mike Ball, Jack Murray, Chris Haft, and John Eckberg and to the AP's Joe Kay. To Hal McCoy, of the *Dayton Daily News*, whose articles were most helpful, as was his 2010 interview about Lou Piniella and Pete Rose; and to Bob Hunter of the *Columbus Dispatch* and the late Ritter Collett, of the *Dayton Daily News*. To Marty Brennaman, who got the ball rolling in a spirited Q&A over English muffins and French toast last December. To Tom Callinan, the *Enquirer*'s executive editor, who opened up the photo library for our use. To *Enquirer* librarian Jeff Suess, who so adeptly carries on the hard-digging work of Ray Zwick, Frank Harmon and Sally Besten, who have breathed life into so many dusty stories for me over the years. To Greg Rhodes, whose initial culling of photos for this book was of immeasurable help, and to Greg Gajus, whose earliest conversa-tions and sharing of John Eisenberg's *That First Season about Vince Lombardi* and the Green Bay Packers, inspired me to pursue this project. To Joe Posnanski, whose book *The Machine* helped inform our approach. To Jack Perconte (for his reminiscences about Mike Scioscia in the minors) and to coach Johnny Reagan and the Murray State 'Breds, especially the '70s guys, whose reunion in October 2009 made for wonderful insight into the '90 Reds reunion two months later. To Bob Quinn and Jimmy Stewart, whose completing and advancing of the '90 Reds has never received enough credit. To baseball's "objective analysts," including my co-author and Mr. Gajus and Justin Merry, all of whom have added greatly to my appreciation of the game. And to my brothers, Greg and Frank, and my sisters, Joanne and Nancy, who have always been such great sounding boards for me—and not just at book-writing time.

To Clerisy Press editorial director Jack Heffron for literally and figuratively keeping it together as we filed one chapter after another in no order whatsoever on deadline. To crack graphic designer Steve Sullivan for making it all look good.

Bibliography

Bass, Mike. *Marge Schott: Unleashed*, 1993.

Browning, Tom. *Tom Browning's Tales from the Reds Dugout*, 2006.

Davis, Eric. *Born to Play: The Eric Davis Story*, 1999.

Erardi, John and Greg Rhodes. *Opening Day: Celebrating Cincinnati's Baseball Holiday*, 2004.

Erardi, John. *Pete Rose, 4,192: Baseball's All-Time Hit Leader*, 1985.

Frost, Mark. *Game Six: Cincinnati, Boston, and the 1975 World Series – The Triumph of America's Pastime*, 2009.

Golenbock, Peter. *George: The Poor Little Rich Boy Who Built The Yankee Empire*, 2009.

Keri, Jonah (editor). *Baseball Between the Numbers: Why Everything You Know About the Game is Wrong*, 2006.

Lyle, Sparky. *The Bronx Zoo*, 1979.

Murcer, Bobby. *Yankee for Life: My 40-Year Journey in Pinstripes*, 2008.

O'Neill, Paul. *Me and My Dad: A Baseball Memoir*, 2003.

Piniella, Lou. *Sweet Lou*, 1986.

Posnanski, Joe. *The Machine: A Hot Team, A Legendary Season, and a Heart-stopping World Series – The Story of the 1975 Cincinnati Reds*, 2009.

Rains, Bob. *Tony LaRussa: Man on a Mission*, 2009.

Rhodes, Greg, and John Erardi. *Big Red Dynasty: How Bob Howsam & Sparky Anderson Built the Big Red Machine*, 1997.

Rhodes, Greg, and John Snyder. *Redleg Journal: Year by Year and Day by Day with the Cincinnati Reds Since 1866*, 2000.

Rose, Pete. *My Prison Without Bars*, 2004.

Also:

Cincinnati Reds, 1990 and 1991 Media Guides.

Magazines: *Baseball Digest, Sports Illustrated, The New Yorker, The Sporting News.*

Newspapers: *Cincinnati Enquirer, Cincinnati Post, Columbus Dispatch, Dayton Daily News, Houston Chronicle, Los Angeles Times, New York Daily News, New York Observer, New York Times, Seattle Post-Intelligencer.*

Internet: Baseball-Almanac.com, BaseballLibrary.com, Baseball-Reference.com, BaseballProjection.com, BaseballProspectus.com, ESPN.com, FanGraphs.com, Retrosheet.org, Wezen-ball.com.

About the Authors

John Erardi, a *Cincinnati Enquirer* reporter, has been chosen three times as Ohio's Best Sports Writer (twice AP, once National Association of Sportscasters and Sportswriters) and has won the APSE award for the best feature story in the country (100,000–250,000 circulation). He resides in Crescent Springs, Kentucky, with his wife, Barb, son, Chris, daughter, Gina, and the best dog in the world, "Milkshake," who sometimes answers to her nickname, "Milky Cabrera."

Joel Luckhaupt is a writer and managing editor for Red Reporter, an online fan community for the Cincinnati Reds. He resides in Cincinnati with his wife, Sara, and son, Alex, who are all looking forward to the arrival of our newest family member in August 2010, and a Reds championship two months later.